International and Regional Politics in the Middle East and North Africa

A GUIDE TO INFORMATION SOURCES

Volume 6 in the International Relations Information Guide Series

Ann Schulz

Associate Professor of Government
Clark University
Worcester, Massachusetts

Gale Research Company
Book Tower, Detroit, Michigan 48226

Library of Congress Cataloging in Publication Data

Schulz, Ann.
 International and regional politics in the Middle
East and North Africa.

   (International relations information guide series ;
v. 6)   (Gale information guide library)
   Includes bibliographical references and index.
   1. Near East--Foreign relations--Bibliography.
2. Africa, North--Foreign relations--Bibliography.
I. Title
Z6465.N35S38   [JX1581.N38]   016.32756   74-11568
ISBN 0-8103-1326-X

Copyright ©1977 by
Ann Schulz

No part of this book may be reproduced in any form without permission in writing from the publisher, except by a reviewer who wishes to quote brief passages or entries in connection with a review written for inclusion in a magazine or newspaper. Manufactured in the United States of America.

International and Regional Politics in the Middle East and North Africa

INTERNATIONAL RELATIONS INFORMATION GUIDE SERIES

Series Editor: Garold W. Thumm, Professor of Government and Chairman of the Department, Bates College, Lewiston, Maine

Also in the International Relations Series:

ARMS CONTROL AND MILITARY POLICY—*Edited by Donald F. Bletz**

EASTERN EUROPE—*Edited by Robin Remington**

ECONOMICS AND FOREIGN POLICY—*Edited by Mark A. Amstutz*

THE EUROPEAN COMMUNITY—*Edited by J. Bryan Collester**

INTELLIGENCE, ESPIONAGE, COUNTERESPIONAGE, AND COVERT OPERATIONS—*Edited by Paul W. Blackstock and Frank Schaf, Jr.**

INTERNATIONAL ORGANIZATIONS—*Edited by Alexine Atherton*

LATIN AMERICA—*Edited by John J. Finan**

THE MULTINATIONAL CORPORATION—*Edited by Helga Hernes*

POLITICAL DEVELOPMENT—*Edited by Arpad von Lazar and Bruce Magid**

SOUTH ASIA—*Edited by Richard J. Kozicki**

SOUTHEAST ASIA—*Edited by Richard Butwell**

SUB-SAHARAN AFRICA—*Edited by W.A.E. Skurnik*

THE STUDY OF INTERNATIONAL RELATIONS—*Edited by Robert L. Pfaltzgraff, Jr.*

U.S.S.R.—*Edited by David Williams and Karen Williams**

*in preparation

The above series is part of the
GALE INFORMATION GUIDE LIBRARY

The Library consists of a number of separate series of guides covering major areas in the social sciences, humanities, and current affairs.

General Editor: Paul Wasserman, Professor and former Dean, School of Library and Information Services, University of Maryland

Managing Editor: Dedria Bryfonski, Gale Research Company

VITA

Ann T. Schulz is associate professor of government at Clark University, Worcester, Massachusetts. She received her B.A. (cum laude) from Miami University, Ohio, and her M.A. and Ph.D. in international relations from Yale University. Schulz coedited (with Onkar Marwah) NUCLEAR PROLIFERATION AND THE NEAR NUCLEAR COUNTRIES (Cambridge, Mass.: Ballinger, 1975) and is presently working on THE POLITICAL ECONOMY OF LOCAL POLITICS. She has written numerous articles on international relations and politics in the Middle East.

CONTENTS

Foreword xi
Preface xiii

Chapter 1 – Introduction: International Politics, The Middle East,
            and Resource Materials 1

Chapter 2 – Regional Issues 9
    Essay 9
    The Middle East in World Politics 13
    Nationalism and the Colonial Experience 18
    Arab State Politics 23
    The Indian Ocean and the Persian/Arab Gulf 27
    North Africa 32
    Documents 34

Chapter 3 – The Foreign Policies of Middle Eastern States 37
    Essay 37
    Country Surveys and Background 42
    Afghanistan 44
    Algeria 44
    Egypt 45
    Iran 47
    Iraq 49
    Israel 50
    Jordan 58
    Lebanon 60
    Libya 60
    Morocco 61
    Saudi Arabia, Yemen, and the Arabian Peninsula 61
    Syria 63
    Tunisia 64
    Turkey 65

Chapter 4 – External Powers in the Middle East 69
    Essay 69

Contents

British Policy in the Middle East 72
    General 72
    Historical 74
Other External Powers 75
Soviet Policy in the Middle East 76
    General 76
    Historical 81
    Internal Communism 82
United States Foreign Policy 83
    General 83
    Iran 88
    Israel/Palestine 89
    Morocco 91
    Turkey 92
    Historical 92
    Documents 93

Chapter 5 - The Arab-Israeli Conflict 97
    Essay 97
    General Works 102
    Historical Background 115
    Documents 126
    Jerusalem 128
    Jordan River 129
    Peacekeeping and Negotiations 130
    Palestinian Nationalism 135
    Military Engagements 141
        1948-49 War 142
        1956 and the Suez Canal 143
        1967 War 146
        1973 War 150

Chapter 6 - Petroleum 153
    Essay 153
    The Economics of Oil 155
    Oil Producer-Consumer Relations 157
    Relations among Oil Producing States 162
    Reference Books 163

Chapter 7 - Reference Materials 165
    Essay 165
    Bibliographies and Indexes 169
    Biographical Indexes 177
    Chronologies 178
    Area Studies in the United States 181
        Guides 181
        Study Programs 181
    Yearbooks and Atlases 183
    Weapons 186

Contents

Chapter 8 – Serials 189
    Essay 189
    Middle East Area 190
    International Politics 193
    Military 195
    Petroleum 198

Author Index 201
Title Index 213
Subject Index 231

FOREWORD

The study of the modern Middle East has been vigorously pursued in the United States only since the conclusion of World War II when the shortage of competent specialists in Asian affairs became evident to government agencies and to the academic community. During the past quarter-century the growth of Middle Eastern studies at American universities has been part of the general development of area studies that was promoted by the setting up of area-centers with federal funding and foundation grants. Where once orientalists concentrated on dead languages and ancient history, the newly-founded centers and departments have launched energetic teaching and research programs in the social sciences to bring an understanding of the contemporary situations of non-Western areas into American higher education.

With the widening of our educational horizons there has come an ever-increasing quantity of publications to satisfy the need for information. Indeed, so well has the scholarly community responded to the need for information that now both the novice and expert need guides through the dense thicket of literature.

While there are a few general bibliographies on the Middle East, a real need exists for in-depth treatments of the literature by discipline. The present bibliography is devoted to political science, and specifically to the subjects of the regional and international politics of the Middle East--topics of first priority to the United States in its efforts to define a constructive foreign policy in that troubled area.

The author of this bibliography, instead of offering up the usual uncritical listing of works, has wisely chosen to present the literature under various headings employed by political scientists. Professor Schulz has, in addition, prefaced each division of the bibliography with an essay designed to provide perspective both to the topic itself and to the literature of the topic. It is my expectation that REGIONAL AND INTERNATIONAL POLITICS IN THE MIDDLE EAST will serve the needs of students, teachers, researchers, and librarians.

David H. Partington
Middle Eastern Librarian
Harvard College Library

PREFACE

With each succeeding month since this bibliography was committed to press, new publications on international politics in the Middle East appeared. Continuing failure to negotiate a settlement to the Arab/Israeli conflict combined with oil politics to create an environment which encouraged greater numbers of publications and, more significantly, fresh approaches to international affairs. Oil price increases and their repercussions, for example, reminded all concerned that world politics is very much influenced by the international distribution of economic resources. Consequently, several of these publications applied concepts from political economy to their topics.

Another discernable trend reflecting the unstable world order has been toward more studies of the foreign policies of small states--a development much to be welcomed. Bibliographies subsequent to this one will be able to achieve a better numerical balance between works on external and regional powers.

Whatever the prospects for future scholarship, those books which were available for this bibliography offer a varied fare for preliminary research and for general library collections. In bringing the materials together, I benefited from the assistance and support of librarians at the universities of New Hampshire, Clark, Brandeis, and Harvard. My friends Kylie and Alida Rothwell confirmed many citations and edited annotations, respectively, with dispatch and care. Anna Cyr hunted for books, which she also managed to put to good use in her seminar papers at Clark. Jeanie Schulz alphabetized the citations with her characteristic attention to detail. Finally, Dorothy Partington applied her skilled editorial hand to the essays. The errors which may be left are despite their contributions, which are sincerely appreciated.

Newton, Massachusetts

Chapter 1

INTRODUCTION: INTERNATIONAL POLITICS, THE MIDDLE EAST, AND RESOURCE MATERIALS

The purpose of this introductory essay is to explain the contents, organization, and style of this guide so that it will be more helpful to users with a variety of backgrounds and needs. The contents and organization were determined by the range of books and monographs available in the English language and by the formal concepts used by students of international politics. The citation and annotation style is fairly standard and is discussed at the end of this section.

The formal concepts of international politics, applied to the Middle Eastern context, can be used to focus research material collections. Researchers work within conceptual frameworks and will look for materials relevant to these frameworks in the libraries that serve them. The categories, or sections, used in this bibliography reflect adaptations of the formal concepts to available materials.

INTERNATIONAL POLITICS AND THE MIDDLE EAST

The impact of international politics as a discipline upon Middle Eastern area studies has been minimal. Few published studies make explicit use of international political concepts to analyze Middle Eastern events. This bibliography reflects this situation, using categories which tend to be more empirically oriented than theoretical. The student of international politics in the Middle East often must integrate materials from many diverse sources.

Most of the works relating to Middle Eastern international politics have been published by area specialists, diplomatic historians, or by practitioners. Before the mid-1960s relatively few area specialists were political scientists and relatively few practitioners have been interested in developing international political theory (some notable exceptions to both points are cited in the bibliography).

International political concepts alone would suggest classification under the headings: (1) international and regional political systems, (2) comparative

International Politics, Middle East, and Resource Materials

foreign policy studies, and (3) decision-making studies.[1] The organization and contents are discussed from that point of view and each of these three approaches to the study of international politics has been considered in the selection of listings for this bibliography and in their classification. However, most of the book-length studies cited are either diplomatic or contemporary history, and the classification used here falls somewhere between the international political concepts and the authors' approaches.

REGIONAL POLITICAL SYSTEMS IN THE MIDDLE EAST

Systems theory as applied to international politics assumes that relationships among nation-states and other nongovernmental actors fall into distinct patterns and are unique. Several of the categories in the bibliography suggest regional political systems: "The Middle East in World Politics"; "Regional Issues"; and the subsections within the latter category--"Arab State Politics," "The Indian Ocean and the Persian/Arab Gulf," and "North Africa." Despite their similar treatment in the bibliography, however, these regions are not equally distinct.

The term "Middle East" came into common usage with the Allied forces' Middle East Supply Centre during World War II. (Near East is an older designation which is still applied by the U.S. government.) The Middle East usually refers to the region from Afghanistan in the east to Turkey in the west and the Arabian Peninsula in the south. Almost all general and survey works refer to the Middle East or to the Middle East and North Africa, reflecting the unifying force of Islam and the Arabic language as well as the imprint of European politics.

Those books which cover the entire Middle East tend to be country-by-country surveys rather than the integrative studies common in more readily defined regions-- such as Western Europe. These works are included in the subsection, "Country Surveys and Background," chapter 3. All of those listed contain information on the countries' foreign policies, and several (where noted) also have introductory material on the region's relationship to the rest of the world.

Books in which the Middle East is discussed as a regional system in the formal sense are listed under the topic "The Middle East in World Politics" in chapter 2. As in the example of the Middle East Supply Center, the Middle East is often described on the basis of extraregional political issues. A number of the studies listed are directed toward American readers, and these emphasize the role played by the Middle East in the cold war.

---

[1] John Spanier uses this classification system in GAMES NATIONS PLAY: ANALYZING INTERNATIONAL POLITICS (New York: Praeger, 1972).

International Politics, Middle East, and Resource Materials

The United Nations has been most visible in its various roles in the Arab-Israeli conflict--supervising truce agreements, administering refugee programs, and serving as a vehicle for negotiations. Books on these UN activities are referenced under "Peacekeeping and Negotiations" in chapter 5.

Some of the more recent studies, such as Ismael [1013] and Hammond and Alexander [1010], discuss the Middle Eastern region from both an external and an internal perspective. If trends in the literature reflect changes in the real world, which they seem to, the predominance of the superpower perspective will probably continue to wane in the future with the increasing salience of regional political issues.

The Middle East is difficult to fit into regional political concepts. But there are less inclusive state groupings which are more readily discussed together. Only one, the Arab States, is formally defined by an organization, the League of Arab States. Arab League meetings are often the scene of joint policy announcements and the central organization has stimulated the creation of a number of subsidiary specialized agencies. Unfortunately, the major study of the league (MacDonald [1214]), while still invaluable, is now somewhat dated. However, primary sources of ongoing information on the activities of the league are often available (see "Chronologies" in chapter 7).

One study (Kerr [1209]), reprinted several times, does analyze inter-Arab politics from a regional perspective and concludes, significantly, that the distinction which is often made in cold-war studies between the "revolutionary" and "conservative" states is not very useful in predicting their foreign policy behavior. Conclusions like this underscore the need for a diversity of approaches.

In addition to belonging to the Arab League, North African states are often grouped together in the literature as a result of their similar French colonial experience, internal Arab-Berber ethnic divisions, and simultaneous orientations toward Africa and the Arab world. Here, too, the definition of region is not one which has been used in a formal way. The listings in the North Africa section are primarily country-by-country studies.

The growth of the petroleum industry and the importance of the nuclear submarine in contemporary military strategy together have stimulated a number of the recent studies which are included in the "Indian Ocean and Persian/Arab Gulf" subsection. The focus of this recent political science literature mirrors shifts in actual international events. The various littoral states do share riparian interests and compete for regional influence. In 1975 these states discussed a possible regional defense pact. Similarly, external powers treat the Gulf and Indian Ocean area as a region in terms of their own interests. If the mutual defense pact proposed in 1975 is concluded by the littoral states, the relationships among the Gulf states will probably increase still further.

International Politics, Middle East, and Resource Materials

Definitions of regions are not always transferred from practical politics to the literature about practical politics. The "northern tier" is a regional term which is a product of the United States's containment policy toward the Soviet Union in the Middle East. The "tier" countries are Turkey, Iran, and Pakistan--members of both the Regional Cooperation for Development (RCD) organization and the Central Treaty Organization (CENTO). The latter organization includes Britain and the United States as ex-officio members, however, neither organization is active enough to provide a major foreign policy focus for any of the member states. The organizations themselves yield few primary sources of information.

Regional perceptions and commitments are not static. Since the mid-1960s the oil-producing states have developed their capacities for acting in concert in a supporting environment. The Organization of Petroleum Exporting Countries (OPEC), which includes members outside of the Middle East, is a major source of industry information for member states as well as being a formal avenue of communication among them. The offshoot, OAPEC (Organization of Arab Petroleum Exporting Countries), has itself held a number of annual Arab Petroleum Congress meetings for which proceedings are also available [5204].

Where historical overviews of regional politics are available, the most widely useful have been included in the relevant regional sections. Few of the works which cover contemporary international political issues also discuss historical issues. But regional relationships often exhibit a remarkable degree of continuity over time. For instance, Iran was actively concerned with the Persian/Arab Gulf in the seventeenth and nineteenth centuries as well as today (Kumar [1319]). Similarly, Iraq and Egypt have competed for influence in the Fertile Crescent over the centuries (Kirk [1212]).

COMPARATIVE FOREIGN POLICY--MIDDLE EAST STATES

International systems concepts emphasize groups of nation-states. Issues concerning individual states' foreign policy goals and the strategies and resources available to pursue those goals are taken up by students of comparative foreign policy. Comparative foreign policy studies consider such factors as cultural and ideological orientations, economic capacity, and political cohesiveness--whatever is thought to shed light upon how foreign policy is made and the policies which result.[2]

Less than two dozen book-length foreign policy studies on Middle Eastern states have been published. None of these is a comparative foreign policy study covering the foreign relations of more than one nation-state. The works which come closest to authentic treaties on comparative foreign policy are the country

---

[2] James N. Rosenau developed this widely-used comparative framework in THE SCIENTIFIC STUDY OF FOREIGN POLICY (New York: Free Press, 1971).

surveys referred to above. The single country foreign policy studies vary widely in the way in which the material is integrated. Brecher's two volumes on Israel are framed in conceptual terms readily usable in a comparative context. The study of Iran's foreign policy by Chubin and Zabih [2403] is remarkably thorough but is organized by chronology and area rather than by comparative foreign policy concepts.

The material available for comparative foreign policy studies has not been exploited. For example, the listings in "Nationalism and the Colonial Experience" contain abundant information on cultural and ideological orientations. The roots of the (ex-colonial) Arab states' ambivalent attitudes toward the Western powers--simultaneously anti-Communist and anticolonialist--are to be found here, as is Arab reaction to Israel as an extension of Western economic and cultural competition. Nonetheless, few foreign policy analyses have developed the topic of images and orientations.

A number of international issues are related to internal relationships among ethnic groups, e.g., the Iraq-Kurdish war and the position of the Druze population in the Golan Heights between Syria and Israel. Moslems in Iraq influence that nation's relations with neighboring Shi'a Iran. "Reference Materials" includes source material on ethnicity, religion, and demography within individual Middle East states.

Because so few books on comparative foreign policy have been written, sources of primary data on individual states' policies are particularly important. Many more of these sources are available in 1975 than there were a decade or more earlier. Listings of sources on international events can be found in the "Chronologies" subsection.

THE DECISION-MAKING APPROACH TO MIDDLE EAST POLITICS

A third approach to the study of international politics focuses on how and why specific decisions are made. Within this area of study, one can distinguish between the traditional, less-structured decision-making framework and the relatively new game theory approach. The latter describes competitive situations in terms of winning strategies and the costs of failure. For example, the most competitive relationships are "zero-sum" games; if one player wins, the other loses. The zero-sum game is that played by a state whose very existence is threatened. For some Palestinians and Israelis the Arab-Israeli conflict is such a game.

No game theory analysis of Middle Eastern international politics has been published in book form. Applied to the Arab-Israeli conflict, game theory stimulates little more than the most simplistic observations. Two-person (or two-state) situations are most amenable to game theory analysis; the Arab-Israeli conflict is an "n-person" game. The 1973 war, for example, was the result of decisions taken in Riyadh, Baghdad, Moscow, and Washington as well as in Damascus, Jerusalem, and Cairo.

International Politics, Middle East, and Resource Materials

The game theory emphasis upon strategy and costs is found in the literature on the Middle East. The changing costs of the conflict are documented in studies of the military capabilities of the adversaries listed in chapter 7 under "Weapons." "Peacekeeping and Negotiations" and "Military Engagements" in chapter 5, also contain materials which either themselves use or lend themselves to game theory analysis.

Diplomatic solutions are created, not found, according to one student of international politics (Fisher [4513]). The need for innovation takes one beyond decisions which have been made and into the area of decisions which might be made. Here, the literature is very sparse.

The traditional decision-making approach itself outlines: (1) the decision-makers' definitions of the general situation in which the decision is to be made, (2) the immediate setting of the decision, (3) the organizational framework, and (4) the decision-makers' psychological makeup.[3] Most of the single-country foreign policy studies available are surveys rather than in-depth analyses of specific decisions. Two exceptions are Copeland's volume on Egyptian foreign policy, THE GAME OF NATIONS [2303] and Brecher's DECISIONS IN ISRAEL'S FOREIGN POLICY [2610].

In the absence of formal decision-making studies, materials on internal politics are useful to describe the domestic political aspects of the setting and the political institutions within which foreign policy decisions are made. For access to this kind of information, researchers should refer to single-country bibliographies. Books on internal politics also are listed in this bibliography where alternative sources of information are sparse.

One approach for those who are interested in decision-making is to explore the literature on specific conflicts. Books on the Yemen civil war, for example, classified in "Saudi Arabia, Yemen, and the Arabian Peninsula" in chapter 3, provide background on specific Saudi Arabian foreign policy decisions. The decisions of Arab and Israeli leaders to go to war (on four occasions) have been written about most frequently. These studies are listed in "Military Engagements" in chapter 5. Articles, accessed through "Serials" in chapter 8, often cover decisions about military strategy and tactics.

Other major sources of information on specific decisions are the biographies and autobiographies of practitioners of international politics. For example, Robert Murphy's DIPLOMAT AMONG WARRIORS [3820] is a little-used source for the United States's decision to become involved in the 1958 Lebanese civil

---

[3]Richard C. Snyder et al., eds. FOREIGN POLICY DECISION-MAKING (New York: Free Press, 1963) and Joseph Frankel, THE MAKING OF FOREIGN POLICY: AN ANALYSIS OF DECISION-MAKING (New York: Oxford University Press, 1963) are major examples of the decision-making approach in the literature of international politics.

International Politics, Middle East, and Resource Materials

conflict. The late American Secretary of State, Dean Acheson, has documented the role of the United States in the 1951-53 British-Iranian oil concession negotiations in PRESENT AT THE CREATION [3801]; the late President Truman's MEMOIRS [3828] review American policy toward the establishment of Israel. Similarly, King Hussein's recollections (UNEASY LIES THE HEAD [2704]) provide material on Jordanian government decisions.

Materials on the decision makers themselves are classified in two different ways. Several individual biographies are entered by subject, either under the specific country or organization which the author served or the event described. Biographical directories are listed separately in "Biography," chapter 7. More contemporary primary material on the explanations offered by leaders for particular decisions is available in press and radio reviews which are listed in "Chronology" in chapter 7.

STYLE

The citations in this volume follow the University of Chicago Press' A MANUAL OF STYLE, as do the other volumes in the International Relations Information Guide Series. The exceptions are that: (1) additional reference material (indexes, maps, etc.) is cited although not listed in the NATIONAL UNION CATALOG; (2) the name of the publishing house is given in shortened form (i.e., omitting incorporation and other similar designations); and, (3) periodicals and serials are cited in the form used by Ulrich's guides, where available.

The annotations cover, wherever possible, the scope of the book, the author's sources (with language information), particularly relevant notes about the author or perspective, and further publishing information. For example, if the contributions to edited volumes are not original, that is noted. Some entries appear without annotation because the volumes themselves or summaries of them were difficult to obtain. Nonetheless, nonannotated entries were included because they represented a publisher or an author of whom users of this bibliography should be aware.

The length of the annotation does not necessarily reflect an implicit evaluation of the author's contribution to the literature. Unique material, though perhaps of limited scholarly value, has received special attention. The essays introducing major sections are also intended to point out differences among books.

Chapter 2

REGIONAL ISSUES

The Middle East region is largely an artificial construct, and few authors have attempted to write about the region as a whole and its place in the international political system. Most limit themselves to some portion of the Middle East, either by region (as the Persian Gulf) or by issue (as the Arab-Israeli conflict).

Those books which are general in scope are classified in "The Middle East in World Politics." The entries vary widely. Jon Kimche's THE SECOND ARAB AWAKENING [1017] is an interpretive study built around the reaction of the Arab states to Israel and to the Western states. Kimiche argues that an accommodation of the conflicting interests in the Arab-Israeli conflict would lessen the small states' dependence upon outside powers. David Kimche also looks at the Middle East from the point of view of the regional state in THE AFRO-ASIAN MOVEMENT [1016], a critique of the post-Bandung period. Both have valuable regional perspectives although their orientations are fundamentally Western.

Banerji (THE MIDDLE EAST IN WORLD POLITICS [1002]), Bustani (DOUBTS AND DYNAMITE [1004] and MARCH ARABESQUE [1005]), and Jansen (NON-ALIGNMENT AND THE AFRO-ASIAN STATES [1014] are three non-Western authors who have written on general international issues in the Middle East. Banerji's writing is the most thorough, and his book provides valuable balance to the more traditional Western approaches.

Lenczowski's THE MIDDLE EAST IN WORLD AFFAIRS [1020], although dated like the former citations, is the most comprehensive monograph available. Lenczowski views the Middle East from the standpoint of the diplomatic historian and has divided his survey by country. POLITICAL DYNAMICS IN THE MIDDLE EAST [1010], edited by Hammond and Alexander, is also divided by country and is more current than Lenczowski. Both surveys denote considerable space to domestic politics. Williams's introduction to BRITAIN AND FRANCE IN THE MIDDLE EAST AND NORTH AFRICA, 1914-1967 [1032] similarly is limited in that the author tends to focus upon internal colonial policies.

Ismael's THE MIDDLE EAST IN WORLD POLITICS [1013] reviews the involvement of external powers in the Middle East and domestic sources of foreign

Regional Issues

policy. Editor Ismael, who also wrote several of the chapters, added an analytical conclusion which was intended to coalesce the various essays into a conceptual framework. However, the volume does not have an integrating theme; and without that, it remains a reader and should be evaluated beside the other readers available.

Among the single-authored monographs, Lewis's (THE MIDDLE EAST AND THE WEST [1021]) and Sachar's (EUROPE LEAVES THE MIDDLE EAST, 1936-52 [1027]) are the most successful in drawing upon a wide range of sources and weaving together the interplay between nationalism in the regional states and external interests. Both trace these forces from the colonial period. Lewis develops regional themes more fully and looks back farther to the Ottoman Empire, but has produced a much shorter book.

The Royal Institute of International Affairs in London published several volumes with Oxford University Press which focus upon the Middle East. All of these are thorough diplomatic chronicles, but they are also dated.

The books brought together in "Nationalism and the Colonial Experience" include historical accounts of Britain and France as colonial powers in the Middle East, collections of writings on contemporary Arab nationalism, and reviews of the independence movements in several of the former mandate territories. The theme which unifies these several topics is the interplay between European policies and political thought and the character of nationalist ideologies and practice in the Middle East.

Monographs such as Abu-Lughod's ARAB REDISCOVERY OF EUROPE: A STUDY IN CULTURAL ENCOUNTERS [1101] develop the link between colonial relations and contemporary patterns of foreign policy. The best-known study of this kind, George Antonius's THE ARAB AWAKENING [1103], traces the roots of Arab nationalism into movements in the provinces of the Ottoman Empire. C. Ernest Dawn's FROM OTTOMANISM TO ARABISM, ESSAYS ON THE ORIGIN OF ARAB NATIONALISM [1108] is a documented study which describes Arab nationalism primarily as a reaction to the defeat of the Ottoman Empire by the European states and the evident need for reforms.

Conflicts within the Ottoman territories were both encouraged by British policies designed to solicit support against the Ottomans during the First World War and, at other times, to unify the erstwhile Ottoman lands (see Marlowe's ARAB NATIONALISM AND BRITISH IMPERIALISM, [1121]).

Against this background of reform movements complicated by the rise of the Saudi dynasty in the Arabian peninsula and the installation of the Hashemite kings in Jordan and Iraq, several themes can be found in expressions of nationalism. Hisham Sharabi views these several threads from the standpoint of the sociology of knowledge, with political thought emerging from the social relations of Europeans and Arab intellectuals (ARAB INTELLECTUALS AND THE WEST [1129]). Nuseibeh produced a longer and more critical study which is also an

Regional Issues

intellectual history (THE IDEAS OF ARAB NATIONALISM, [1125]).

Either of these volumes can be supplemented with Haim's anthology ARAB NATIONALISM [1114], which offers original statements of Arab spokesmen with various viewpoints--Islamic, pan-Arab, and Arab state conceptions of the nation. As a counterpoint, Tutsch's introductory review of nationalist thought juxtaposes the lack of support for the Islamic community with the promise of communism. Tutsch's FACETS OF ARAB NATIONALISM [1133] successfully integrates a variety of material, but his observations on communism need to be balanced with one of the studies of internal communism to be found in the section on Soviet policy.

The other face of colonialism, that of European power politics and global strategies, is briefly described in Henry Cumming's FRANCO-BRITISH RIVALRY IN THE POST-WAR NEAR EAST [1107] and more extensively by William Hocking in THE SPIRIT OF WORLD POLITICS [1115]. Another early work, written as an undocumented essay, is Hans Kohn's WESTERN CIVILIZATION IN THE NEAR EAST [1118]. Published more recently, Nevakivi's BRITAIN, FRANCE AND THE ARAB MIDDLE EAST 1914-1920 [1124] focuses upon continuing British-French rivalry for influence, using a number of new sources. Finally, Elie Kedourie combines an interest in Arab nationalism and European political strategies in the lengthy THE CHATHAM HOUSE VERSION AND OTHER MIDDLE-EASTERN STUDIES [1116]. Kedourie's bibliography is extensive and unusually well-balanced.

None of the books listed here considers Turkish or Iranian nationalism in more than passing fashion. Nationalist movements and thought in these countries were less complicated by the impact of colonialism upon territory, and less immediately relevant to international political objectives. A few studies on nationalism in these two non-Arab states are included in the sections on Iranian and Turkish foreign policy.

Studies of nationalism and colonialism in specific countries are listed. Among these, the records of Britain in Egypt (Marlowe [1122] and al-Sayyid [1128]) are likely to be used most widely as background to contemporary international political issues. Most of the books in the section on historical background to the Arab-Israeli conflict also could be appropriately classified here as studies of the British Palestine Mandate.

Although aspects of pan-Arab ideas continue to play a part in contemporary inter-Arab state politics, Malcolm Kerr documents the simultaneous hardening of interests dividing Arab state leaders in THE ARAB COLD WAR [1209]. Kerr draws upon the records of the 1963 unification talks among Syria, Iraq, and Egypt to develop the theme that pan-Arab thought overlay a myriad of practical political differences and mutual antagonisms.

Hopes to develop joint activities among Arab states centered upon the League of Arab States, one of the first regional organizations to be created after World War II. Robert MacDonald (THE LEAGUE OF ARAB STATES [1214]) relates the

Regional Issues

league's history, structure, and functional activities as well as the political competition which has limited the league's growth.

The conflicts over the Fertile Crescent have a long history, at least partly covered by several books (Holt, EGYPT AND THE FERTILE CRESCENT [1206]; Saab, THE ARAB FEDERALISTS OF THE OTTOMAN EMPIRE [1218]; and Sayegh, ARAB UNITY [1219]). Saab's book is a more specialized study of unification movements and strategies, with extremely useful documentation. Holt has written a general history including the European political record.

With the late President Nasser's assumption of power in 1954, Egypt began to play a role in regional politics more active than it had for almost a century, mirroring an earlier period in its Ottoman history which Holt has described. Cremeans' sympathetic THE ARABS AND THE WORLD, NASSER'S ARAB NATIONALIST POLICY [1203] suggests that Nasser's developing foreign policy represented a new approach to the international political arena, that of positive neutralism.

In regional issues, however, positive neutrality has little meaning. Leila Kadi presents the record of Arab conferences on Palestine in ARAB SUMMIT CONFERENCES AND THE PALESTINE PROBLEM [1208]. Patrick Seale's THE STRUGGLE FOR SYRIA [1221], describes the reactions of the Syrian regime to Iraqi and Egyptian interference in Syrian affairs. Both are partisans of their subjects--Palestine and the Syrian Bath--but offer a different view and new materials.

With the formal withdrawal of the British from the Persian Gulf states in 1971, the possibility arose of regional interests taking precedence over those of external states. These potential shifts in regional power stimulated the writing of books which covered the Gulf, the neighboring Indian Ocean, and in some cases, the Red Sea and the Arabian Sea. These are cited in "The Indian Ocean and the Persian Gulf." In most cases, the authors bring either Western or Indian perspectives to their topics.

The precursor of the books of the 1970s is John Marlowe's 1962 study, THE PERSIAN GULF IN THE TWENTIETH CENTURY [1320]. Marlowe documents British-American competition in the Gulf. His study is useful background to the extension of U.S. involvement in the region in the mid-1970s. The strategic interests of external states in the region are further explored in the various writings of Burrell and Cottrell [1307-8, 1316], and Bernard Reich's THE PERSIAN GULF [1324].

The writing on the Gulf and the Indian Ocean available in English is unique among the regions in that a totally different perspective is added by regional authors. Kaushik's THE INDIAN OCEAN [1317] and Singh's POLITICS OF THE INDIAN OCEAN [1326] are both concerned with regional conflicts which are exacerbated, they argue, by superpower intervention. Little has been written, however, on India's growing military presence in the area.

Iran's prospects for greater influence are the subject of Ramazani's THE PERSIAN GULF [1324] and in the U.S. Committee on Foreign Affairs' hearing NEW PERSPECTIVES ON THE PERSIAN GULF [1328]. Chubin and Zabih's more comprehensive study of Iranian foreign policy (THE FOREIGN RELATIONS OF IRAN [2403]) also considers Iran's regional role and is thus also cited in chapter 3.

Most of the books written during the early 1970s emphasize contemporary diplomatic history. Other short, focused analyses usually are appended to the U.S. congressional hearings on the region. These hearings also can be very useful sources of economic and military data.

Several books on the Gulf states are included in this section and, although domestic issues predominate, each discusses British and other external interests. Here too are historical accounts of British policies toward the region, pathway to its Indian empire. Kumar (INDIA AND THE PERSIAN GULF REGION [1319]) and Hawley (THE TRUCIAL STATES [1313]) are especially useful backgrounds.

THE MIDDLE EAST IN WORLD POLITICS

1001 Azzam, Abdel Rahman. THE ETERNAL MESSAGE OF MUHAMMAD. Translated by Caesar E. Farah. New York: Devin-Adair, 1964. 297 p.

> Islamic thought on public affairs including war and the United Nations.

1002 Banerji, J.K. THE MIDDLE EAST IN WORLD POLITICS. Calcutta: World Press, 1960. 390 p. Bibliog. Index. Maps.

> Overview of the Middle East during the twentieth century-- colonial relations and nationalism--and the great power confrontation in the region. Documents pertaining to external relationships appended. Based upon secondary and primary sources and the author's firsthand observations. Short bibliography.

1003 Blaxland, Gregory. OBJECTIVE: EGYPT. London: Frederick Muller, 1966. EGYPT AND SINAI: EXTERNAL BATTLEGROUND. New York: Funk and Wagnalls, 1966. 319 p. Bibliog. Notes. Maps. Photos. Ports.

> Egypt as a region of external conflict throughout history, focusing on the nineteenth and twentieth centuries and particularly the 1956 Suez invasion.

1004 Bustani, Emile. DOUBTS AND DYNAMITE: THE MIDDLE EAST TODAY. London: Allan Wingate, 1958. 159 p. Illus.

> A Lebanese businessman and politician describes the fundamentals of Arab nationalism, external powers in the Middle East, and

the conflict over Israel. Without documentation, but with first-hand observations.

1005 _____. MARCH ARABESQUE. London: Robert Hale, 1961. 216 p. App. Index. Photos.

Survey of the Middle East during the twentieth century and of outstanding sources of conflict among Middle Eastern states and external powers. No documentation.

1006 Childers, Erskine B. THE ROAD TO SUEZ: A STUDY IN WESTERN-ARAB RELATIONS. London: MacGibbon and Kee, 1962. 416 p. Bibliog. Chron. Index.

Historical background of the relations of the West to the Arab Middle East prior to World War II and an analysis of the Suez invasion and Eisenhower Doctrine. Critical of external pressures against Arab state neutralism. No footnotes; short bibliography; based upon primary and secondary sources.

1007 Fisher, Carol Ann, and Krinsky, Fred. MIDDLE EAST IN CRISIS; A HISTORICAL AND DOCUMENTARY REVIEW. Syracuse, N.Y.: Syracuse University Press, 1959. 213 p. Apps. Index.

Brief survey of Middle Eastern states and international politics in the region. Nearly two-thirds of the volume consists of documents concerning the Arab-Israeli conflict and U.S./USSR competition in the region.

1008 Frye, Richard Nelson, ed. THE NEAR EAST AND THE GREAT POWERS. Cambridge, Mass.: Harvard University Press, 1951. 214 p.

Papers from a conference entitled "The Great Powers and the Near East" held at Harvard University, August 1950. Includes Israel-U.S. relations, Soviet policy in the Middle East, inter-Arab politics, oil, and Palestine.

1009 Georgetown University. Institute of Ethnic Studies. THE ARAB MIDDLE EAST AND MUSLIM AFRICA. Edited by Tibor Kerekes. New York: Praeger, 1961. 126 p. Bibliog. refs.

Islam, nationalism, and prospects for a unified Maghreb.

1010 Hammond, Paul Y., and Alexander, Sidney S., eds. POLITICAL DYNAMICS IN THE MIDDLE EAST. New York: American Elsevier, 1972. 702 p. Bibliog.

Essays on internal politics in individual nations, relations among the Middle Eastern states, and the role of external powers in the Middle East. A section on the Palestinian refugees by Don Peretz and the Palestinian movement by William Quandt.

Regional Issues

Oil issues and the cold war are included. A major collection, although many of the contributions are not original.

1011 Hatem, Abdel-Hatem. INFORMATION AND THE ARAB CAUSE. New York: Longman, 1974. 344 p. Index.

A deputy prime minister of Egypt reviews public opinion formation techniques and case histories of events in the Middle East as they were perceived by world public opinion.

1012 Hoskins, Halford Lancaster. THE MIDDLE EAST; PROBLEM AREA IN WORLD POLITICS. New York: Macmillan, 1954. 311 p. Bibliog. notes. Index. Maps.

International issues in the Middle East--the Suez Canal, Arab state unity, the creation of Israel, and oil--through English language sources and western security perspectives. Little documentation.

1013 Ismael, Tareq [Y.], ed. THE MIDDLE EAST IN WORLD POLITICS. Syracuse, N.Y.: Syracuse University Press, 1974. 297 p. Bibliog. fnn. Index.

Original essays covering, individually, the major powers' Middle East policies, Africa and the Middle East, the United Nations, domestic sources of foreign policy, oil, and an analytical conclusion. The bibliographies were organized by the chapter authors as background readings--duplicative, unfocused, but extensive.

1014 Jansen, Godfrey H. NON-ALIGNMENT AND THE AFRO-ASIAN STATES. New York: Praeger, 1966. 432 p. Apps.

Includes references to the Middle East. By a proponent of the Afro-Asian Movement.

1015 Khadduri, Majid [D.], ed. MAJOR MIDDLE EASTERN PROBLEMS IN INTERNATIONAL LAW. Washington, D.C.: American Enterprise Institute for Public Policy Research, 1972. 139 p. Paper. Bibliog. fnn. Index. Maps.

Description of the formal legal aspects of regional collective security arrangements, the Palestine conflict, international waterways, and territorial jurisdictional disputes. Ten useful maps.

1016 Kimche, David. THE AFRO-ASIAN MOVEMENT: IDEOLOGY AND FOREIGN POLICY OF THE THIRD WORLD. The Monograph Series of the Shiloah Center for Middle Eastern and African Studies, Tel Aviv. New York: Halsted, 1973. 296 p. Apps. Bibliog.

A review of the Bandung conference and the post-Bandung era.

Regional Issues

Covers, specifically, "Cairo and Algiers: The Demise of Afro-Asianism." Useful bibliography.

1017 Kimche, Jon. THE SECOND ARAB AWAKENING. London: Thames and Hudson, 1970. 288 p. Bibliog. Chron. Index. Maps.

Develops the theme that Israel and the Arab states have the potential to become independent from the great powers if accommodation to Israeli statehood and Palestinian nationalism is accomplished. Little documentation.

1018 Kirk, George Eden. THE MIDDLE EAST IN THE WAR. Survey of International Affairs 1939-46, vol. 2. London: Oxford University Press for the Royal Institute of International Affairs, 1954,[c1952]. xiii, 511 p. Bibliog. refs. Index. Maps.

Relations among the European powers and the Middle East during the war, including a section on the Soviet Union. Extensive documentation.

1019 _____. THE MIDDLE EAST 1945-1950. Survey of International Affairs, 1939-1946, vol. 5. London and New York: Oxford University Press, 1954. 338 p. Bibliog. fnn. Index. Maps.

Traces the shift from European colonial relationships with the Middle Eastern states to the pursuit of cold war objectives by the United States, the disintegration of the European colonies, the cold war in Turkey and Iran, and the Palestinian War. Palestine partition maps. Thorough documentation.

1020 Lenczowski, George. THE MIDDLE EAST IN WORLD AFFAIRS. 3d ed. Ithaca, N.Y.: Cornell University Press, 1962. xxvi, 723 p. Apps. Bibliog. Index. Maps.

Country survey of domestic and foreign issues, historical background and conflicts over strategic waterways. Oil and trade data appended; extensive English language bibliography; little documentation in text.

1021 Lewis, Bernard. THE MIDDLE EAST AND THE WEST. New York: Harper and Row, 1966; London: Weidenfeld and Nicolson, 1968. 164 p. Bibliog. refs. Index.

Arab nationalism in the context of the Ottoman Empire and Western imperialism pre-World War II and the post-war orientation of Arab states toward world affairs. Arabic and European language sources in an extensive bibliography.

1022 Miller, John Donald B. THE POLITICS OF THE THIRD WORLD. Chatham House Essays, 15. New York: Oxford University Press for the Royal Institute of International Affairs, 1967. 128 p.

Regional Issues

1023 Qubain, Fahim I. CRISIS IN LEBANON. Washington, D.C.: Middle East Institute, 1961. 243 p. Apps. Bibliog. refs. Index. Maps.

> Background to and analysis of the 1958 Lebanese civil war-- the involvement of Egypt, the United States, the Soviet Union, and the United Nations. United Nations Documents and Arab press excerpts appended. Extensively documented.

1024 Ramazani, Rouhollah K. THE MIDDLE EAST AND THE EUROPEAN COMMON MARKET. Charlottesville: University Press of Virginia, 1964. xxii, 152 p. Bibliog. fnn. Illus. Index.

> The effects of the European Common Market on the economies of Middle Eastern states. Considered by sector. Some attention to the influence of politics.

1025 Rondot, Pierre. THE CHANGING PATTERNS OF THE MIDDLE EAST. Translated by Mary Dilke. New York: Frederick A. Praeger, 1959. 221 p. Apps. Index. Maps.

> A long-time student of Middle Eastern affairs reviews and synthesizes the pre-independence and post-World War II experience of the external powers in the Middle East--through the first Soviet arms agreement (1955) and the Suez invasion (1956).

1026 Royal Institute of International Affairs, Information Department. THE WESTERN POWERS AND THE MIDDLE EAST, 1959: A DOCUMENTARY RECORD. Oxford: Oxford University Press for the Royal Institute of International Affairs, 1959. 51 p.

> The second portion relates particularly to Britain and the Arabian Peninsula.

1027 Sachar, Howard M. EUROPE LEAVES THE MIDDLE EAST, 1936-1954. New York: Alfred A. Knopf, 1972. xviii, 687 p. Bibliog. Maps.

> A study of British, French, Italian, German, Russian, and American political involvement in the Middle East. The author sees the objectives of the European powers in the region as ranging from strategic bases and control over oil to their desire to "modernize and liberalize." The history is comprehensive; the coverage given to the competition among these several objectives is not. Almost one-third of the volume deals with the establishment of Israel and the Palestine question.

1028 Sands, William, ed. NEW LOOK AT THE MIDDLE EAST. Washington, D.C.: Middle East Institute, 1957. 84 p.

> The institute's eleventh annual conference. Addresses on topics including the Soviet Union and the United States in the Middle East. Essays by J.C. Hurewitz, Fayez Sayegh, and others.

Regional Issues

1029 _____. TENSIONS IN THE MIDDLE EAST: A SERIES OF ADDRESSES. Washington, D.C.: Middle East Institute, 1956. 67 p.

> The institute's tenth conference on Middle Eastern affairs.

1030 U.S. Congress. House. Committee on Foreign Affairs. THE MIDDLE EAST, 1974: NEW HOPES, NEW CHALLENGES. Hearings before the Subcommittee on the Near East and South Asia, 93d Cong., 2d sess., April 9-June 27, 1974. Washington, D.C.: Government Printing Office, 1974. 202 p. Apps. Illus.

> Testimony on a variety of topics--the United States and the Soviet Union in the Middle East, the oil embargo, and Israeli foreign policy. Mostly nonofficial. Discussion of nuclear reactor exchanges.

1031 U.S. AND SOVIET POLICY IN THE MIDDLE EAST, 1945-56. Edited by John Donovan. New York: Facts on File, 1972. 282 p. Index. Map.

> The book is based upon FACTS ON FILE records and the editor's own materials which he collected as a journalist in the Middle East. The information presented goes beyond U.S. and Soviet policy into domestic political processes in Iran, Egypt, Iraq, and Israel. No references are used, so the volume is largely limited to introductory use.

1032 Williams, Ann. BRITAIN AND FRANCE IN THE MIDDLE EAST AND NORTH AFRICA, 1914-1967. London: Melbourne and Macmillan; New York: St. Martins, 1968. xiv, 194 p. Bibliog. Facsims. Illus. Maps. Plates. Ports.

> An introductory work, based upon secondary material, dealing with the internal aspects of colonial policy more than with strategic affairs. Lengthy bibliography.

1033 Wilmington, Martin W. THE MIDDLE EAST SUPPLY CENTRE. Edited by Lawrence Evans. Albany: State University of New York Press, 1971. 248 p.

> The operation of the supply agency created by the Allies during World War II.

NATIONALISM AND THE COLONIAL EXPERIENCE

1101 Abu-Lughod, Ibrahim. ARAB REDISCOVERY OF EUROPE: A STUDY IN CULTURAL ENCOUNTERS. Princeton Oriental Studies 22. Princeton, N.J.: Princeton University Press, 1964. 188 p. Bibliog.

> The impact of Western European culture on the Arab world and its reactions toward the West--especially French-Egyptian relations.

Regional Issues

1102 Anderson, M.S., ed. THE GREAT POWERS AND THE NEAR EAST, 1774-1923. London: Arnold, 1970. x, 182 p. New York: St. Martins, 1972. viii, 181 p. Bibliography.

    The Crimean War and the latter nineteenth century. Extracts from letters and books of the period. Includes documents. See also No. 1502.

1103 Antonius, George. THE ARAB AWAKENING; THE STORY OF THE ARAB NATIONAL MOVEMENT. 1938. Reprint. New York: Capricorn Books, 1965. 471 p. App. Illus. Index. Map.

    Arab national movements and pan-Arabism from the end of the eighteenth century through the interwar mandate period. Eight major post-World War I documents appended. Few footnotes or references.

1104 al-Bazzaz, Abdul Rahman. ON ARAB NATIONALISM. Translated by Edward Atiyah. London: Embassy of the Republic of Iraq, 1965. 92 p.

    A selection from the writings of a former prime minister of Iraq. Islam and Arab nationalism are linked and regional (Syrian) nationalism disparaged. A few of al-Bazzaz's writings have been published in anthologies.

1105 Bentwich, Norman. THE MANDATES SYSTEM. London and New York: Longmans, Green, 1930. 200 p.

    The mandates in Palestine, Syria, and Iraq by the attorney general in Palestine in the early Mandate period.

1106 Carmichael, Joel. THE SHAPING OF THE ARABS: A STUDY IN ETHNIC IDENTITY. New York: Macmillan, 1967. 407 p. Bibliog. Maps.

    The meaning of Arab nationalism from the rise of Islam and the Arab empires to the turn of this century. Secondary sources.

1107 Cumming, Henry H. FRANCO-BRITISH RIVALRY IN THE POST-WAR NEAR EAST; THE DECLINE OF FRENCH INFLUENCE. London and New York: Oxford University Press, 1938. 229 p. Bibliog. Index. Fold. map.

    World War I and the Middle Eastern settlement against the European background--primarily British-French competition. Short bibliography on European issues.

1108 Dawn, C. Ernest. FROM OTTOMANISM TO ARABISM, ESSAYS ON THE ORIGINS OF ARAB NATIONALISM. Urbana, Chicago, and London: Bibliog. refs.

    The development of Ottomanism, nationalism, and modernization as seen through the works of Arab intellectuals and emerging from European military victories over the Ottoman Empire.

Regional Issues

1109 Fanon, Frantz. TOWARD THE AFRICAN REVOLUTION. Translated by Hoakon Chevalier. Hammondsworth, Eng.: Penguin, Pelican Books, 1970. 207 p.

> The psychological repercussions of colonialism.

1110 Gabrielli, Francesco. THE ARAB REVIVAL. New York: Random House, 1961. 178 p. Illus.

> Nationalism and democracy in the Arab states and relations with the Soviet Union.

1111 Gallagher, Charles F. THE UNITED STATES AND NORTH AFRICA: MOROCCO, ALGERIA, AND TUNISIA. The American Foreign Policy Library. Cambridge, Mass.: Harvard University Press, 1963. xii, 275 p. Bibliog. Maps.

> A study of the growth of the independence movements in Morocco, Algeria, and Tunisia. Little on U.S.-North African relations.

1112 Glubb, [Sir] John Bagot. BRITAIN AND THE ARABS: A STUDY OF FIFTY YEARS, 1908-1958. London: Hodder and Stoughton, 1959. 496 p. Apps. Index. Maps.

> Excellent collection of maps which illustrate the former commander of the Arab Legion's argument that British policy vacillated while Arab nationalism grew. Overview of Iraqi, Syrian, Jordanian, and Egyptian politics.

1113 Hahn, Lorna. NORTH AFRICA: NATIONALISM TO NATIONHOOD. Washington, D.C.: Public Affairs Press, 1960. 264 p. Bibliog.

> A sketchy background of the independence movements in Tunisia, Morocco, and Algeria.

1114 Haim, Sylvia G. ARAB NATIONALISM, AN ANTHOLOGY. Berkeley and Los Angeles: University of California Press, 1962. 255 p. Bibliog.

> Arab leaders' and writers' statements on Arab nationalism. A varied collection on Islamic and Arab nationalism.

1115 Hocking, William Ernest. THE SPIRIT OF WORLD POLITICS, WITH SPECIAL STUDIES OF THE NEAR EAST. New York: Macmillan, 1932. xiv, 571 p.

> Focuses upon Egypt, Syria, and Palestine; nationalism and imperialism.

1116 Kedourie, Elie. THE CHATHAM HOUSE VERSION AND OTHER MIDDLE-EASTERN STUDIES. New York: Praeger, 1970. 488 p. App. Bibliog.

Index.

Revised, previously published scholarly essays focusing on the mandate system and Arab nationalism. The bibliography is extensive and refers to Arabic, English, and French language sources.

1117 Kelly, George Armstrong. LOST SOLDIERS: THE FRENCH ARMY AND EMPIRE IN CRISIS, 1947-1962. Cambridge, Mass.: M.I.T. Press, 1965. x, 404 p. Bibliog.

French strategy in Algeria (and Indo-China) and its impact on the army's loyalties. Periodical sources. Also cited in No. 3605.

1118 Kohn, Hans. WESTERN CIVILIZATION IN THE NEAR EAST. New York: Columbia University Press, 1936. 329 p. Bibliog. Illus. Index.

Nationalism and colonialism in the 1920s and '30s, with little documentation. A different perspective of French and British interests in the region.

1119 Ling, Dwight L. TUNISIA, FROM PROTECTORATE TO REPUBLIC. Indiana University International Studies. Bloomington: Indiana University Press, 1967. xi, 273 p. Bibliog. Bibliog. ref. Illus. Map. Chron. Index.

Tunisia's protectorate history. A variety of sources. Also cited in No. 3301.

1120 Mansfield, Peter. THE BRITISH IN EGYPT. New York: Holt, Rinehart & Winston, 1972 [c1971]. xiv, 351 p. 8 plates. Bibliog. Illus. Index. Ports.

Documents seventy years of British presence in Egypt, from the occupation to the Suez invasion. Traces the major events in Egypt's struggle for independence.

1121 Marlowe, John. ARAB NATIONALISM AND BRITISH IMPERIALISM: A STUDY IN POWER POLITICS. London: Cresset Press, 1961. 236 p. Bibliog. Index.

Covers Arab nationalism in the nineteenth century, independence movements, and British unification strategies. Discusses the Eisenhower Doctrine and the post-Suez period.

1122 _____. CROMER IN EGYPT. New York: Praeger, 1971. xi, 332 p. Bibliog. Illus. Index. Maps.

A portrait of the British Consul-General in Egypt from 1883-1907, based upon European language sources, especially British and French documents. Pseudonymous, Marlowe's book is a balanced view of Cromer's personality, not a history of the period.

Regional Issues

1123 Morris, James. ISLAM INFLAMED: A MIDDLE EAST PICTURE. New York: Pantheon, 1957. 326 p. Illus. Index.

    An unsympathetic, journalistic picture of Arab nationalism and its provocation (author's term) of the 1956 war.

1124 Nevakivi, Jukka. BRITAIN, FRANCE AND THE ARAB MIDDLE EAST 1914-1920. London: University of London, Athlone Press (distr. Oxford University Press, New York), 1969. 284 p. Bibliog. Index. Maps.

    A summary record of the beginning of the Mandate system in the Middle East focusing upon conflicts within British circles and between Britain and France. Bibliography includes notes on unpublished primary sources.

1125 Nuseibeh, Hazem Zaki. THE IDEAS OF ARAB NATIONALISM. Ithaca, N.Y.: Cornell University Press, 1956. 227 p. Index.

    An intellectual history of Arab nationalism and political thought. Discusses Islam, European expansionism, pan-Turanism, and contemporary political trends in this connection. Critical.

1126 Royal Institute of International Affairs. Information Department. GREAT BRITAIN AND EGYPT, 1914-51. Information Papers, 14. London and New York: Oxford University Press for the Institute, 1952. 216 p. Bibliog. Maps.

    Largely chronological, using official British sources.

1127 Saleh, Zaki. BRITAIN AND MESOPOTAMIA (IRAQ TO 1914); A STUDY IN BRITISH FOREIGN AFFAIRS. Rev. ed. Baghdad: al-Ma'aref Press, 1966. 350 p.

    European rivalries in Iraq.

1128 al-Sayyid, Afaf Lutfi. EGYPT AND CROMER; A STUDY IN ANGLO-EGYPTIAN RELATIONS. New York: Praeger, 1969 [c.1968]. xiii, 236 p. Bibliog. Illus. Ports.

    A thoroughly documented analysis of British proconsul Cromer's policies and their effect upon Egyptian nationalism.

1129 Sharabi, Hisham. ARAB INTELLECTUALS AND THE WEST: THE FORMATIVE YEARS, 1875-1914. Baltimore and London: Johns Hopkins Press in cooperation with the Middle East Institute, 1970. x, 139 p. Bibliog. refs.

    Analysis of a period of intellectual ferment from a sociology of knowledge approach. Political ideologies--Islamism, Ottomanism, and Nationalism. The conclusion is concerned with Arab modernization, traditionalism, and Western imperialism.

Regional Issues

1130 _____. NATIONALISM AND REVOLUTION IN THE ARAB WORLD, THE MIDDLE EAST AND NORTH AFRICA. New York: Van Nostrand Reinhold, 1966. ix, 176 p. Paper. Bibliog. notes.

> Survey of Arab history, European domination, and post-independence domestic political structures and ideologies in the Arab states. Constitutional documents and official proclamations appended.

1131 Sorensen, Reginald. ADEN, THE PROTECTORATES AND THE YEMEN. Fabian Tract 332. London: Fabian Society, International and Commonwealth Bureau, 1961. 31 p. Paper. Bibliog. Illus.

> A brief review of British colonial policy and social and economic conditions in the Protectorates.

1132 Steiner, Morris Jacob. INSIDE PAN-ARABIA. Chicago: Packard, 1947. xv, 237 p. Bibliog. Index.

> Popularly written survey of the colonial interwar period and World War II--European policies and Arab nationalism. English language bibliography; no documentation.

1133 Tutsch, Hans E. FACETS OF ARAB NATIONALISM. Detroit: Wayne State University Press, 1965. 157 p. Bibliog. Index.

> An introduction to the various themes in Arab nationalism including unification in North Africa and the Fertile Crescent. Develops the theme that communism is appealing where religion has "lost its hold." Helpful bibliography.

1134 Zeine, Zeine N. THE EMERGENCE OF ARAB NATIONALISM; WITH A BACKGROUND STUDY OF ARAB-TURKISH RELATIONS IN THE NEAR EAST. 3d ed. Delmar, N.Y.: Caravan, 1973. viii, 192 p. Apps. Bibliog. Index.

> Arab nationalist or independence movements at the turn of the century and through World War I. Examines themes of secular and Islamic thought in the context of diplomatic events. Thoroughly documented from primary and secondary sources. First published in 1958 under the title ARAB-TURKISH RELATIONS AND THE EMERGENCE OF ARAB NATIONALISM.

ARAB STATE POLITICS

1201 Adams, Michael. CHAOS OR REBIRTH: THE ARAB OUTLOOK. London: BBC Publications, 1968. x, 170 p. Maps.

> Post-1967 war view of the Arab states by a sympathetic British correspondent.

Regional Issues

1202 Afifi, Mohamed El-Hadi. THE ARABS AND THE UNITED NATIONS. London: Longmans, Green, 1964. xii, 202 p.

    The United Nations in the Arab Middle East and the Arab states in the United Nations. Covers United Nations action on self-determination in Palestine, Libya, Morocco, Tunisia, and Algeria, as well as economic and social assistance programs in the area. Relates the Arab nationalist movement to the United Nations Charter.

1203 Cremeans, Charles D. THE ARABS AND THE WORLD; NASSER'S ARAB NATIONALIST POLICY. New York and London: Frederick A. Praeger for the Council on Foreign Relations, 1963. xi, 338 p. Bibliog. Illus. Index.

    A beginning theory of the foreign policy of Arab nationalism. Arab states in the postcolonial context, focusing upon the late President Nasser's positive neutralism and U.S. policy alternatives. Primary and secondary European and Arabic language sources.

1204 Dib, G. Moussa. THE ARAB BLOC IN THE UNITED NATIONS. Amsterdam: Djambatan, 1956. 128 p. Paper. Bibliog. Index.

    Middle-Eastern and non-Middle-Eastern issues raised in the United Nations and the voting and diplomatic responses of regional states. No aggregated voting data. Based primarily upon UN documents; short bibliography.

1205 Faris, Nabih Amin, and Husayn, Mohammed Tawfik. THE CRESCENT IN CRISIS: AN INTERPRETIVE STUDY OF THE MODERN ARAB WORLD. Lawrence: University of Kansas Press, 1955. 191 p. Bibliog. fnn.. Index. Map.

    Official and secondary English and Arabic language sources. Interpretation of Arab state domestic and international politics focusing upon Israel and European colonialism.

1206 Holt, P.M. EGYPT AND THE FERTILE CRESCENT, 1516-1922: A POLITICAL HISTORY. Ithaca, N.Y.: Cornell University Press, 1966. 337 p. Apps. Bibliog. Index.

    Background to Egyptian-Syrian-Iraqi relations focusing upon the nineteenth century--political currents within the Ottoman Empire and growing European dominance.

1207 Hurewitz, Jacob Coleman. UNITY AND DISUNITY IN THE MIDDLE EAST. International Conciliation 481. New York: Carnegie Endowment for International Peace, May 1952. Pp. 197-260.

    Summary introduction to social and political impediments to integration with survey of great power rivalry.

Regional Issues

1208 Kadi, Leila S. ARAB SUMMIT CONFERENCES AND THE PALESTINE PROBLEM (1936-1950), (1964-1966). Palestine Books, 4. Beirut Research Center, Lebanon: Palestine Liberation Organization, 1966. 221 p. Bibliog.

> The author has integrated the conference proceedings with contemporary events, including the activities of Palestinian leaders. Short bibliography of Arabic and English language titles; mainly newspaper and document sources.

1209 Kerr, Malcolm [H.]. THE ARAB COLD WAR: GAMAL ABD AL-NASIR AND HIS RIVALS, 1958-1970. 3d ed. London and New York: Oxford University Press for the Royal Institute of International Affairs, 1971. 166 p. Paper. Bibliog. Index.

> Interpretive analysis of the relations among Arab states--particularly Egypt, Syria, and Iraq. Based upon Arabic press reports as well as secondary sources; short bibliography. Unique coverage of 1963 Cairo unification negotiations.

1210 _____. REGIONAL ARAB POLITICS AND CONFLICT WITH ISRAEL. RM-5966-FF. Santa Maria, Calif.: Rand Corporation, 1969. 50 p.

> The section on Arab state relations with Israel describes what the author views as the Arab states' lack of initiative in either military preparedness or in diplomacy. Also cited in No. 4047.

1211 Khalil, Muhammad, ed. THE ARAB STATES AND THE ARAB LEAGUE, A DOCUMENTARY RECORD. 2 vols. Beirut: Khayats, 1962. 705, 1,019 p.

> Volume 1 documents constitutional developments in Middle-East states; volume 2, inter-Arab state politics and relations with external powers. Almost six hundred documents from World War I on.

1212 Kirk, George E[den]. CONTEMPORARY ARAB POLITICS: A CONCISE HISTORY. New York: Praeger, 1961. 231 p.

> A critique of Arab nationalism since World War II.

1213 Koury, Enver [M.]. THE SUPER-POWERS AND THE BALANCE OF POWER IN THE ARAB WORLD. Beirut: Catholic Press, 1970. 208 p. Bibliog. refs. Map.

> Arab state international politics. Looks at Middle East politics from an unaccustomed regional perspective. The author urges policymakers in the United States to overcome cold war perspectives which are irrelevant to the independent Arab world and to be receptive to new ideas, such as Arab state-European Common Market cooperation.

Regional Issues

1214 MacDonald, Robert W. THE LEAGUE OF ARAB STATES; A STUDY IN THE DYNAMICS OF REGIONAL ORGANIZATION. Princeton, N.J.: Princeton University Press, 1965. xiii, 407 p. Bibliog. Illus.

Surveys of Arab League activities during its first two decades of existence. The author argues that the League has been hindered by several major cleavages in the Arab world--the Egyptian-Iraqi competition, the Sunni-Shi'ite conflict and those differences arising from the Arab-Israeli conflict. The League's functional activities have centered primarily upon independent professional interest groups rather than the League's own agencies.

1215 Musrey, Alfred G. AN ARAB COMMON MARKET: A STUDY IN INTER-ARAB TRADE RELATIONS, 1920-67. Special Studies. New York: Frederick A. Praeger, 1969. xii, 274 p. Apps. Bibliog. Illus.

Analysis of past performance and future potential in regional economic cooperation among the Arab states of the Middle East. Trade data and agreements appended; primary and secondary sources in Arabic and European languages.

1216 Proctor, Jesse Harris, ed. ISLAM AND INTERNATIONAL RELATIONS. New York: Praeger, 1965. 221 p. Bibliog. ref. Map.

Papers originally presented at a conference at Duke University, June 10-13, 1963. Political and social characteristics of Islam, nationalism, communism, and the relations among Arab and African states.

1217 Rikabi-Succari, Elizabeth Hart. REGIONAL SYSTEM AND POLITICAL DEVELOPMENT IN THE ARAB WORLD. New Series, 88. Louvain, Belgium: Universite Catholique de Louvain, 1971. 219 p. Bibliog.

Reviews inter-Arab politics and unification attempts from the standpoint of the impact of internal politics and political development. Based upon secondary sources.

1218 Saab, Hassan. THE ARAB FEDERALISTS OF THE OTTOMAN EMPIRE. Amsterdam: Djambatan, 1958. xii, 322 p. Apps. Bibliog.

Arab federal movements in Arab Asia and Egypt from medieval times to the First World War. Includes federalists' views of their strategic interests and religious ideology. Extensively documented, includes a lengthy bibliography.

1219 Sayegh, Fayez Abdullah. ARAB UNITY: HOPE AND FULFILLMENT. New York: Devin-Adair, 1958. 272 p. Apps.

The growth of Arab nationalism from the nineteenth century and proposals for pan-Arab unions by a Palestinian scholar and member of the Palestine National Council. Documents related to unification are appended.

Regional Issues

1220 _____, ed. THE DYNAMICS OF NEUTRALISM IN THE ARAB WORLD: A SYMPOSIUM. San Francisco: Chandler for the Council on International Perspectives, 1964. xiv, 275 p. Bibliog. fnn. Index.

>Original essays by Arab scholars on the theory of Arab neutralism and neutralism in practice vis-a-vis the Western powers. Majority of references are to works on U.S. foreign policy rather than to Arab sources.

1221 Seale, Patrick. THE STRUGGLE FOR SYRIA: A STUDY OF POST-WAR ARAB POLITICS, 1945-1958. New York and London: Oxford University Press, 1965. Bibliog. Illus. Maps. Ports.

>The Iraqi-Egyptian rivalry in Syria which created the background to the formation of the United Arab Republic in 1958. The author's perspective is that of an involved observer, sympathetic to the Ba'th Party leadership. Little documentation.

1222 Stephens, Robert H. THE ARABS' NEW FRONTIERS. London: Temple Smith, 1973. 256 p.

>The Kuwait Fund for Arab Economic Development and contemporary development problems.

THE INDIAN OCEAN AND PERSIAN/ARAB GULF

1301 Abir, Mordechai. OIL, POWER AND POLITICS: CONFLICT IN ARABIA, THE RED SEA AND THE GULF. London: Frank Cass; Portland, Oreg.: International Scholarly Book Services, 1974. xiii, 221 p. Maps.

>Nationalism and Soviet and Chinese involvement in southern Arabia and the Horn of Africa. Based upon press reviews, including Arabic, with extensive documentation. Little development of Arab perspectives.

1302 Adamiyat, Fereydun. BAHREIN ISLANDS: A LEGAL AND DIPLOMATIC STUDY OF THE BRITISH-IRANIAN CONTROVERSY. New York: Frederick A. Praeger, 1955. x, 268 p. Bibliog.

>The legal and political basis for Iran's claim to sovereignty over Bahrain focusing on the nineteenth-century controversy with Britain and the case at the league and the United Nations. Well-documented background for British policies in the Gulf by an Iranian historian.

1303 Adie, W.A.C. OIL, POLITICS, AND SEAPOWER: THE INDIAN OCEAN VORTEX. Strategy Papers, 4. New York: Crane, Russack for the National Straregy Information Center, 1975. 97 p. Map.

>Brief survey of the interests of external powers and the littoral states in the Indian Ocean region. Focuses on a criticism of

Regional Issues

Australian Labor Party policy.

1304 THE ARABIAN PENINSULA: SOCIETY AND POLITICS. Edited by Derek Hopwood. Studies on Modern Asia and Africa. Totawa, N.J.: Rowman and Littlefield; London: George Allen and Unwin, 1972. 320 p. Bibliog. ref. Maps.

Fourteen papers from a seminar and conference held jointly by the University of London Centre of Middle Eastern Studies and the Oxford University Middle East Centre. "The Arabian Peninsula in Arab and Power Politics" (inter-Arab rivalries), British and Iranian interests in the Persian Gulf, and the relationship between the oil companies and the producer states (especially Saudi Arabia and Kuwait) provide a focus on the Arab Gulf states. A short bibliographical essay by Hopwood has been superseded by his book-length bibliography. Also cited in No. 3105.

1305 al-Bahama, Husain M. THE LEGAL STATUS OF THE ARABIAN GULF STATES. Manchester, Eng.: Manchester University Press, 1968. THE ARABIAN GULF STATES: THEIR LEGAL AND POLITICAL STATUS AND THEIR INTERNATIONAL PROBLEMS. 2d ed. Beirut: Librairie du Liban, 1973. 351 p. Apps.

Internal and external relations from a legal viewpoint. Boundary agreements and other treaties appended.

1306 Becker, Abraham S. OIL AND THE PERSIAN GULF IN SOVIET POLICY IN THE 1970'S. Papers. Santa Monica, Calif.: Rand Corporation, 1972. 49 p. Refs.

Soviet interests in the Gulf region in the future, focusing on oil import potential.

1307 Burrell, Robert Michael. THE PERSIAN GULF. Washington Papers, 1. New York: Library Press, 1972. 81 p. Paper. Map.

Descriptive survey of local politics, oil, and the superpowers. No references.

1308 Burrell, Robert Michael, and Cottrell, Alvin J. IRAN, THE ARABIAN PENINSULA, AND THE INDIAN OCEAN. Strategy Papers, 14. New York: National Strategy Information Center, 1972. 46 p. Bibliog.

Oil, Gulf State politics, the U.S.-USSR naval rivalry, Iran's foreign policy.

1309 Curzon, George Nathaniel. PERSIA AND THE PERSIAN QUESTION. 2 vols. London and New York: Longmans, Green & Co., 1892.

A view of the Persian Gulf and Britain's strategic needs by the former Governor of India.

Regional Issues

1310 "Focus on Iran, Ethiopia and the Indian Ocean." ORBIS 8 (Winter 1975): entire issue.

   Includes five articles on international politics in the Indian Ocean region--Iranian foreign policy, Iran and Israel, Ethiopia, international politics in the Indian Ocean, and Soviet-U.S. naval competition in the Indian Ocean.

1311 Foroughy, Abbas. THE BAHREIN ISLANDS, 750-1951; A CONTRIBUTION TO THE STUDY OF POWER POLITICS IN THE PERSIAN GULF, AN HISTORICAL, ECONOMIC AND GEOGRAPHICAL SURVEY. New York: Verry, Fisher, 1951. 128 p. Apps. Bibliog. Illus. Map. Plates.

   Surveys society and economy in Bahrein and Gulf power politics with little documentation in text, but fairly extensive historical bibliography.

1312 THE GULF: IMPLICATIONS OF BRITISH WITHDRAWAL. Special Report Series, 8. Washington, D.C.: Center for Strategic and International Studies, Georgetown University, 1969. 110 p. Paper. Fold. map.

   Regional politics from perspective of U.S.-Soviet competition. No references.

1313 Hawley, Donald. THE TRUCIAL STATES. London: George Allen and Unwin, 1970; New York: Twayne Publishers, 1971, [c1970]. 379 p. Apps. Bibliog. Maps.

   History of British involvement in the Persian Gulf and background to Saudi Arabian-Trucial states boundary disputes. Discusses oil concessions, seabed rights, and political competition among the members of the United Arab Emirates (which was not in existence when the book was written).

1314 Hay, Rupert. THE PERSIAN GULF STATES. Washington, D.C.: Middle East Institute, 1959. 160 p. Illus. Index.

   Description of social, economic, and political conditions in the Arab littoral states.

1315 Hurewitz, Jacob C[oleman]. THE PERSIAN GULF: PROSPECTS FOR STABILITY. Headline Series 220. New York: Foreign Policy Association, 1974. 63 p. Bibliog. Illus. Maps.

   Reviews the diplomatic history of the region and examines Soviet and American policies. Little attention is given to the regional states' foreign policies.

1316 THE INDIAN OCEAN: ITS POLITICAL, ECONOMIC, AND MILITARY IMPORTANCE. Edited by Alvin J. Cottrell and Robert M[ichael]. Burrell. Special Studies Series. New York: Praeger for the Center for Strategic

Regional Issues

and International Studies, Georgetown University, 1972. xxiv, 457 p. Bibliog. refs. Illus. Index. Map.

Twenty-three papers from a 1971 conference--geopolitics, economic issues, foreign policies of littoral states, and naval strategy.

1317 Kaushik, Devendra. THE INDIAN OCEAN: TOWARDS A PEACE ZONE. New Delhi: Vikas, 1972. 225 p. Apps. Bibliog. Index. Maps.

The superpowers and India in the Indian Ocean region, including a chapter on the Persian Gulf. Extensive documentation and bibliography. Records of Indian public debates over that country's strategic interests appended.

1318 Koury, Enver M. OIL AND GEOPOLITICS IN THE PERSIAN GULF AREA: A CENTER FOR POWER. Beirut: Catholic Press, 1973.

1319 Kumar, Ravinder. INDIA AND THE PERSIAN GULF REGION, 1858-1907. New York: Asia Publishing House, 1965. 259 p. Bibliog.

Focuses upon a time period during which Iran (Persia), Britain, and Russia were vying for influence in the Persian Gulf. Discusses naval competition and Iran's claim to sovereignty over Bahrain. Thoroughly documented.

1320 Marlowe, John. THE PERSIAN GULF IN THE TWENTIETH CENTURY. New York: Praeger, 1962. 280 p. Bibliog. Illus.

Focuses on oil, regional development, and competition between United States and Britain for influence in the area.

1321 Millar, T[homas].B. THE INDIAN AND PACIFIC OCEANS: SOME STRATEGIC CONSIDERATIONS. Adelphi Papers, 57. London: Institute for Strategic Studies, 1969. 20 p. Illus. Map.

The superpowers in the Western Pacific and Indian Oceans in light of British withdrawal. Information on mutual defense treaties, oil agreements.

1322 Monroe, Elizabeth. THE CHANGING BALANCE OF POWER IN THE PERSIAN GULF. Center for Mediterranean Studies, Rome, June 26 to July 1, 1972. New York: American Universities Field Staff, 1972. 79 p. Bibliog. Map.

Report from an international seminar covering internal development problems of Gulf states and the international significance of this region to the West.

Regional Issues

1323 THE PERSIAN GULF. By Bernard Reich et al. McLean, Va.: Research Analysis Corporation for the Department of the Army, 1971. 94 p.

Briefly summarizes the probable consequences of the 1971 British withdrawal from the Gulf.

1324 Ramazani, Rouhollah K. THE PERSIAN GULF; IRAN'S ROLE. Charlottesville: University Press of Virginia, 1972. xiv, 157 p. Apps. Bibliog. Illus. Index. Maps.

Historical and contemporary analysis of the Gulf in Iran's foreign policy--relations with littoral Arab states and oil issues. English, Persian, and Arabic language sources and documentation; military capability and oil data; (five) documents and statements appended.

1325 Sadik, Mohammad T., and Snavely, William P. BAHRAIN, OATAR AND THE UNITED ARAB EMIRATES: COLONIAL PAST, PRESENT PROBLEMS AND FUTURE PROSPECTS. Lexington, Mass.: D.C. Heath, 1972. xxii, 255 p. Bibliog. Illus.

Internal development and regional issues. Prospects for the federation.

1326 Singh, K. Rajendra. POLITICS OF THE INDIAN OCEAN. New Delhi, India: Ekta Press; Columbia, Mo.: South Asia Books, 1974. 252 p. Apps. Bibliog. Map.

Superpower military competition in the Indian Ocean from 1945 (military data appended) and regional conflicts among the littoral states. Extensive bibliography; non-Western perspective.

1327 U.S. Congress. House. Committee on Foreign Affairs. THE INDIAN OCEAN: POLITICAL AND STRATEGIC FUTURE. Hearings before the Subcommittee on National Security Policy and Scientific Developments, 92d Cong., 1st sess., July 20-28, 1971. Washington, D.C.: Government Printing Office, 1971. 242 p. Bibliog. ref. Index.

Ten statements regarding Indian Ocean littoral states' and external powers' strategic interests and military capacities. Appended statements, articles, and documents with references and useful index.

1328 _____. NEW PERSPECTIVES ON THE PERSIAN GULF. Hearings before the Subcommittee on the Near East and South Asia, 93d Cong., 1st sess., June 6-November 28, 1973. Washington, D.C.: Government Printing Office, 1973. 227 p. Apps. Figures.

Official and academic testimony covering regional politics,

Regional Issues

U.S. policy, oil and arms transfers, and CENTO activities. Articles on Iran in the Gulf and the Dhofar war appended; military and oil data included.

1329 _____. PROPOSED EXPANSION OF U.S. MILITARY FACILITIES IN THE INDIAN OCEAN. Hearings before the subcommittee on the Near East and South Asia, 93d Cong., 2d sess., February 21-March 20, 1974. Washington, D.C.: Government Printing Office, 1974. 219 p. Illus. Maps.

Eight statements, seven by government officials, on the strategic reasons for and material detail of the development of Diego Garcia. No index, military detail appended.

NORTH AFRICA

1401 Amin, Samir. THE MAGHREB IN THE MODERN WORLD: ALGERIA, TUNISIA, MOROCCO. Translated by Michael Perl. Harmondsworth, Eng. and Baltimore, Md.: Penguin, 1970. 256 p. Bibliog. Index. Maps.

French rule, economic and social change, and some attention to foreign relations.

1402 Berque, Jacques. FRENCH NORTH AFRICA: THE MAGHREB BETWEEN TWO WORLD WARS. Translated by Jean Stewart. New York: Praeger, 1967. 422 p.

First published in France in 1962. Basic background to the area.

1403 Brace, Richard M. MOROCCO, ALGERIA, TUNISIA. Englewood Cliffs, N.J.: Prentice-Hall, 1964. 184 p. Bibliog. Index. Maps.

Overview of political change in the three countries which are developing unique national cultures in the wake of the declining importance of Islam. Little possibility seen for a Maghreb federation.

1404 Burrell, Robert M[ichael]., and Cottrell, Alvin J. POLITICS, OIL, AND THE WESTERN MEDITERRANEAN. Washington Papers, 7. Beverly Hills, Calif.: Sage Publications for the Center for Strategic and International Studies, Georgetown University, 1973. 80 p. Paper. Illus. Maps.

U.S.-USSR military and economic competition in the region, with brief attention to the littoral states. Relates the demand for North African oil to the foreign policies of consumer states.

1405 Cottrell, Alvin [J.], and Theberge, J., eds. THE WESTERN MEDITERRANEAN: ITS POLITICAL, ECONOMIC AND STRATEGIC IMPORTANCE. Special

Regional Issues

Studies. New York: Praeger, in cooperation with Georgetown University, Center for Strategic and International Studies, 1974. 256 p.

Fifteen papers from a 1972 conference on the Western Mediterranean covering oil economics, U.S. and USSR policies and the Maghreb. Little examination of basic policy constraints or alternatives, or of the foreign policies of the North African states themselves, beyond economic cooperation with the European Community.

1406 EUROPE AND THE MAGHREB. By C. Gasteyger et al. Atlantic Papers, 1. Paris: Atlantic Institute, 1972. 72 p.

Five brief sections on topics including North African integration and Europe and North Africa.

1407 Hermassi, Elbak. LEADERSHIP AND NATIONAL DEVELOPMENT IN NORTH AFRICA: A COMPARATIVE STUDY. Berkeley: University of California Press, 1973 [c1972]. xi, 241 p. Bibliog.

Political leadership and institutions in precolonial, colonial, and postcolonial periods in Morocco, Algeria, Tunisia.

1408 Liska, George. THE GREATER MAGHREB: FROM INDEPENDENCE TO UNITY? Washington, D.C.: Washington Center of Foreign Policy Research, 1963. 75 p. Bibliog.

Briefly reviews the prospects for unity.

1409 Moore, Clement H. POLITICS IN NORTH AFRICA: ALGERIA, MOROCCO AND TUNISIA. Boston: Little, Brown, 1970. xix, 360 p. Bibliog. ref.

Summarizes the colonial period and contemporary political development. Explores the possibility of Maghreb unity.

1410 Robanna, Abderrahman. THE PROSPECTS FOR AN ECONOMIC COMMUNITY IN NORTH AFRICA: MANAGING ECONOMIC INTEGRATION IN THE MAGHREB STATES. Special Studies. New York: Praeger, 1973. xv, 206 p. Bibliog. Map.

The theory and practice of economic integration in North Africa.

1411 Touval, Saadia. THE BOUNDARY POLITICS OF INDEPENDENT AFRICA. Cambridge, Mass.: Harvard University Press, 1972. xii, 334 p. Bibliog. ref.

1412 U.S. Congress. House. Committee on Foreign Affairs. THE STATES OF NORTH AFRICA IN THE 1970'S. Joint hearings before the Subcommittee on Africa and the Subcommittee on the Near East, July 18-August 2, 1972. Washington, D.C.: Government Printing Office, 1972. 244 p.

Regional Issues

DOCUMENTS

1501 Agwani, Mohammed S[hafi]. THE LEBANESE CRISIS, 1958; A DOCU-
MENTARY STUDY. New York: Asia Publishing House, 1965. xiv,
407 p. Bibliog. Index.

> Documents, chronologically ordered, are mainly addresses by
> and correspondence among government leaders. Also includes
> U.N. resolutions and reports.

1502 Anderson, M.S., ed. THE GREAT POWERS AND THE NEAR EAST, 1774-
1923. London: Arnold, 1970. x, 182 p. New York: St. Martins, 1971.
viii, 181 p. Bibliography.

> Annotated collection of documents from the nineteenth and
> early twentieth centuries. Highly selective. See also No.
> 1102.

1503 Arab Republic of Egypt. Ministry of Information. ARAB POLITICAL
ENCYCLOPEDIA: DOCUMENTS AND NOTES. Cairo: Documentation
Research Centre, 1952-66.

> An irregular series in which political and economic documents
> were published. Intended to be monthly.

1504 DOCUMENTS ON INTERNATIONAL AFFAIRS, 1962. Selected and edited
by D.C. Watt et al. London and New York: Oxford University Press
for the Royal Institute of International Affairs, 1971.

> The most recent volume of a series which began in 1928 and
> which has been published irregularly since then. Supplements
> the Royal Institute of International Affairs' SURVEY.

1505 Hurewitz, Jacob C[oleman]., comp. DIPLOMACY IN THE NEAR AND
MIDDLE EAST: A DOCUMENTARY RECORD. Vol. 1, 1535-1914; Vol. II,
1914-1956. Princeton, N.J.: Van Nostrand, 1956. Reprint. New
York: Octagon, 1972. 290, 427 p.

> Over 200 documents from the Middle Ages, through the Ottoman
> empire to the cold war. Includes landmark petroleum agreements.
> Chronologically organized.

1506 Keesing's Research Report. TREATIES AND ALLIANCES OF THE WORLD:
A SURVEY OF INTERNATIONAL TREATIES IN FORCE AND COMMUNI-
TIES OF STATES. Bristol, Eng.: Keesing's Publications; New York:
Scribner's, 1968. 158 p. Illus. Index. Maps.

> Classified by region and time period. Coverage of Middle
> East minimal; includes Arab League, CENTO, and Constanti-
> nople Convention documents, and general Bandung and Afro-
> Asian documents.

Regional Issues

1507 Permanent Organization for Afro-Asian People's Solidarity. Permanent Secretariat. DOCUMENTS OF THE Xth EXECUTIVE COMMITTEE SESSION OF THE AFRO-ASIAN PEOPLES' SOLIDARITY ORGANIZATION, DAMASCUS SYRIA, 23-24 JUNE 1971. Cairo: Permanent Secretariat, 1971. 202 p.

Statements, reports, and resolutions especially concerning Palestine, Korea, and Indo-China. Earlier conference proceedings available.

Chapter 3
THE FOREIGN POLICIES OF MIDDLE EASTERN STATES

COUNTRY SURVEYS AND BACKGROUND

Until there are more studies on the foreign policies of Middle Eastern states, country surveys which emphasize domestic politics will continue to be an important source of information for initial research. Domestic political studies are also important because by stressing the rapidity of political changes and the recentness of independence in the Middle East, they indicate the influence of internal politics on international orientations.

The more recent surveys differ from those of the 1950s and 60s which focused on diplomatic history. The later volumes reflect the development of a conceptual framework of comparative politics which is relatively new. Each approach is useful. The diplomatic histories portray patterns of international involvement. The comparative studies offer insight into foreign policy constraints and, less often, decision-making processes.

In addition to the Hammond and Alexander volume [1010], several exceptional surveys are: al-Marayati, THE MIDDLE EAST: ITS GOVERNMENTS AND POLITICS [2007]; Sharabi's GOVERNMENT AND POLITICS OF THE MIDDLE EAST IN THE TWENTIETH CENTURY [2009]; and Hurewitz's MIDDLE EAST POLITICS [2006]. Hurewitz's approach is essentially chronological rather than analytic, but includes many military references. Sharabi offers a less Western perspective. And, al-Marayati offers outstanding chapter authors, a good set of bibliographies, and often a regional outlook.

The overlap between domestic and international politics expresses itself in many ways. The intervention of the military in civilian government in most of the Middle Eastern states influences decision-making patterns as well as military performance. Haddad's REVOLUTIONS AND MILITARY RULE IN THE MIDDLE EAST [2004] is a thorough treatment of the states covered. Be'eri (ARMY OFFICERS IN ARAB POLITICS AND SOCIETY [2002]) concentrates on the army as an instrument of social change in three countries. The extensive social background information for army officers which he presents also could be used for other types of studies.

Foreign Policies of Middle Eastern States

EGYPT

The constraints which internal issues placed upon President Nasser's foreign policy are the chief focus of Copeland's THE GAME OF NATIONS [2303]. Copeland's book is an unusual gaming analysis of Egypt's reactions to the United States's cold war perspectives and to the Arab world. Dekmejian [2304] and Little [2309] give more information about Egypt in their respective volumes than does Copeland. Little does not cover the last years of Nasser's regime but does treat foreign policy problems in more detail.

Egypt was more involved in African politics, relative to the Middle East, during the early years of Nasser's presidency. Unity between Sudan and Egypt was a continuing issue during British rule and after independence (Baddour, SUDANESE-EGYPTIAN RELATIONS [2301]). A later book by Ismael (THE U.A.R. IN AFRICA [2307]) looks beyond the federation potential to inter-African relations and to Egypt's involvement in the Organization of African Unity, which the late president described as one of Egypt's "circles of influence." Mohammed Heikal's THE CAIRO DOCUMENTS [2306] is one of the few English-language discussions of Egyptian foreign policy written by an Egyptian, who was, incidentally, a strong supporter of Nasser. Heikal's book in conjunction with either the Wheelock or Wynn biographies of Nasser would provide basic coverage of one of the most active neutralist leaders in the Third World.

THE FERTILE CRESCENT

Despite the centrality of the Fertile Crescent to Middle Eastern politics throughout history, there is no current analysis of Iraq's foreign relations or of Syria's, past or present. Al-Marayati's A DIPLOMATIC HISTORY OF MODERN IRAQ [2506] looks at Iraq's role in the League of Nations. But since that time, Iraq has developed different foreign policy concerns--and these new concerns have been a major transformation from the standpoint of Soviet relations. By 1975 Iraq and Syria were the two primary recipients of Soviet military supplies and the Iraqi regime had approved a mutual defense pact with the Soviet Union. However, Western news coverage of these two countries is slight and neither regime supports internal political research.

In 1969 Majid Khadduri published a major study, REPUBLICAN IRAQ [2504]. Khadduri writes about the Balthist leadership and, in the course of that, about Iraq's international perspectives. Ireland's 1937 volume (IRAQ: A STUDY IN POLITICAL DEVELOPMENT [2502]), republished in 1970, is a thorough background. Kimball's version of contemporary Iraqi politics (THE CHANGING PATTERN OF POLITICAL POWER IN IRAQ, 1958-1971 [2505]) is concept-heavy, but advances the current view that national development is a primary priority and foreign issues secondary to that concern.

Petran (SYRIA [3205]) wrote a useful guide to contemporary Syrian politics. She discusses the aftermath of the 1967 war and the loss of the Golan Heights. Zeine's THE STRUGGLE FOR ARAB INDEPENDENCE [3209] and Hourani's SYRIA

AND LEBANON [3204] both give perspective to Syria's regional relationships and to the historical development of its international perspectives.

Military involvement in Syrian politics is intense. Although primarily concerned with domestic issues, the studies of the role of the military are useful also for foreign policy background. Rabinovich's SYRIA UNDER THE BA'TH 1963-66 [3206] includes biographical information on Syrian leaders; Torrey's SYRIAN POLITICS AND THE MILITARY, 1945-1958 [3207] covers the parliamentary period following the war.

A number of books on Lebanese internal politics are available, but no study specifically on foreign policy has yet been written. Meo (LEBANON: IMPROBABLE NATION [2803]) reviews the mandate background, internal politics, and Lebanon's position in world politics. Binder (POLITICS IN LEBANON [2801]) includes seventeen essays in his edited volume including two on Lebanon's international position.

Jordan's internal politics, like Lebanon's, are inextricably interwoven with its foreign relations, particularly through its Palestinian population. Vatikiotis' POLITICS AND THE MILITARY IN JORDAN: A STUDY OF THE ARAB LEGION 1921-1957 [2707] discusses the integration of Palestinians into the military, and West- and East-Bank relations. Sir John Glubb, who commanded the Jordanian Arab Legion until 1956, examines Jordan's foreign relations during his service in A SOLDIER WITH THE ARABS [2703].

These two books along with the more recently published works (Snow, HUSSEIN, A BIOGRAPHY [2705] and Faddah, THE MIDDLE EAST IN TRANSITION [2702]) cover Jordan's foreign policy quite thoroughly. None develops primary source material, however. Abidi's JORDAN, A POLITICAL STUDY [2701] uses Jordanian primary sources to document Jordanian-Palestinian conflict and Soviet-American competition in Jordan. The Vance and Lauer interviews with King Hussein [2706] give the monarch's opinions on these issues.

ISRAEL

Books on Egyptian politics devote much attention to the perspective and actions of the late President Nasser. Conversely, only a few studies of Israel's foreign policy emphasize leadership roles. Brecher's THE FOREIGN POLICY SYSTEM OF ISRAEL [2611] defines Israel's policy alternatives partly in terms of elite views. The author goes on in DECISIONS IN ISRAEL'S FOREIGN POLICY [2610] to specific cases to analyze the interplay of these constraints. Wagner's CRISIS DECISION-MAKING [2652] uses the same type of approach to explain, in more limited space, Israel's decisions to go to war in 1967 and, more briefly, in 1973.

By contrast, most of the other books on Israel emphasize trends in Israel-other country bilateral relations, concepts of Israeli nationalism and their linkage to foreign policy issues, and military-strategic problems. Of the military studies, Michael Handel's ISRAEL'S POLITICAL-MILITARY DOCTRINE [2626] is the most current and thorough. Ernest Stock's ISRAEL ON THE ROAD TO SINAI [2648] evaluates changes in the regional military balance and its contribution to the Suez invasion decision. Two major books on military issues have been published by Israeli leaders: Yigal Allon's THE MAKING OF ISRAEL'S ARMY [2601] and Shimon Peres's DAVID'S SLING [2640]. Allon devotes more attention to strategy; Peres to the history of the military establishment.

Very little is available which considers borders and military tactics specifically. The pamphlet ISRAEL AND ELATH [2619], a speech by Eliahu Elath given in 1966, is included in the list because it discusses the inclusion of the port in partitioned Israel. Many of the books on the four military engagements are also good sources for territorial views.

Territorial questions are related to the foundations of Zionist thought as well as to military security policy. Arie Eliav brings the two together in LAND OF THE HART [2621]. Halpern's THE IDEA OF THE JEWISH STATE [2625] includes a longer period of history and is more thoroughly documented. In ISRAEL AMONG THE NATIONS [2649], Talmon, a political philosopher, takes up the same questions as Halpern but from an ideological vantage point rather than a historical perspective.

Halpern sees Israel as ideally a nonaligned state. Developing this theme, the major studies of Israel's bilateral relations with other states are: Sylvia Crosbie's A TACIT ALLIANCE [2613]; Dagan's MOSCOW AND JERUSALEM [2614] takes Soviet-Israeli relations up to the 1967 war; and Deutschkron reviews West German-Israeli relations in a work which is long but tends toward generalities (BONN AND JERUSALEM [2615]). Books on United States-Israel relations are listed in "United States Foreign Policy" in chapter 4. Deutschkron's topic is important more because of the atrocities committed by the German Third Reich than because of West Germany's present role in Israeli strategic concerns.

The last type of source which should be mentioned are the memoirs of Israeli statesmen. Official and unofficial views of former Prime Ministers Ben-Gurion [2606-7], Eshkol [2623], and Meir [2638] are available. And former Foreign Minister Abba Eban's views have been published in several places [2616-18].

THE NORTHERN TIER STATES

The Arab-Israeli conflict occupies only a limited position in Iran's foreign policy horizons. Interest in Iran's foreign relations has heightened with the increasing salience of competition over petroleum resources and regional power struggles in the wake of the British Empire's decline. Influence over Iran has been a source of competition between first Russia and Britain and then the Soviet Union and the United States. But Britain's relationship with Iran was quite different from the approach of the United States, which is to arm Iran as a surrogate.

Foreign Policies of Middle Eastern States

The direct clash between Russian and British interests at the turn of the present century is the subject of a major study by Firuz Kazemzadeh, RUSSIA AND BRITAIN IN PERSIA [2407]. Kazemzadeh's book, extensively documented and detailed, is helpful background to Iran's present policy of formally balancing its relationships with the Soviet Union and the United States. An indirect outcome of that competition was the nationalization of Iran's oil in 1951 and the subsequent renewal of production by the consortium in which the United States participated. Nirumand's IRAN: THE NEW IMPERIALISM IN ACTION [2408] covers that period critically.

By far the most comprehensive analysis of Iranian foreign policy in which Iranian interest and policies are identified is Chubin and Zabih's THE FOREIGN RELATIONS OF IRAN [2403]. This volume, like Brecher's on Israel, analyzes Iran's foreign relations in terms of decision-making styles and gives a chronological development of diplomatic events.

Turkey, like Iran, has been only tangentially involved in the Arab-Israeli conflict. Turkish foreign policy has been involved more with Western European politics and NATO. The most comprehensive study of Turkish foreign policy is Vali's BRIDGE ACROSS THE BOSPORUS [3414] which looks at Turkey and NATO, and also discusses Turkey's regional relationships in the Middle East. TROUBLED ALLIANCE [3405] is good background for the 1974 conflict over the Turkish invasion of Cyprus which placed new stress on NATO.

Turkey's location at the Dardanelles Straits has inevitably made it a focal point for great power conflict. Several studies specifically focus on the Straits and Turkey in international affairs. The most recent of these is Vali's study, THE TURKISH STRAITS AND NATO [3415]. Shotwell and Deak published a useful, short history, TURKEY AT THE STRAITS [3412], which also includes documents relevant to control over the Straits. One volume in French is listed which emphasizes the Soviet Union's interest in the Straits and its relations with Turkey (Erkin [3404]).

Turkey's transition from empire to republic is covered in Harry Howard's THE PARTITION OF TURKEY [3408]. Balfour's ATATURK [3402] reviews subsequent changes in his biography of the first president of the Republic. Bernard Lewis's THE EMERGENCE OF MODERN TURKEY [3410] gives a more general picture of the diplomatic background.

Afghanistan is the third "northern tier" state. Its monarchy was overthrown in 1973, but the new regime had not evidenced a major international reorientation by 1975. Little material on Afghanistan's politics, foreign or internal, is published. Nonetheless, one careful study of its foreign relations is available (Adamec, AFGHANISTAN'S FOREIGN AFFAIRS TO THE MID-TWENTIETH CENTURY [2101]). In addition to Adamec's book, an edited volume was published in 1969 (Grassmuck, et al., AFGHANISTAN [2102]), which offers a review of internal and foreign problems, an extensive bibliography, and a political chronology for the past century and one-half.

Foreign Policies of Middle Eastern States

SAUDI ARABIA, YEMEN, AND THE ARABIAN PENINSULA

Little is available on the foreign relations of the peninsula states. The books listed in this section are largely accounts of history and domestic issues. The list does not include the Gulf sheikhdoms (the UAE, Qatar, Bahrein) which have been classified under the Persian Gulf.

The lack of materials on Saudi Arabian foreign policy can be overcome somewhat by using materials about the conflicts and issues in which Saudi Arabia has been involved. Of the three books on the Yemen civil war, in which Saudi Arabia supported the royalists, two are by journalists and the third by a military writer. On the other side of the peninsula, one volume on KUWAIT AND HER NEIGHBORS (Dickson [3103]) and two accounts of boundary disputes involving Saudi Arbia have been published: (Brown [3101] and Kelly [3107]). David Holden's FAREWELL TO ARABIA [3104] is a survey of politics and personalities written by a British journalist. Its focus is internal politics.

NORTHERN AFRICA

The materials available for these states are scant. The few books listed are studies of internal politics.

COUNTRY SURVEYS AND BACKGROUND

2001 Abboushi, W.F. POLITICAL SYSTEMS OF THE MIDDLE EAST IN THE 20TH CENTURY. New York: Dodd, Mead, 1970. 345 p. Bibliog. Index.

>A country-by-country survey with an introductory chapter on the region. Omits North Africa and the Arabian Peninsula. Includes separate descriptions of foreign policy (excepting Iraq). Useful bibliography.

2002 Be'eri, Eliezer. ARMY OFFICERS IN ARAB POLITICS AND SOCIETY. Translated by Dov Ben-Abba. New York: Praeger, 1970. 514 p. Bibliog. Index.

>Focuses on the history of army intervention in domestic politics and the social backgrounds of army officers in Egypt, Syria, Iraq.

2003 Berger, Morroe. THE ARAB WORLD TODAY. Garden City, N.Y.: Doubleday, 1962. 480 p. Bibliog. Illus.

>Survey of social structure and social change in the Arab states with emphasis on Egypt, Syria, Lebanon, Jordan, and Iraq.

2004 Haddad, George M. REVOLUTIONS AND MILITARY RULE IN THE MIDDLE EAST. VOL. III: THE ARAB-STATES. PART II: EGYPT, SUDAN, YEMEN, AND LIBYA. New York: Robert Speller and Sons, 1973. 444 p. App. Bibliog. Index.

> Although primarily concerned with the military-socialist regimes' internal behavior, the author also criticizes their ineptness in supporting Palestine. Part I (1965, 251 p.) covers the northern tier states.

2005 Harari, Maurice. GOVERNMENT AND POLITICS OF THE MIDDLE EAST. Englewood Cliffs, N.J.: Prentice-Hall, 1962. 179 p. Index. Map. Sel. bibliog.

> Twentieth-century political and diplomatic history by country with a summary chapter.

2006 Hurewitz, Jacob Coleman. MIDDLE EAST POLITICS: THE MILITARY DIMENSION. New York: Praeger for the Council on Foreign Relations, 1969. 553 p. Bibliog. fnn. Illus. Index.

> A country survey which focuses upon military-civilian relationships, arms and troop capabilities, intra- and inter-regional relations.

2007 al-Marayati, Abid A., et al. THE MIDDLE EAST: ITS GOVERNMENTS AND POLITICS. Belmont, Calif.: Duxbury/Wadsworth, 1972. 491 p. Bibliog. Glossary. Index.

> Social and economic background of the region, country surveys including summaries of foreign policies, and international politics.

2008 Rivlin, Benjamin, and Szyliowicz, Joseph S. THE CONTEMPORARY MIDDLE EAST: TRADITION AND INNOVATION. New York: Random House, 1965. 576 p.

> Collection of essays covering economic, cultural, and political issues. Many by Middle Eastern authors.

2009 Sharabi, Hisham. GOVERNMENT AND POLITICS OF THE MIDDLE EAST IN THE TWENTIETH CENTURY. Princeton, N.J.: D. Van Nostrand, 1962. 296 p. Index.

> Country-by-country review of recent political history with varying, but generally limited, references to foreign relations.

2010 Spencer, William. POLITICAL EVOLUTION IN THE MIDDLE EAST. Philadelphia and New York: B. Lippincott, 1962. 440 p. Apps. Index. Sel. bibliog.

> Political and diplomatic histories of the Middle East states.

Foreign Policies of Middle Eastern States

2011 Tutsch, Hans E. FROM ANKARA TO MARRAKESH: TURKS AND ARABS IN A CHANGING WORLD. Library of International Studies. London: George Allen and Unwin, 1964. 224 p. Bibliog. Index. Maps.

> Country surveys of Turkey and the Arab states. Includes descriptions of general foreign policy orientations. Not documented; based upon personal interviews and secondary sources.

AFGHANISTAN

2101 Adamec, Ludwig W. AFGHANISTAN'S FOREIGN AFFAIRS TO THE MID-TWENTIETH CENTURY: RELATIONS WITH THE USSR, GERMANY, AND BRITAIN. Tucson: University of Arizona Press, 1974. 324 p. Bibliog. Illus. Index.

> Useful bibliography of archival and secondary material. Sources include recently released political files and were drawn from libraries in several countries. Relates foreign policies to internal reforms.

2102 Grassmuck, George; Adamec, Ludwig W.; and Irwin, Frances H., eds. AFGHANISTAN: SOME NEW APPROACHES. Ann Arbor: University of Michigan Press, 1969. 405 p. Bibliog. Chron.

> A collection of articles on social and political issues in contemporary Afghanistan. Includes an essay entitled "Germany, Third Power in Afghanistan's Foreign Relations" by Adamec. The volume is most useful for its bibliography, which covers materials in Persian and Russian as well as English and other Western languages, and its chronology of events covering 220 years from 1747 through June 1969.

ALGERIA

2201 Alwan, Mohamed. ALGERIA BEFORE THE UNITED NATIONS. New York: R. Speller, 1959. 121 p.

> A documented study of the Algerian case for independence by an Iraqi diplomat.

2202 Gordon, David C. THE PASSING OF FRENCH ALGERIA. London and New York: Oxford University Press, 1966. 265 p. Bibliog.

> The independence movement and the problems encountered in renewing Algeria's Moslem heritage after more than a century of colonization.

2203 Humbaraci, Arslan. ALGERIA: A REVOLUTION THAT FAILED: A POLITICAL HISTORY SINCE 1954. London: Pall Mall, 1966; New York:

Praeger, 1966. 308 p. Maps.

>Reviews the problems that prevented the revolution from attaining the two goals of national development and North African unity. Based on interviews with Algerian nationalists.

2204 O'Ballance, Edgar. THE ALGERIAN INSURRECTION: 1954-1962. Hamden, Conn.: Archon, 1967. 231 p.

>A military writer's view of the conflict. Emphasis upon military tactics, diplomatic strategy, and unconventional warfare.

EGYPT

2301 Baddour, Abd el-Fattah Ibrahim el-Sayed. SUDANESE-EGYPTIAN RELATIONS: A CHRONOLOGICAL AND ANALYTICAL STUDY. The Hague: M. Nijhoff, 1960. 264 p. App. Bibliog. Illus. Index. Map.

>Historical review from the pre-Arab period to British dominance and independence. Based upon official documents (British, Egyptian, United Nations), and English and Arabic language sources. The case for unification.

2302 Collins, Robert O., and Tignor, Robert L. EGYPT AND THE SUDAN. Englewood Cliffs, N.J.: Prentice-Hall, 1967. 180 p. Map. Sel. bibliog.

>Documented background of the Nile Valley and relations between Egypt and Sudan during President Nasser's regime.

2303 Copeland, Miles. THE GAME OF NATIONS: THE AMORALITY OF POWER POLITICS. New York: Simon and Schuster, 1970. 318 p. Bibliog. Index.

>A study of the late President Nasser's foreign policy in the context of the cold war and Arab politics. By a former CIA officer who worked with Nasser.

2304 Dekmejian, R. Hrair. EGYPT UNDER NASIR; A STUDY IN POLITICAL DYNAMICS. Albany: State University of New York Press, 1972. 368 p. Index.

>Includes a discussion of President Nasser's international political perspectives, focusing on the 1965-69 period.

2305 EGYPT AND NASSER. 3 vols. New York: Facts on File, 1973. 264, 226, and 298 p. Index. Maps.

>A chronological summary of Egyptian foreign relations under the late President Nasser. Volume I: 1952-56; volume II: 1957-66; volume III: 1967-72.

2306 Heikal, Mohammed Hassanein. THE CAIRO DOCUMENTS. New York: Doubleday, 1973. 357 p.

    The late President Nasser, his perspectives on Egyptian foreign policy, and his relations with world leaders from the Suez invasion to his death. Recounted by an adviser and editor of AL-AHRAM.

2307 Ismael, Tareq Y. THE U.A.R. IN AFRICA: EGYPT'S POLICY UNDER NASSER. Evanston, Ill.: Northwestern University Press, 1971. xiv, 258 p. Apps. Maps.

    Three basic principles of Egypt's African policy--anti-imperialism, African unity and Egyptian preeminence. Based on Egyptian newspapers, journals, government publications, and foreign policy textbooks.

2308 al-Jamiyah al-Misriyah lil-Qanun al-Duwali. EGYPT AND THE UNITED NATIONS. Report of a Study Group, Egyptian Society of International Law. New York: Manhattan Publishing for the Carnegie Endowment for International Peace, 1957. 197 p.

    Part of a series which also includes volumes on Israel and Turkey. Emphasizes legal and official attitudes rather than political issues.

2309 Little, Tom. HIGH DAM AT ASWAN. New York: John Day, 1965. 248 p.

    History of the project and its international aspects.

2310 _____. MODERN EGYPT. New York: Praeger, 1967. xiii, 300 p. Fold. map. Bibliog.

    First published in 1958 under the title EGYPT. Deals with Nasser, Arab unity, and the Arab-Israel conflict. Director of Cairo's Arab News Agency at the time.

2311 Mansfield, Peter. THE BRITISH IN EGYPT. New York: Holt, Rinehart & Winston, 1972 [c1971]. xiv, 351 p. Bibliog. Illus. Index. Ports.

    See No. 1120.

2312 el-Naggar, Said. FOREIGN AID AND THE ECONOMIC DEVELOPMENT OF THE U.A.R. Princeton, N.J.: Princeton University Press, 1965. 93 p. Illus.

2313 Vatikiotis, P[anayiotis].J. THE EGYPTIAN ARMY IN POLITICS: PATTERN FOR NEW NATIONS? Bloomington: Indiana University Press, 1961. 300 p.

Internal politics focusing on the military's involvement.

2314 Wheelock, Keith. NASSER'S NEW EGYPT; A CRITICAL ANALYSIS. Foreign Policy Research Institute Series, 8. New York: Frederick A. Praeger, 1960. 326 p. Bibliog. fnn. Index.

One-half of the volume is devoted to an analysis of the late President Nasser's "positive neutralism," which emphasizes his personal role and international pragmatism. Based mainly on news dispatches.

2315 Wynn, Wilton. NASSER OF EGYPT; THE SEARCH FOR DIGNITY. London: Arlington, 1959. 213 p.

A popularly written account of the early years of President Nasser's regime. Covers the Czechoslovakian arms agreement.

2316 Zayid, Mahmud Y. EGYPT'S STRUGGLE FOR INDEPENDENCE. Beirut: Khayats, 1965. x, 258 p. App. Bibliog.

Uses Arabic and European sources to describe the period from 1882-1936. Provides an explanation of Egypt's perspectives concerning the 1936 treaty establishing new relationship with England.

IRAN

2401 Amuzegar, Jahangir. TECHNICAL ASSISTANCE IN THEORY AND PRACTICE: THE CASE OF IRAN. Special Studies. New York: Praeger, 1966. 275 p.

Discusses the U.S. Point Four program in Iran, concentrating on its economic aspects. By an oil adviser to the Iranian government.

2402 Burrell, Robert Michael, and Cottrell, Alvin J. IRAN, AFGHANISTAN AND PAKISTAN: TENSIONS AND DILEMMAS. Washington Papers, vol. 2, no. 20. Beverly Hills, Calif.: Sage, 1974. 68 p. Bibliog. Maps.

Publications for the Center for Strategic and International Studies, Georgetown University.

2403 Chubin, Shahram, and Zabih, Sepehr. THE FOREIGN RELATIONS OF IRAN, A DEVELOPING STATE IN A ZONE OF GREAT POWER CONFLICT. Berkeley: University of California Press, 1974. 362 p. Bibliog. Index. Map.

Iran's foreign policy--international and regional--since World War II analyzing the relationship between international strategies and internal political processes. Comprehensive bibliography; primary and secondary English and Persian language sources.

2404 Cottam, Richard W. NATIONALISM IN IRAN. Pittsburgh, Pa.: University of Pittsburgh Press, 1964. 319 p.

Still the definitive study of the practical politics of Iranian nationalism and various themes in national thought.

2405 Fatemi, Nasrollah Saifpour. DIPLOMATIC HISTORY OF PERSIA, 1917-1923: ANGLO-RUSSIAN POWER POLITICS IN IRAN. New York: R.F. Moore, 1952. xiii, 331 p. Bibliog. fnn.

2406 Kazemian, Gholam H. THE IMPACT OF U.S. TECHNICAL AID ON THE RURAL DEVELOPMENT OF IRAN. Brooklyn: Theodore Gaus, 1968. xiii, 129 p. Bibliog.

Brief survey, focusing upon the role of international assistance.

2407 Kazemzadeh, Firuz. RUSSIA AND BRITAIN IN PERSIA, 1844-1914. New Haven, Conn.: Yale University Press, 1968. 711 p. Bibliog. Maps.

Details the diplomatic confrontation between Britain and Russia in the region of Persia (Iran) and internal Iranian politics. Draws upon varied primary and secondary sources in several languages, including Russian.

2408 Nirumand, Bahman. IRAN: THE NEW IMPERIALISM IN ACTION. Translated by Leonard Mins. New York: Monthly Review Press, 1969. 192 p.

Iran as a client state to the United States; a critique of Iran's internal politics and external affairs.

2409 Ramazani, Rouhollah K. THE FOREIGN POLICY OF IRAN, A DEVELOPING NATION IN WORLD AFFAIRS, 1500-1941. Charlottesville: University Press of Virginia, 1966. Bibliog. fnn. Index.

The foreign policies of three dynasties--Safavid, Qajar, and Pahlavi--in regional and international conflicts, including economic relations. Primary and secondary English and Persian language sources. Also see Ramazani, under the Persian Gulf.

2410 Reppa, Robert B., Sr. ISRAEL AND IRAN: BILATERAL RELATIONSHIPS AND EFFECT ON THE INDIAN OCEAN BASIN. Special Studies in International Politics and Government. New York: Praeger, 1974. 187 p. Bibliog. Maps.

Brief survey of domestic and international political issues in Israel and Iran prior to Iran's rapprochement with the Arab states. Little documentation, numerous errors, and extensive bibliography.

2411 Upton, Joseph M. THE HISTORY OF MODERN IRAN: AN INTERPRETATION. Cambridge, Mass.: Harvard University Press for the Center for Middle Eastern Studies, 1960. 163 p. Illus.

> A concise summary of Iran's internal and foreign politics during the twentieth century.

2412 Van Wagenen, Richard W. THE IRANIAN CASE, 1946. United Nations Action Case Histories, 2. New York: Carnegie Endowment for International Peace, 1952. 119 p.

> The withdrawal of Soviet troops from Iran after World War II. U.N. and secondary sources.

IRAQ

2501 Adamson, David. THE KURDISH WAR. London: George Allen and Unwin, 1964. 215 p.

> An account by a LONDON SUNDAY TELEGRAPH correspondent of the Kurdish-Iraq war based upon interviews with Barzani and other Kurdish leaders. Publicizes the Kurds' case and recommends U.S. support for Kurdish demands.

2502 Ireland, Philip W. IRAQ: A STUDY IN POLITICAL DEVELOPMENT. London: Cape, 1937. Reprint. New York: Russell and Russell, 1970. 510 p. Apps. Bibliog.

> The British Mandate--the rebellion of 1920, British interests, and problems of administration. Primary and secondary sources; excellent bibliography.

2503 Khadduri, Majid [D.]. INDEPENDENT IRAQ, 1932-58, A STUDY IN IRAQI POLITICS. 2d ed. London and New York: Oxford University Press, 1960. 388 p.

> Largely events up to 1955. Sources include personal interviews and unpublished documents.

2504 _____. REPUBLICAN IRAQ, A STUDY IN IRAQI POLITICS SINCE THE REVOLUTION OF 1958. London and New York: Oxford University Press, 1969. xii, 318 p. Bibliog. fnn. Map.

> Focuses upon the 1958 revolution, Qassem's regime and the subsequent Ba'th government. Devotes much attention to Iraq's relations with other Arab states and oil issues. Uses numerous Arabic language primary sources.

2505 Kimball, Lorenzo K. THE CHANGING PATTERN OF POLITICAL POWER IN IRAQ, 1958-1971. New York: Speller, 1972. 246 p. Bibliog.

Describes the development of Iraq's role as a small state in the United Nations within the context of Iraqi nationalism.

2506 al-Marayati, Abid A. A DIPLOMATIC HISTORY OF MODERN IRAQ. New York: R. Speller, 1961. 222 p.

Focuses upon Iraq in the League of Nations and the United Nations. A discussion of the emergence of a small state's role in international organizations.

2507 Schmidt, Dana Adams. JOURNEY AMONG BRAVE MEN. Boston: Little, Brown, 1964. xiv, 298 p.

A NEW YORK TIMES correspondent gives his firsthand observations on the Kurdish-Iraq war, predicting an eventual Kurdish victory.

ISRAEL

2601 Allon, Yigal. THE MAKING OF ISRAEL'S ARMY. New York: Universe Books, 1970. 273 p. Apps. Illus. Maps. Ports.

Summary of Israeli military strategy and organization as it emerged from the prestatehood period. Speeches by military leaders are appended as are maps of the major operations during the first three wars. No documentation or detail of military capabilities.

2602 Avnery, Uri. ISRAEL WITHOUT ZIONISTS: A PLEA FOR PEACE IN THE MIDDLE EAST. New York: Macmillan, 1968. 215 p.

A member of the Knesset and a binationalist surveys Israel's foreign policy and foreign policy makers and his own recollections of the Mandate and independence. Popularly written.

2603 Balabkins, Nicholas. WEST GERMAN REPARATIONS TO ISRAEL. New Brunswick, N.J.: Rutgers University Press, 1971. 384 p. Apps. Bibliog. fnn.

The negotiations leading up to the reparations agreements with the surrounding domestic political and economic issues in both countries; Israel's interest in reparations viewed in terms of the economic pressures which it faced during the early 1950s.

2604 Bar-Zohar, Michel. SUEZ: ULTRA-SECRET. Paris: Fayard, 1964. 317 p. Bibliog. refs. Maps.

Also cited in No. 4715.

2605 Begin, Menahem. THE REVOLT: STORY OF THE IRGUN. Translated by Samuel Katz. Tel Aviv: Hadar, 1972. 386 p. Maps.

Foreign Policies of Middle Eastern States

The author's personal memoirs as a former Irqun leader during the 1944-47 period of the Jewish revolt against the British Mandate and during the 1948 war.

2606 Ben-Gurion, David. ISRAEL: A PERSONAL HISTORY. Translated by Nechemia Meyers and Uzy Nystar. New York: Funk and Wagnalls, 1971. xxii, 862 p. Illus. Maps.

Internal and external affairs from the establishment of the nation of Israel through the 1967 war, recounted chronologically and focused upon the late prime minister's relationship to the events. Little on the foreign policy-making process.

2607 _____. ISRAEL: YEARS OF CHALLENGE. New York: Holt, Rinehart and Winston, 1963. 240 p. Illus. Ports. Maps.

Military and diplomatic activity from the establishment of Israel through the 1956 war.

2608 Blum, Yehuda Z. SECURE BOUNDARIES AND MIDDLE EAST PEACE IN LIGHT OF INTERNATIONAL LAW AND PRACTICE. Jerusalem: Hebrew University, Faculty of Law, Institute for Legislative Research and Comparative Law, 1971. 134 p. Paper. Apps. Bibliog. Index. Maps.

Draws upon past international practice to establish an appropriate definition of "secure" boundaries as contrasted with "natural" boundaries and to establish the intent of relevant U.N. resolutions.

2609 Bober, Arie, comp. THE OTHER ISRAEL: THE RADICAL CASE AGAINST ZIONISM. Garden City, N.Y.: Anchor Books, 1972. 264 p. Paper. Apps. Bibliog. refs.

Statements issued by the Israeli Socialist Organization and articles written by its members on Israel's regional and international relationships and internal conflicts. Not edited for accuracy of references.

2610 Brecher, Michael. DECISIONS IN ISRAEL'S FOREIGN POLICY. London: Oxford University Press; New Haven, Conn.: Yale University Press, 1974. x, 639 p. App. Bibliog. Illus. Index.

The "structured" empirical research design developed in the earlier volume, see below, is applied to seven decision-making areas--Jerusalem, German reparations, Korean War and China, Sinai campaign, Jordan waters, the 1967 war, and Rogers proposals--using elite statements about contextual images. Extensive bibliography, divided by issue area.

2611 _____. THE FOREIGN POLICY SYSTEM OF ISRAEL: SETTINGS, IMAGES,

PROCESS. London: Oxford University Press, 1972. xx, 693 p. Apps. Bibliog. Illus. Index.

>The structure of Israel's foreign policy-making institutions, military and economic capabilities of the state, and the world views of relevant elites based upon a content analysis of public statements and interviews. Data on economic, demographic, communication, and elite characteristics.

2612 _____. ISRAEL, THE KOREAN WAR, AND CHINA: IMAGES, DECISIONS AND CONSEQUENCES. Jerusalem: Jerusalem Academic Press for the Institute of Asian and African Studies, Hebrew University, 1974. 148 p. Bibliog.

2613 Crosbie, Sylvia K. A TACIT ALLIANCE: FRANCE AND ISRAEL FROM SUEZ TO THE SIX DAY WAR. Modern Middle East Series, 7. Princeton, N.J.: Princeton University Press, 1974. xii, 280 p. Bibliog. Index.

>A well-documented study of French-Israeli relations focusing upon French policy and the military technology and weapons transfers resulting from the alliance. Based upon interviews with military leaders and diplomats in France and Israel and numerous written sources in French and English. Useful bibliography of periodical sources, especially military issues. Also cited in No. 3603.

2614 Dagan, Avigdor. MOSCOW AND JERUSALEM: TWENTY YEARS OF RELATIONS BETWEEN ISRAEL AND THE SOVIET UNION. London and New York: Adelard-Schuman, 1970. 255 p. Bibliog. Index. Ports.

>A chronological description of relations between Soviet Union and Israel from the time of the latter's independence to the 1967 war. With emphasis placed upon Soviet policy shifts. Little documentation.

2615 Deutschkron, Inge. BONN AND JERUSALEM--THE STRANGE COALITION. Philadelphia: Chilton Book Co., 1970. x, 357 p.

>Relations between West Germany and Israel from 1945-65, based upon newspapers and periodicals, interviews, and personal observations. The official documents for this period are confidential, and the study is limited by their absence, as well as by the fact that Israel is described as being free from the imperatives of realpolitik.

2616 Eban, Abba Solomon. ISRAEL IN THE WORLD: TWO TELEVISION INTERVIEWS WITH ABBA EBAN. South Brunswick, N.Y.: London: Thomas Yoseloff, 1966. 70 p.

>Text of discussions with Israel's former Foreign Minister on "Open End," March 1965, and "Meet the Press," March 1965. Major foreign issues raised were Jordan River water rights, arms flows, and Israel's nuclear capacity.

2617 _____. MY COUNTRY: THE STORY OF MODERN ISRAEL. London: Weidenfeld and Nicolson, 1973. 304 p. Illus. Maps. Ports.

2618 _____. VOICE OF ISRAEL. New York: Horizon, 1969. 398 p.

> An expanded version of a 1957 edition by the same publisher. Contains statements made by the former foreign minister of Israel before public and private audiences on topics ranging from the Suez blockade to the future position of Israel in the Middle East.

2619 Elath, Eliahu. ISRAEL AND ELATH: THE POLITICAL STRUGGLE FOR THE INCLUSION OF ELATH IN THE JEWISH STATE. London: Weidenfeld and Nicolson, 1966. 24 p. Index.

> Address delivered to the Jewish Historical Society (June 1966) by the President of Hebrew University and former Israeli ambassador to the United States, concerning the history of the negotiations to include Elath in partitioned Israel.

2620 _____. ISRAEL AND HER NEIGHBORS. Cleveland, N.Y.: World Publishing, 1957. 89 p. Map.

> Lectures delivered at Brandeis University in 1956 by Israel's ambassador to Great Britain and, formerly, to the United States. He discusses Israel's internal Arab population and his views on the domestic problems within the Arab states.

2621 Eliav, Arie Lova. LAND OF THE HART: ISRAELIS, ARABS, THE TERRITORIES, AND A VISION OF THE FUTURE. Translated by Judith Yalon. Philadelphia: Jewish Publication Society of America, 1974. 381 p.

> An Israeli diplomat surveys the background of Zionism, Israel's relations with neighboring Arab states, and the involvement of the external powers in the Arab-Israeli conflict. Good source for Israeli images of its regional setting. No documentation.

2622 Ellis, Harry B. THE DILEMMA OF ISRAEL. Analysis 18. Washington, D.C.: American Enterprise Institute for Public Policy Research, 1970. 110 p. Bibliog. ref.

> Israel's international position--vis-a-vis the Arab states, the United States, Europe, and the United Nations; little on foreign policy-making process in Israel.

2623 Eshkol, Levi. THE STATE PAPERS OF LEVI ESHKOL. Edited, with an introduction, by Henry M. Christman. New York: Funk and Wagnalls, 1969. xiv, 153 p. Port.

> Fifteen public statements covering the six-year period the late Prime Minister Eshkol was in office (1963-69).

Foreign Policies of Middle Eastern States

2624 Eytan, Walter. THE FIRST TEN YEARS: A DIPLOMATIC HISTORY OF ISRAEL. New York: Simon and Schuster, 1958. 239 p. Illus. Maps. Ports.

>Israel's foreign policy during the 1950s. By a former director general of the Foreign Ministry of Israel. Analyzes the armistice, the Jerusalem settlement, and the Palestinian refugee population.

2625 Halpern, Ben. THE IDEA OF THE JEWISH STATE. Harvard Middle Eastern Studies, 3. Cambridge, Mass.: Harvard University Press, 1961. 492 p. Bibliog. Illus. Index. Maps.

>The evolution of the Jewish state idea in practical terms as expressed by its relations with the external environment from the nineteenth century to 1956. Note especially the discussion of nonalignment in the superpower conflict. The reference notes include many League and UN documents, the latter from armistice negotiations.

2626 Handel, Michael I. ISRAEL'S POLITICAL-MILITARY DOCTRINE. Occasional Papers in International Affairs, 30. Cambridge, Mass.: Harvard University, Center for International Affairs, 1973. 101 p. Paper. Bibliog. ref. Illus.

>Israeli military doctrine from 1947-73. The author documents the shift from ground forces to air power to advanced electronic technology and missiles. The analysis does not extend to the relationship between Israeli occupation policies and military strategy nor to its adversaries' military doctrines.

2627 Hodes, Aubrey. DIALOGUE WITH ISHMAEL: ISRAEL'S FUTURE IN THE MIDDLE EAST. New York: Funk & Wagnalls, 1968. 258 p. Bibliog. ref.

>The author sees an end to the Arab-Israeli conflict when Israeli leaders view the state as Middle Eastern rather than European. Includes discussions of prior peace plans and of political tensions within Egypt, Israel, Jordan, and Syria.

2628 ISRAEL AND THE UNITED NATIONS. Report of a study group set up by the Hebrew University of Jerusalem prepared for the Carnegie Endowment for International Peace. New York: Manhattan Publishing, 1956. 322 p. Apps.

>Report of a study of Israel's foreign policy objectives and the performance of the United Nations--general Israeli-Arab relations, the Jerusalem question, Arab refugees, regional cooperation, the cold war, and Third World independence movements.

2629 Jabber, Fuad [A.]. ISRAEL AND NUCLEAR WEAPONS: PRESENT OPTIONS

AND FUTURE STRATEGIES. London: Chatto and Windus for the International Institute for Strategic Studies, 1971. 164 p. Bibliog. Index.

Israel's nuclear capacity--costs, organization, military potential. Comprehensive bibliography.

2630 Jacob, Abel. "The Political Outcomes of Foreign Aid: Israel's Foreign Aid Program to Africa." Doctoral dissertation, University of California at Los Angeles, 1969. xi, 577 p.

Foreign aid as a strategy for recipients and donors, contact among Israeli and African experts and recipient state behavior in international organizations. Extensive bibliography.

2631 Jansen, Godfrey H. ZIONISM, ISRAEL, AND ASIAN NATIONALISM. Monograph series, 29. Beirut: Institute for Palestine Studies, 1971. xv, 347 p. Paper. Bibliog. ref. Index.

Israel's relations with other Asian states by a former correspondent for HA'ARETZ and an Indian diplomat in Cairo who criticizes Israel's western ties. Unique account of numerous Asian states' policies toward Israel.

2632 Kagan, Benjamin. THE SECRET BATTLE FOR ISRAEL. Translated by Patsy Southgate. Cleveland: World Publishing Co., 1966. xv, 299 p. Maps.

An Israeli Air force officer's recollections of the military aspects of the Jewish resistance movement in Palestine, including arms acquisitions.

2633 Kahler, Erich. THE JEWS AMONG THE NATIONS. New York: F. Ungar, 1967. 149 p. Bibliog. fnn.

2634 Kisch, Frederick H. PALESTINE DIARY. London: Victor Gollancz, 1938. 478 p. Front. Illus. Plates. Ports.

Favorable picture of Zionist leaders' attempts to improve Jewish-Arab relations in Palestine during the early years of the Mandate. Also cited in No. 4135.

2635 Krammer, Arnold. THE FORGOTTEN FRIENDSHIP: ISRAEL AND THE SOVIET BLOC, 1947-53. Urbana: University of Illinois Press, 1974. 224 p. Bibliog. Index.

Covers the Soviet Union's decision to support statehood for Israel, later conflict over emigration, and the trials of accused Israeli spies. Describes early military assistance from Czechoslovakia to Israel. Hebrew and English language sources. Based upon the author's doctoral dissertation.

2636 Laufer, Leopold. ISRAEL AND THE DEVELOPING COUNTRIES: NEW

APPROACHES TO COOPERATION. New York: Twentieth Century Fund, 1967. xiii, 298 p. Apps. Bibliog. fnn. Illus. Map.

> Description of Israel's foreign technical assistance programs from 1957-67--their structure and composition, recipients, and the characteristics of Israeli participants.

2637 Litvinoff, Barnet. ROAD TO JERUSALEM: ZIONISM'S IMPRINT ON HISTORY. London: Weidenfeld and Nicolson, 1966. 311 p. Bibliog. Maps. Plates.

> Published in 1965 under the title: TO THE HOUSE OF THEIR FATHERS.

2638 Meir, Golda. THIS IS OUR STRENGTH: SELECTED PAPERS. Edited, and with an introduction, by Henry M. Christman. New York: Macmillan, 1962. xviii, 158 p.

> Nineteen public statements by Israel's prime minister from 1969-74.

2639 Oden, David H. "Israel's Foreign Policy in the United Nations 1948-1967: Security Aspects." Doctoral dissertation, University of Pennsylvania, 1970. 347 p. Apps. (Available from University Microfilm.)

> Survey of Israeli positions in the United Nations on issues related to Palestine and more general questions, based upon U.N. records.

2640 Peres, Shimon. DAVID'S SLING. New York: Random House, 1971 [c1970]. 332 p.

> Narrative of the growth of Israel's defense establishment. One-third of the book is devoted to a discussion of arms supplies' negotiations with France, West Germany, and the United States. The author, Israel's defense minister, also describes the indigenous armaments industry from the standpoint of Israel's military strategic needs and capabilities and the 1956 and 1967 conflicts. No mention of advanced weapons.

2641 Peretz, Don. ISRAEL AND THE PALESTINE ARABS. Washington, D.C.: Middle East Institute, 1958 [c1956]. 264 p. Bibliog. Index.

> A long-time student of the Arab refugee problem discusses the history of various refugee policies, Israel's internal security and the Arab minority, and compensation and integration issues. Also cited in No. 4623.

2642 Perlmutter, Amos. MILITARY AND POLITICS IN ISRAEL; NATION-BUILDING AND ROLE EXPANSION. London: Frank Cass, 1969. xiv, 161 p. Bibliog. Index.

> The history of pre-independence defense units and post-indepen-

dence relations between the army and the Ministry of Defense. Extensive bibliography on Israel and military organizations in politics.

2643 Roberts, Samuel J. SURVIVAL OR HEGEMONY? THE FOUNDATIONS OF ISRAELI FOREIGN POLICY. Studies in International Affairs, 20. Baltimore, Md.: Johns Hopkins University Press, 1973. x, 163 p. Bibliog.

    A short history of Judaism from earliest times and an analysis of Zionism in the Middle East today. The author envisages accommodation between Egyptian and Israeli imperialism in which each state recognizes the other's respective sphere of influence.

2644 Sayegh, Fayez Abdullah. THE RECORD OF ISRAEL AT THE UNITED NATIONS. Information Papers, 3. New York: Arab Information Center, 1957. 124 p. Paper.

    The author cites U.N. resolutions on Palestine and related Israeli policy using U.N. documents and Israeli sources.

2645 _____. THE ZIONIST DIPLOMACY. Palestine Monographs, 13. Beirut: Palestine Liberation Organization Research Center, 1969. 160 p.

2646 Schiff, Zeev. A HISTORY OF THE ISRAELI ARMY (1870-1974). Translated by Raphael Rothstein. San Francisco: Straight Arrow Books (distr. Simon and Schuster, New York), 1974. 338 p. Bibliog. Illus. Index. Maps. Ports.

    A popularly written and largely pictorial history of the Israeli army which nonetheless contains useful information concerning military strategy, arms transfers, and the army in Israeli politics. Large collection of contemporary maps.

2647 Selzer, Michael, comp. ZIONISM RECONSIDERED; THE REJECTION OF JEWISH NORMALCY. New York: Macmillan, 1970. xxii, 259 p. Bibliog. fnn.

2648 Stock, Ernest. ISRAEL ON THE ROAD TO SINAI, 1949-1956. Ithaca, N.Y.: Cornell University Press, 1967. x, 284 p. Bibliog. Fold. map.

    The origins of the second Arab-Israeli war in disunity within the Israeli cabinet and Soviet support for Egypt which upset unacceptably the arms balance. Sequel chapter on 1967 war concludes that Israel's battlefield strategies were better prepared than its occupation strategies.

2649 Talmon, Jacob. L. ISRAEL AMONG THE NATIONS. New York: Macmillan, 1971 [c1970]. 199 p. Bibliog. ref. Index.

Foreign Policies of Middle Eastern States

Previously published, revised essays by an Israeli political philosopher on Jewish self-awareness within and outside of Israel. Includes essay which focuses upon Israel's international relationships and ideology.

2650 Teveth, Shabtai. THE CURSED BLESSING: THE STORY OF ISRAEL'S OCCUPATION OF THE WEST BANK. Translated by Myra Bank. N.Y.: Random House, 1971 [c1970]. 372 p. Illus. Index. Map.

The 1967 war and the two years afterwards on the West Bank, written from the perspective that stability contributes to accommodation. Based upon discussions with West Bank Jews and Arabs which concern Israeli occupation policies.

2651 Vogel, Rolf, ed. THE GERMAN PATH TO ISRAEL; A DOCUMENTATION. London: Oswald Wolff, 1969. 325 p. Index. Photos.

Foreword by Konrad Adenauer. Statements and correspondence of West German and Israeli leaders tracing the approval of the reparations agreements and the eventual establishment of diplomatic relations (list of documents appended).

2652 Wagner, Abraham R. CRISIS DECISION-MAKING: ISRAEL'S EXPERIENCE IN 1967 AND 1973. New York: Praeger, 1974. 186 p.

Decision-making constraints focusing upon the 1967 war and Israel. A brief chapter on 1973. Psychology, personalities, environment, and alternatives combining to make war a rational choice (author's assessment).

2653 Walichnowski, Tadeusz. THE TEL AVIV-BONN AXIS AND POLAND. Warsaw: Interpress Publishers, 1968. 88 p. Paper. Bibliog. fnn. Photos.

The author argues that the amicable relations between Israel and West Germany help to reinstate the latter's moral standing after World War II at Poland's expense while providing material benefits to Israel.

2654 ZIONISM: THE DREAM AND THE REALITY, A JEWISH CRITIQUE. Edited by Gary V. Smith. New York: Barnes and Noble, Harper and Row, 1975. 325 p.

Twenty-one essays by Jewish writers representing Zionist, anti-Zionist, and non-Zionist positions; covers years from 1917-74.

JORDAN

2701 Abidi, Aqil H. H. JORDAN, A POLITICAL STUDY. New York: Asia Publishing House, 1965. x, 251 p. App. Bibliog.

Foreign Policies of Middle Eastern States

Relations between the Jordanian monarchy and pre-1948 Palestinian leaders. The interplay between domestic and foreign (Arab nationalist) issues. Material on the United States-Soviet cold war in a Middle Eastern context.

2702 Faddah, Mohammad Ibrahim. THE MIDDLE EAST IN TRANSITION: A STUDY OF JORDAN'S FOREIGN POLICY. New York: Asia Publishing House, 1974. 339 p.

Secondary, published sources focused upon Jordan's relations with other Arab states and the West.

2703 Glubb, Sir John Bagot. A SOLDIER WITH THE ARABS. London: Hodder and Stoughton, 1957. 460 p. Maps. Ports.

Jordan's international position from World War II until 1956 based upon the recollections of the British commander of the Arab Legion (the Jordanian Army).

2704 King Hussein. UNEASY LIES THE HEAD: THE AUTOBIOGRAPHY OF HIS MAJESTY KING HUSSEIN OF THE HASHEMITE KINGDOM OF JORDAN. New York: Geis, 1962. 306 p.

Personal and public recollections.

2705 Snow, Peter. HUSSEIN, A BIOGRAPHY. Washington, D.C.: Robert B. Luce, 1972. 256 p. Bibliog. Illus.

An enthusiastic account of King Hussein's political and personal life. Hussein's perceptions of and reactions to neighboring Arab regimes. More motive than events. Information on members of the decision-making circles around the king.

2706 Vance, Vick, and Lauer, Pierre. HUSSEIN OF JORDAN: MY "WAR" WITH ISRAEL. Translated by June P. Wilson and Walter B. Michaels. New York: William Morrow and Co., 1969. 170 p. Map.

An analysis of the events in the Arab world and Jordan leading up to the 1967 war, according to King Hussein. Problems of Arab unity and the conflict between Palestinian leaders and the Hashemite monarchy.

2707 Vatikiotis, P[anayiotis].J. POLITICS AND THE MILITARY IN JORDAN: A STUDY OF THE ARAB LEGION, 1921-1957. New York: Frederick A. Praeger, 1967. xvi, 169 p. App. Maps.

The diffuse tribal and village backgrounds of the Arab Legion. Military organization and the assimilation of Palestinians into the Jordanian polity. The withdrawal of direct British involvement in the Legion (1956-57) has meant that it relies on technical support from within Jordan. This, plus new recruiting procedures, meant that obtaining the support of the Palestinian West Bank for the Jordanian State and the Hashemite dynasty was a crucial task for the 1960s. Important background for understanding the 1970 civil war as well as the 1967 defeat, in which technical disparities among the adversaries were critical. Careful attention to detail.

LEBANON

2801 Binder, Leonard, ed. POLITICS IN LEBANON. New York: John Wiley, 1966. 345 p. Index.

> Seventeen essays on various aspects of Lebanese politics including "The Personality of Lebanon in Relation to the Modern World" by Kamal Salibi and "Lebanese Democracy in the International Setting" by Jacob C. Hurewitz.

2802 Hudson, Michael C. THE PRECARIOUS REPUBLIC; POLITICAL MODERNIZATION IN LEBANON. New York: Random House, 1968. xvi, 364 p. Bibliog. Illus. Maps.

> Emphasizes internal politics--elites, organizations, and political processes--but also discusses foreign policy.

2803 Meo, Leila M.T. LEBANON: IMPROBABLE NATION. International Studies Series. Bloomington: Indiana University Press, 1965. 346 p.

> Internal politics and Lebanon in world politics and the Mandate system. The Eisenhower Doctrine and Arab state nationalism. Based on interviews and primary sources.

2804 Salibi, Kamal S. THE MODERN HISTORY OF LEBANON. London: Weidenfeld and Nicolson, 1965. 227 p. Bibliog. Index. Maps.

> The historical development of Lebanon from the seventeenth century to the 1958 civil war. Focuses upon social and economic conditions.

LIBYA

2901 Khadduri, Majid [D.]. MODERN LIBYA: A STUDY IN POLITICAL DEVELOPMENT. Baltimore: Johns Hopkins Press, 1963. 404 p. Apps. Bibliog. fnn. Index. Map. Ports.

> Devotes considerable attention to the issue of Libya's independence before the United Nations and to later foreign policies. Constitution and foreign agreements appended. Written prior to the overthrow of King Idris.

2902 Pelt, Adrian. LIBYAN INDEPENDENCE AND THE UNITED NATIONS, A CASE OF PLANNED DECOLONIZATION. New Haven, Conn. and London: Yale University Press for the Carnegie Endowment for International Peace, 1970. xxviii, 1,016 p. Apps. Bibliog. Index. Refs. Map.

> The author, United Nations commissioner preceding Libya's independence, discusses Libya's integration, the strategies of the administering powers, and the General Assembly's initiative in overcoming the "big four" deadlock over Libya's future status. Based upon reminiscences, interviews, and documents.

2903 Rivlin, Benjamin. THE UNITED NATIONS AND THE ITALIAN COLONIES. New York: Carnegie Endowment for International Peace, 1950. 114 p.

> Includes Libya. By a former officer in the U.N. Trusteeship Department.

MOROCCO

3001 Zartman, I. William. PROBLEMS OF NEW POWER: MOROCCO. New York: Atherton, 1964. 276 p. Maps.

> Looks at international issues confronting Morocco in addition to internal development problems.

SAUDI ARABIA, YEMEN, AND THE ARABIAN PENINSULA

3101 Brown, Edward Hoagland. THE SAUDI ARABIA-KUWAIT NEUTRAL ZONE. Middle East Oil Monograph, 4. Beirut: Middle East Research and Publishing Center, 1963. 150 p.

> The history and legal aspects of oil concessions and production in the neutral zone.

3102 DeGaury, Gerald. FAISAL, KING OF SAUDI ARABIA. London: Barber, 1966; New York: Praeger, 1967. 191 p. Bibliog. Illus.

> Personal and official details from a sympathetic vantage point.

3103 Dickson, Harold R.P. KUWAIT AND HER NEIGHBORS. London: George Allen and Unwin, 1956. 627 p. Illus. Maps. Ports.

> Reminiscences and historical description.

3104 Holden, David. FAREWELL TO ARABIA. New York: Walker, 1966. 268 p.

> Popularly written, critical account of politics and the problems of political change in the Arabian peninsula states. By a British journalist.

3105 THE ARABIAN PENINSULA: SOCIETY AND POLITICS. Edited by Derek Hopwood. Studies on Modern Asia and Africa. Totawa, N.J.: Rowman and Littlefield; London: George Allen and Unwin, 1972. 320 p. Bibliog. ref. Maps.

> The Gulf states, Saudi Arabia, Yemen, and the peninsula. Covers social and economic topics as well as politics and foreign policy. Fourteen essays presented at a 1968-69 seminar held jointly by the Oxford University Middle East Centre and the University of London Centre of Middle Eastern Studies. Also cited in No. 1304.

3106 Ingrams, William Harold. THE YEMEN: IMANS, RULERS, AND REVOLUTIONS. London: J. Murray; New York: Frederick Praeger, 1963. xi, 164 p. Illus. Map. Ports.

> A survey of the Yemen's recent history by a former British colonial officer. Includes favorable references to the colonial experience and evaluations of future political alternatives.

3107 Kelly, John Barrett. EASTERN ARABIAN FRONTIERS. New York: Praeger, 1964. 319 p. Bibliog. fnn.

> Eastern frontier disputes of Saudi Arabia from 1935, from the British perspective. Focuses upon the Buraimi Oasis.

3108 Landen, Robert G. OMAN SINCE 1856: DISRUPTIVE MODERNIZATION IN A TRADITIONAL ARAB SOCIETY. Princeton, N.J.: Princeton University Press, 1967. xv, 488 p. Bibliog. Maps.

3109 Little, Tom. SOUTH ARABIA: ARENA OF CONFLICT. New York: Frederick A. Praeger, 1968. 196 p. Index. Maps.

> External state involvement, Arab and non-Arab, in the collapse of the Federation of South Arabia and the establishment of the Yemen Republic. Little documentation; short bibliography.

3110 Macro, Eric. YEMEN AND THE WESTERN WORLD SINCE 1571. New York: Praeger, 1968. xvi, 150 p. Bibliog. Index. Map.

> Primarily twentieth-century inter-Arab state politics and external involvement in the Yemen region with little documentation. European language sources.

3111 O'Ballance, Edgar. THE WAR IN YEMEN. Hamden, Conn.: Archon, 1971. 218 p. Index.

> Description of the civil war and external intervention, undocumented and critical of the late Egyptian President Nasser. Detailed journalism.

3112 Sanger, Richard H. THE ARABIAN PENINSULA. Ithaca, N.Y.: Cornell University Press, 1954. Reprint. Freeport, N.Y.: Books for Libraries Press, 1970. 295 p.

> A general survey concerned with the influence of the United States. Based upon firsthand observations and official U.S. sources.

3113 Schmidt, Dana Adams. THE YEMEN: UNKNOWN WAR. New York: Holt, Rinehart & Winston, 1968. 316 p. Illus. Maps. Ports.

> The Yemen war from the overthrow of Imam Ahmad al-Badr (1962). By a NEW YORK TIMES correspondent.

3114 Trevaskis, Sir Gerald Kennedy Nicolas. SHADES OF AMBER: A SOUTH ARABIAN EPISODE. London: Hutchinson, 1968. xv, 256 p. Illus. Maps. Plates. Ports.

> The plan for the Federation of South Arabia, authored by its diplomat-architect.

3115 Waterfield, Gordon. SULTANS OF ADEN. London: John Murray, 1968. xiii, 267 p. Bibliog. refs. Illus. Maps. Plates. Ports.

> The history of southern Arabia. Detailed and documented.

3116 Wenner, Manfred W. MODERN YEMEN: 1918-66. Baltimore: Johns Hopkins Press, 1967. 257 p. Bibliog. Maps.

> Independent Yemen in international affairs, including its relations with the United States.

SYRIA

3201 Abu Jaber, Kamel S. THE ARAB BA'TH SOCIALIST PARTY: HISTORY, IDEOLOGY, AND ORGANIZATION. Syracuse, N.Y.: Syracuse University Press, 1966. 218 p.

> The party's history, ideology, and regional organization. Focuses on the Syrian Ba'th Party.

3202 al-Akhrass, Safouh. REVOLUTIONARY CHANGE AND MODERNIZATION IN THE ARAB WORLD: A CASE FROM SYRIA. Damascus: Atlas, 1972. xv, 264 p.

3203 Burrowes, Robert, and Spector, Bert. "The Strength and Direction of Relationships between Domestic and External Conflict and Cooperation: Syria, 1961-1967." In CONFLICT BEHAVIOR AND LINKAGE POLITICS, compiled by Jonathan Wilkenfeld. New York: McKay, 1973.

> The quantitative use of event data to explore foreign policy patterns.

Foreign Policies of Middle Eastern States

3204 Hourani, Albert H. SYRIA AND LEBANON: A POLITICAL ESSAY. 1946. Reprint. London: Oxford University Press, 1968. 402 p. Apps. Bibliog. Maps.

    Background on social, political and diplomatic issues. European colonial interests and Greater Syria's place in the Arab world. Mandate documents appended.

3205 Petran, Tabitha. SYRIA. New York: Praeger Publishers, 1972. 284 p. Bibliog. Maps.

    Not specifically a foreign policy study, but includes the international dimension of Syria's statehood and Syria's role in the Arab-Israeli conflict. The conflict within Syrian leadership circles over the 1967 defeat in the Golan.

3206 Rabinovich, Itamar. SYRIA UNDER THE BA'TH 1963-66. THE ARMY-PARTY SYMBIOSIS. Monograph Series, Shiloah Center for Middle Eastern and African Studies, Tel Aviv University. Jerusalem: Israeli Universities Press, 1972. xix, 276 p. Apps. Bibliog.

    Domestic politics and Syrian-Egyptian relations. Appendixes include biographical information on Syrian leaders.

3207 Torrey, Gordon H. SYRIAN POLITICS AND THE MILITARY, 1945-1958. Columbus: Ohio State University Press, 1964. 438 p. Apps. Bibliog. Index.

    Domestic politics and the union with Egypt.

3208 Yamak, Labib Zuwiyya. THE SYRIAN SOCIAL NATIONALIST PARTY: AN IDEOLOGICAL ANALYSIS. Cambridge, Mass.: Harvard University Press, 1966. 177 p.

    Lebanese history from the mid-nineteenth to mid-twentieth century. The party's organization and doctrine of Syrian nationalism.

3209 Zeine, Zeine N. THE STRUGGLE FOR ARAB INDEPENDENCE: WESTERN DIPLOMACY AND THE RISE AND FALL OF FAISAL'S KINGDOM IN SYRIA. Beirut: Khayats, 1960. 297 p.

    The First World War and immediately thereafter--Anglo-French conflict and Arab nationalism.

TUNISIA

3301 Ling, Dwight L. TUNISIA, FROM PROTECTORATE TO REPUBLIC. Indiana University International Studies. Bloomington: Indiana University Press, 1967. xi, 273 p. Bibliog. Bibliog ref. Chron. Illus. Index. Map.

Tunisia's protectorate history and the institutionalization of the post-independence regime. A variety of sources: government documents, interviews, periodicals. Also cited in No. 1119.

TURKEY

3401 Ata'ov, Turkkaya. TURKISH FOREIGN POLICY, 1939-1945. Ankara: Ankara University, 1965. 148 p. Bibliog.

3402 Balfour, John Patrick Douglas, Baron Kincross. ATATURK: A BIOGRAPHY OF MUSTAFA KEMAL, FATHER OF MODERN TURKEY. New York: Morros, 1965. 614 p.

Public actions are emphasized--internal reforms and international diplomacy. Mustafa Kemal's rise as a Turkish leader during the First World War.

3403 Cemal, Ahmed Pasha. MEMOIRS OF A TURKISH STATESMAN, 1913-1919. 1922. Reprint. New York: Arno, 1973. 302 p.

3404 Erkin, Feridun Cemal. LES RELATIONS TURCO-SOVIETIQUES ET LA QUESTION DES DESTROITS. Ankara: Basnur Matbassi, 1968. 540 p.

Focuses upon Soviet-Turkish relations and the straits. The memoirs of a former Turkish foreign minister and ambassador to the United States.

3405 Harris, George Sellers. TROUBLED ALLIANCE; TURKISH-AMERICAN PROBLEMS IN HISTORICAL PERSPECTIVE, 1945-1971. AEI-Hoover Policy Studies, 2. Washington, D.C.: American Enterprise Institute for Public Research, 1972. 263 p. Bibliog. Illus.

The Turkish view of the alliance as a source of development assistance and military backing against the Soviet Union.

3406 Heyd, Uriel. FOUNDATIONS OF TURKISH NATIONALISM, THE LIFE AND TEACHINGS OF ZIYA GOKALP. London: Luzac, 1950. 174 p.

Originally written in Hebrew for the Hebrew University in Jerusalem as a Ph.D. thesis.

3407 Hostler, Charles W. TURKISM AND THE SOVIETS: THE TURKS OF THE WORLD AND THEIR POLITICAL OBJECTIVES. London: Allen and Unwin; New York: Frederick A. Praeger, 1957. xiv, 214 p. Bibliog. Illus. Maps.

3408 Howard, Harry N. THE PARTITION OF TURKEY: A STUDY IN DIPLOMATIC HISTORY, 1913-1923. 1931. Reprint. New York: Howard

Fertig, 1966. 486 p. Bibliog. refs.

> Pre-World War I and the post-War peace conferences. The Middle East settlement.

3409 Kilic, Altemur. TURKEY AND THE WORLD. Introduction by William O. Douglas. Washington, D.C.: Public Affairs Press, 1959. 224 p. Bibliog. Index.

> A survey of the foreign relations of Turkey from the end of the nineteenth century by a Turkish correspondent and diplomat. A short but useful bibliography. Justifies occasional differences between Turkey and the United States.

3410 Lewis, Bernard. THE EMERGENCE OF MODERN TURKEY. 2d ed. New York and London: Oxford University Press for the Royal Institute of International Affairs, 1968. xi, 530 p. Bibliog. Maps.

> General political and economic background to contemporary Turkey since the Ottoman reform movements.

3411 Romeril, P. E. A. WAR DIPLOMACY AND THE TURKISH REPUBLIC: A STUDY IN NEUTRALITY. Leiden: Brill, 1970. 150 p.

> Turkey's position in World War II, written by a Canadian diplomat.

3412 Shotwell, James T., and Deak, Francis. TURKEY AT THE STRAITS; A SHORT HISTORY. 1940. Reprint. Freeport, N.Y.: Books for Libraries Press, 1971. xii, 196 p. Bibliog.

> Includes texts of treaties and conventions with Turkey.

3413 TURKEY AND THE UNITED NATIONS. National Studies on International Organization. New York: Manhattan Publishing Co. for the Carnegie Endowment for International Peace, 1961. 228 p. Apps. Index.

> Turkey's international commitments and the activities of the League of Nations, NATO, and the United Nations. Based upon press reviews, official statements, and opinion polls.

3414 Vali, Ferenc A. BRIDGE ACROSS THE BOSPORUS: THE FOREIGN POLICY OF TURKEY. Baltimore: Johns Hopkins Press, 1971. xiv, 410 p. Bibliog. Map.

> The first comprehensive study of Turkish foreign policy, based upon both Western and Turkish sources. Focuses primarily upon the post-World War II period and analyzes the historical, geopolitical, and cultural elements in the Republic's policies toward NATO, the Arab states, Israel, Iran, and others.

Foreign Policies of Middle Eastern States

3415 _____. THE TURKISH STRAITS AND NATO. Stanford, Calif.: Hoover Institution, 1972. 348 p. Apps. Bibliog. Maps.

> Reviews the place of the straits in NATO strategy. More than thirty documents are appended.

3416 Weisband, Edward. TURKISH FOREIGN POLICY, 1943-1945: SMALL STATE DIPLOMACY AND GREAT POWER POLITICS. Princeton, N.J.: Princeton University Press, 1973. xiii, 377 p. Bibliog.

> Seeks to explain Turkish policy during World War II. Useful bibliography of primary and secondary sources. Discusses Turkey's tactics of national preservation in the face of possible external intervention.

Chapter 4
EXTERNAL POWERS IN THE MIDDLE EAST

The great majority of the entries in this section are studies of U.S. and Soviet policies in the Middle East. The imbalance is partly a function of the English language coverage. More important, it is a reflection of the reduction in British and French power in the Middle East following World War II and the 1956 Suez invasion and the simultaneous intensification of US-Soviet competition in the region. Many of the books listed under "Nationalism and the Colonial Experience" cover pre-World War II British and French foreign policy. The listings in this section focus upon the interests of specific external powers. More general discussions of the role of external powers can be found in the sections on "The Middle East in World Politics" and in "The Foreign Policies of Middle Eastern States."

BRITAIN

The most comprehensive study of recent British policy in the Middle East is Darby's BRITISH DEFENSE POLICY EAST OF SUEZ, 1947-1968 [3504]. Darby links the retrenchment of British involvement to internal constraints and the growth of nationalism in the region. The material referenced in the section on the Mandate period forms the background to his claims that a presence in the Middle East was simply too costly.

Epstein's BRITISH POLITICS IN THE SUEZ CRISIS [3505] illustrates Darby's theme in the specific case of the Suez invasion and British parliamentary politics. Epstein is primarily interested in the workings of the British system in foreign policy making. Few studies with this kind of focus are available.

Looking back over Britain's experience in the Middle East during this century, Fitzsimons concludes that the mandate and protectorate systems were fundamentally unworkable [EMPIRE BY TREATY [3512]). The delineation of the treaty system in the Fertile Crescent at the 1921 Cairo Conference is thoroughly detailed in Klieman's 1970 study, FOUNDATIONS OF BRITISH POLICY IN THE ARAB WORLD [3513].

External Powers in the Middle East

OTHER EXTERNAL POWERS

Among the few entries here, Crosbie's A TACIT ALLIANCE [3603] and Khalili's COMMUNIST CHINA'S INTERACTION WITH ARAB NATIONALISTS [3606] are particularly useful. Crosbie has written an analytical case study of the almost incidental overlapping of French-Israeli interests during the 1950s. Her approach is likely to be of interest to nonarea specialists as well as students of Middle East politics. Khalili's book is brief but important because of its subject. China's entry into Middle Eastern politics is a relatively unexplored topic.

UNITED STATES FOREIGN POLICY

United States foreign policy in the Middle East prior to World War II is covered by several volumes, each of which has a limited time span. However, in combination, these studies extend from the eighteenth century onward. Early contacts between the United States and the Middle East were more often religious and economic than official.

The major official commitments to the Middle East were made after the Second World War and, of these, one of the earliest was American involvement in the Palestine conflict and the establishment of Israel. Sufficient time has elapsed since the Truman administration to allow access to more materials on its policy decisions. Snetsinger's TRUMAN, THE JEWISH VOTE AND THE CREATION OF ISRAEL [3851] and Schechtman's THE UNITED STATES AND THE JEWISH STATE MOVEMENT [3849] are both extensive analyses of the domestic political climate at that time. The latter book also provides some historical background in terms of U.S. relations with the Mandate and President Roosevelt's discussions with King Saud. For later American-Israeli relations, the most comprehensive study is Safran's THE UNITED STATES AND ISRAEL [3848]. Safran's book was published in 1963, however, and U.S. policy has changed considerably since then.

Sheehan's description of U.S.-Iran relations, published in 1968, is more current (IRAN [3836]) but is a somewhat limited view of the variety of U.S. interests in Iran. Cottam's COMPETITIVE INTERFERENCE AND TWENTIETH CENTURY DIPLOMACY [3834] is essentially a case study of U.S. commitment to Iran's internal political stability. It is more thorough than Sheehan's work, but undocumented.

Surprisingly few general studies of American policy toward the Middle East are available. One of the most provocative is Badeau's THE AMERICAN APPROACH TO THE ARAB WORLD [3805]. Badeau, a former U.S. ambassador to Egypt, writes about positive neutralist roles for the United States toward the region. Badeau is concerned particularly about the effect of American pressure upon nationalist regimes. From a different approach, Lenczowski (UNITED STATES INTERESTS IN THE MIDDLE EAST [3804]) details the variety of U.S. interests which explain its involvement in the area. "America and the Middle East" [3802], similar in coverage, was published as a single issue of the journal serial, THE ANNALS.

Congressional hearings and staff reports are an extremely useful source of information about American policy and critiques of American policies. A few of the most recent hearings are listed. The number of hearings tends to be greatest during periods of intense American activity in the region. Thus, numerous other titles are to be found in the periods from 1955-58 (the Baghdad Pact, Suez, and the Lebanese action), 1969-71 (the Rogers Plan), and 1973 to the present with the Kissinger negotiations and the oil embargo.

A substantial number of documents relating to U.S. policy in the Middle East are available in general documents series. Current and very general statements of U.S. interests and objectives in the Middle East are included in the President's now annual "State of the World" message to Congress. In addition, Magnus (DOCUMENTS ON THE MIDDLE EAST [3867] has compiled a collection of statements and agreements which is unusually even in terms of geographic coverage, not focusing exclusively on the Arab-Israeli conflict.

SOVIET POLICY IN THE MIDDLE EAST

The amount of published material on Soviet policy in the Middle East has increased significantly in recent years. Soviet policy has shifted from an emphasis upon domestic communist parties to interstate relations. The relative number of books on foreign policy vis-a-vis internal communism has grown along with this shift in Soviet strategy.

Several general studies place Soviet policies in the Middle East into the context of other commitments, domestic and foreign. Becker's section in SOVIET POLICY IN THE MIDDLE EAST (Becker and Horelick [3702]) enumerates those constraints on Soviet Middle Eastern policy that come from the Communist world, its military capabilities, detente, and the possibility of nuclear proliferation in the region. THE USSR AND THE MIDDLE EAST (Confino and Shamir [3730]) is also an overview in which foreign policy decision-making and internal Communist party activities are described. A similar overview is given by Laqueur in THE STRUGGLE FOR THE MIDDLE EAST [3716].

A shorter and slightly older volume reviews USSR-U.S. competition across a range of activities--economic, cultural, and military (Hurewitz [3708]). It provides a good bibliography, but much less detailed information about Soviet policy.

Several books discuss specific focuses of Soviet interest. Freedman [3704] describes the chronology of USSR involvement in the Arab-Israeli conflict since the Second World War. THE SOVIET UNION AND THE OCTOBER 1973 MIDDLE EAST WAR (Kohler, Goure, and Harvey [3713]) is a much shorter look at the questions posed for detente with the United States by the Soviet Union's indirect participation in the war.

Similarly specific, Ra'anan's THE USSR ARMS THE THIRD WORLD [3722] documents the sequence of events which led to the Egyptian-Czechoslovakian arms agreement in 1955 in order to determine whether Egypt's action was a reaction to the West or whether Egypt and the Soviet Union had been planning the arms transfers for some time.

The Soviet Union began to supply arms to Egypt and Syria in the mid-1950s. A more recent issue is the growth of Soviet-U.S. interest in the Indian Ocean. SOVIET NAVAL DEVELOPMENTS is a collection of papers which includes analyses of naval forces in the Mediterranean and Indian Ocean (MccGwire [3725]). Several of the volumes listed in the Persian Gulf and Indian Ocean section also cover Soviet activities there.

Documents relating to the Soviet Union in the Middle East are compiled and woven together chronologically in Ro'i [3723]. Ro'i's is the most complete documentary published. For other references, THE SOVIET UNION AND THE MIDDLE EAST contains a bibliographic essay (Lederer and Vucinich [3728]).

Few books have been published on the history of Soviet policy in the Middle East. THE SOVIET UNION AND THE MUSLIM WORLD (Spector [3740]) is the most comprehensive historical survey. Persia (Iran) and the other northern tier states were a major emphasis in Russian policy which continues to the present. Kapur describes the shift in tactics which followed the 1917 revolution (SOVIET RUSSIA AND ASIA, 1917-1927 [3736]) and Nollau and Wiehe [3739] and Lenczowski [3738] trace Soviet policies in that region into the subsequent decades.

INTERNAL COMMUNISM

The compatibility of communism, nationalism, and Arab socialism in the Middle East is often at issue. WARY PARTNERS (Buss [3703]) looks at doctrinal differences. Agwani argues that ideological and practical conflicts between Arab nationalism and Soviet foreign policy are not insurmountable (COMMUNISM IN THE ARAB EAST [3742]).

Focusing upon more specific contexts, Harris [3743] and Zabih [3746] both illustrate sources of tension or conflict between Communist parties and the post-World War I nationalist regimes in Turkey and Iran. Laqueur's COMMUNISM AND NATIONALISM IN THE MIDDLE EAST [3744] covers a more recent period than Harris or Zabih, but emphasizes ideology rather than a range of political behavior.

BRITISH POLICY IN THE MIDDLE EAST

General

3501 BACKGROUND TO THE MIDDLE EAST SITUATION 1958. New York and
    Washington, D.C.: British Information Services, April 1958. 29 p. Maps.

This pamphlet covers the Baghdad Pact, the Eisenhower Doctrine, Suez invasion, and the 1950 Tripartite Convention.

3502 Blaxland, Gregory. EGYPT AND SINAI: ETERNAL BATTLEGROUND. New York: Funk, 1968. 327 p.

    A history of British-Egyptian relations, with little coverage of the post-Suez period.

3503 Bullard, Sir Reader William. BRITAIN AND THE MIDDLE EAST FROM EARLIEST TIMES TO 1963. 3d rev. ed. London: Hutchinson, 1964. 200 p.

    A general survey by a former British diplomat in Tehran.

3504 Darby, Phillip. BRITISH DEFENSE POLICY EAST OF SUEZ, 1947-1968. London and New York: Oxford University Press for the Royal Institute for International Affairs, 1973. 366 p.

    The effects of domestic financial constraints, ideology, and nationalism upon British policy. Military issues also explored.

3505 Epstein, Leon D. BRITISH POLITICS IN THE SUEZ CRISIS. Urbana: University of Illinois Press, 1964. xi, 220 p. Bibliog. fnn.

    A study of British parliamentary politics, using the 1956 Suez invasion as a case study. Finds partisan loyalties persistent in foreign policy.

3506 King, Gillian. IMPERIAL OUTPOST-ADEN: ITS PLACE IN BRITISH STRATEGIC POLICY. Chatham House Essays, 6. London and New York: Oxford University Press, 1964. 93 p. Maps.

    Summary of Britain's strategic interests in the Arabian Peninsula and Indian Ocean in light of Arab state politics. Primary sources; little documentation.

3507 Monroe, Elizabeth. BRITAIN'S MOMENT IN THE MIDDLE EAST, 1914-1956. Baltimore: Johns Hopkins Press, 1963. 254 p. Bibliog. Index. Refs.

    A largely uncritical rendition of British policy toward the Arab Middle East—marked by the "straightforward pursuit of British interests." Bibliography includes notes on sources, including periodicals and unpublished papers.

3508 Royal Institute of International Affairs. BRITISH INTERESTS IN THE MEDITERRANEAN AND MIDDLE EAST. Chatham House Report. London: Oxford University Press for the Royal Institute of International Affairs, 1958. 123 p.

Undocumented report of a group formed in 1956. Overview of external and Arab state interests in the region and conclusions for British foreign policy.

3509 Woodhouse, Christopher M. BRITAIN AND THE MIDDLE EAST. Publications de l'Institut Universitaire de Hautes Etudes Internationales, 30. Geneva: Librarie E. Droz, 1959. 59 p.

"Three lectures by Director General of the Royal Institute for International Affairs." Summary of relations between Great Britain and the Middle East.

Historical

3510 Amin, Abdul Amir. BRITISH INTERESTS IN THE PERSIAN GULF. Leiden: E.J. Brill, 1967. 163 p. Apps. Bibliog. Maps.

Covers British policies toward the Gulf principalities in the eighteenth century. Extensive documentation from primary sources.

3511 Busch, Briton Cooper. BRITAIN, INDIA, AND THE ARABS, 1914-1921. Berkeley: University of California Press, 1971. 522 p. Bibliog. Index. Maps.

A continuation of the author's earlier book on Britain and the Persian Gulf, 1894-1914. The author provides a detailed analysis of the impact of the British government in India upon Whitehall's Arab policy during the premandate period.

3512 Fitzsimons, Matthew A. EMPIRE BY TREATY: BRITAIN AND THE MIDDLE EAST IN THE TWENTIETH CENTURY. International Studies. Notre Dame, Ind.: Notre Dame University Press, 1964. 235 p. Index. Maps.

Arab history and British diplomacy in the twentieth century. Britain's effort to maintain order was doomed to failure. Based upon secondary and primary sources and the press.

3513 Klieman, Aaron S. FOUNDATIONS OF BRITISH POLICY IN THE ARAB WORLD: THE CAIRO CONFERENCE OF 1921. Baltimore and London: Johns Hopkins Press, 1970. xiv, 322 p. Apps. Bibliog. Maps.

A first comprehensive history of the Cairo Conference and its contest. British mandate decisions based on primary sources. The establishment of Faisal in Iraq, Abdullah in Jordan, and a policy of "drift" in Palestine. Extensive documentation.

OTHER EXTERNAL POWERS

3601 Ahmad, S. Maqbul. INDO-ARAB RELATIONS: AN ACCOUNT OF INDIA'S RELATIONS WITH THE ARAB WORLD FROM ANCIENT UP TO MODERN TIMES. New Delhi: Indian Council for Cultural Relations, 1969. 187 p.

    Political, cultural, and economic relations.

3602 Baulin, Jacques [pseud.]. THE ARAB ROLE IN AFRICA. Baltimore: Penguin African Library, 1962. 144 p.

    A journalist's survey of relations among the states bordering the Sahara.

3603 Crosbie, Sylvia K. A TACIT ALLIANCE: FRANCE AND ISRAEL FROM SUEZ TO THE SIX DAY WAR. Modern Middle East Series, 7. Princeton, N.J.: Princeton University Press, 1974. xii, 280 p. Bibliog. Index.

    A well-documented study of French-Israeli relations focusing upon French policy and the military technology and weapons transfers resulting from the alliance. Based upon interviews with military leaders and diplomats in France and Israel and numerous written sources in French and English. Useful bibliography of periodical sources, especially military issues. Also cited in No. 2613.

3604 Glick, Edward B. LATIN AMERICA AND THE PALESTINE PROBLEM. New York: Theodor Herzl Foundation, 1958. 199 p. Apps. Bibliog. Index.

    The positions taken by Latin American states in the United Nations debates on the disposition of Palestine, based upon interviews with delegates and official sources. Little account is taken of regional political realities in the author's explanations of Latin American state policies.

3605 Kelly, George Armstrong. LOST SOLDIERS: THE FRENCH ARMY AND EMPIRE IN CRISIS, 1947-1962. Cambridge: M.I.T. Press, 1965. x, 404 p. Bibliog.

    French strategy in Algeria (and Indochina) and its impact on the army's loyalties. Periodical sources. Also cited in No. 1117.

3606 Khalili, Joseph E. COMMUNIST CHINA'S INTERACTION WITH ARAB NATIONALISTS SINCE THE BANDUNG CONFERENCE. Jericho, N.Y.: Exposition, 1970. 121 p.

    Conflict and cooperation between the Arab states and China. Disputes the notion that competition for influence in the Middle East is the exclusive prerogative of the Soviet Union and the United States.

External Powers in the Middle East

3607 Sulzberger, Cyns Leo. THE TEST: DEGAULLE AND ALGERIA. London and New York: Harcourt, Brace & World, 1962. 228 p.

A journalist's account of de Gaulle's leadership which is only partly concerned with Algeria.

SOVIET POLICY IN THE MIDDLE EAST

General

3701 Baczkowski, Wlodzimierz. SOVIET POLICY IN THE MIDDLE EAST. Washington, D.C.: Georgetown University, Institute of Ethnic Studies, 1958. 27 p.

Growing Soviet penetration into the Middle East since 1955 based upon the common ethnic background of Soviet Eurasians and peoples of the Middle East. Cold war perspective.

3702 Becker, Abraham S., and Horelick, Arnold I. SOVIET POLICY IN THE MIDDLE EAST. Santa Monica, Calif.: Rand Corporation, 1970. xiii, 115 p. Bibliog. ref.

Two sections: (1) historical patterns in which deepening Soviet involvement is a result of the declining salience of the Baghdad pact and shifts in United States's weapons technology (Horelick) and (2) Soviet foreign policy decisions reflecting developments within the communist world, the Soviet Union's military capabilities, detente, and nuclear proliferation in the area (Becker).

3703 Buss, Robin. WARY PARTNERS: THE SOVIET UNION AND ARAB SOCIALISM. Adelphi Papers, 73. London: Institute for Strategic Studies, 1970. 28 p. Bibliog. ref.

Class conflict in Marxism and its absence in Arab socialist theory. Based upon the cases of the (Egyptian) Arab Socialist Union, the Ba'th Party, the FLN (Algeria), and the Palestinian fedayeen.

3704 Freedman, Robert O. SOVIET POLICY TOWARD THE MIDDLE EAST SINCE 1970. New York: Praeger, 1975. 224 p. Bibliog.

Chronological approach focusing upon the Arab-Israeli conflict with review of Soviet policy since World War II and ending with the 1974 Vladivostok Summit.

3705 Giritli, Ismet. SUPERPOWERS IN THE MIDDLE EAST. Istanbul: Fakulteler Matbaasi, 1972. 202 p. Bibliog. notes.

Focuses upon the Soviet Union's interests and policies in several areas, including Turkey and Iran, and upon Sino-Soviet rivalry in the Middle East. Mainly English language sources. Useful references.

3706 Golan, Galia. THE SOVIET INVOLVEMENT IN THE MIDDLE EAST. Jerusalem: Hebrew University, Soviet and East European Research Center, 1971. 19 p. Bibliog. ref.

   Egypt's place in Soviet foreign policy and the Arab-Israeli conflict.

3707 Hunter, Robert E. THE SOVIET DILEMMA IN THE MIDDLE EAST. 2 vols. Adelphi Papers, 59, 60. London: Institute for Strategic Studies, 1969. Map.

   Two volumes: (1) PROBLEMS OF COMMITMENT; (2) OIL AND THE PERSIAN GULF. An introduction to Soviet policy in the Middle East--military commitments, economic and strategic interests, and ideological dilemmas.

3708 Hurewitz, Jacob Coleman, ed. SOVIET-AMERICAN RIVALRY IN THE MIDDLE EAST. New York: Praeger, 1967. 250 p. Paper. Bibliog.

   Fifteen essays on military competition, economic policies, cultural relations, and regional strategic issues. Good bibliography.

3709 Israel. Ministry of Foreign Affairs. THE USSR AND ARAB BELLIGERENCY. Jerusalem: Information Division, 1967. 87 p. Paper.

   Excerpts from the Soviet and Arab State press and radio broadcasts illustrating the high level of antagonism toward Israel prior to the 1967 war.

3710 Joshua, Wynfred. SOVIET PENETRATION INTO THE MIDDLE EAST. New York: National Strategy Information Center, 1970. 45 p. Bibliog. Map.

   Soviet policy constraints and competition between Egypt and Iraq for Soviet support.

3711 Jukes, Geoffrey. THE INDIAN OCEAN IN SOVIET NAVAL POLICY. Adelphi Papers, 87. London: International Institute for Strategic Studies, 1972. 30 p. Apps. Refs.

   A thorough analysis of published evidence on the extent and purposes of the Soviet naval presence in the Indian Ocean. Useful references.

3712 Klieman, Aaron S. SOVIET RUSSIA AND THE MIDDLE EAST. Washington Center of Foreign Policy Research. Studies in International Affairs, 14. Baltimore, Md.: Johns Hopkins Press, 1970. 107 p. Paper. Bibliog.

Summary of the Soviet Union's position in the Middle East and its policy implications for the United States.

3713 Kohler, Foy D.; Goure, Leon; and Harvey, Mose L. THE SOVIET UNION AND THE OCTOBER 1973 MIDDLE EAST WAR: THE IMPLICATIONS FOR DETENTE. Monographs in International Affairs. Coral Gables, Fla.: University of Miami, Center for Advanced International Studies, 1974. xi, 131 p. Bibliog. ref.

The immediate postwar period up to the Egyptian-Israeli cease-fire. Well-documented, brief, deals only sketchily with the United States' approach to detente in the Middle East context. Foy Kohler is a former U.S. Ambassador to the Soviet Union.

3714 Kulski, W. W. THE SOVIET UNION IN WORLD AFFAIRS. A DOCUMENTED ANALYSIS, 1964-1972. Syracuse, N.Y.: Syracuse University Press, 1973. xiv, 526 p. Bibliog.

Soviet nuclear and regional strategy with a section on the Middle East.

3715 Landis, Lincoln. POLITICS AND OIL, MOSCOW IN THE MIDDLE EAST. New York: Dunellen, 1973. 201 p. Apps. Bibliog. Illus. Index. Map.

Soviet relations with oil-producing states. Concludes that the primary Soviet role in the international oil industry will be that of a middleman. Oil data and several official statements appended. Extensive bibliography.

3716 Laqueur, Walter Ze'ez. THE STRUGGLE FOR THE MIDDLE EAST: THE SOVIET UNION IN THE MEDITERRANEAN, 1958-1968. New York: Macmillan, 1969. 360 p. App. Bibliog. ref. Index.

Soviet diplomatic relations with the northern tier and Arab countries during the pre-1967-war period; Soviet economic interests in the Middle East and the activities of Communist, Maoist, and Arab Socialist organizations. Sources are chiefly Soviet periodicals. Statements of Soviet and Middle Eastern leaders appended.

3717 Lenczowski, George. SOVIET ADVANCES IN THE MIDDLE EAST. Washington, D.C.: American Enterprise Institute for Public Policy Research, 1972. 176 p. Bibliog. ref. Index. Maps.

Country studies and arms flows from a descriptive, historical perspective. Primary sources.

3718 McLane, Charles B. SOVIET-THIRD WORLD RELATIONS. VOL. 1: SOVIET MIDDLE EAST RELATIONS. London: Central Asian Research

Centre (dist. by Columbia University Press, New York), 1973. 126 p. Apps. Bibliog.

> A chronological record of Soviet relations with sixteen Middle Eastern states, including North Africa. Classified by country.

3719 Millar, Thomas B. SOVIET POLICIES IN THE INDIAN OCEAN AREA. Canberra Papers on Strategy and Defence, 7. Canberra: Australian National University Press, 1970. 136 p.

3720 Page, Stephen. THE USSR AND ARABIA: THE DEVELOPMENT OF SOVIET POLICIES AND ATTITUDES TOWARDS THE COUNTRIES OF THE ARABIAN PENINSULA, 1955-1970. London: Central Asian Research Centre in association with Canadian Institute of International Affairs, 1971. 149 p. Bibliog. Index. Map.

> Originally presented as the author's thesis, University of Reading. National interests and communist ideology overlap in the Middle East. Thoroughly documented, primarily Soviet sources.

3721 Pennar, Jaan. THE USSR AND THE ARABS: THE IDEOLOGICAL DIMENSION, 1917-1972. London: C. Hurst; New York: Crane Russak, 1973. 180 p. Bibliog. ref.

> Soviet foreign policy and Arab socialist thought from the standpoint of Soviet perspectives on national liberation.

3722 Ra'anan, Uri. THE USSR ARMS THE THIRD WORLD: CASE STUDIES IN SOVIET FOREIGN POLICY. Cambridge: M.I.T. Press and the Research Institute on Communist Affairs, Columbia University, 1969. x, 256 p. Bibliog. fnn.

> One section of this volume is devoted to the arms agreement between Egypt and Czechoslovakia in 1955. Egyptian, Soviet, and Western sources.

3723 Ro'i, Y. FROM ENCROACHMENT TO INVOLVEMENT. New York: Halsted Press, 1975. 616 p.

> Soviet policy in the Middle East from 1945 to 1973 (prewar), built on a collection of documents with integrating essays.

3724 Smolansky, Oles M. THE SOVIET UNION AND THE ARAB EAST UNDER KHRUSHCHEV. Modern Middle East Series, 6. Lewisburg, Pa.: Bucknell University Press, 1974. 326 p. Bibliog.

> Summary of Soviet publications, with analysis, covering the period of the Soviet Union's initial involvement with Egypt, Syria, and Iraq.

3725 SOVIET NAVAL DEVELOPMENTS: CAPABILITY AND CONTEXT; PAPERS

External Powers in the Middle East

RELATING TO RUSSIA'S MARITIME INTERESTS. Edited by Michael Mcc-Gwire. New York: Praeger, 1973. 555 p.

> Thirty-six papers given at a 1972 seminar sponsored by the Maritime Warfare School, Halifax. Several papers cover topics related to Soviet policy in the Mediterranean and the Indian Ocean. Also includes information on Soviet naval strength.

3726 SOVIET OBJECTIVES IN THE MIDDLE EAST: REPORT OF A STUDY GROUP OF THE INSTITUTE FOR THE STUDY OF CONFLICT. London: Institute for the Study of Conflict, 1974. 27 p. Illus. Maps.

3727 THE SOVIET UNION AND THE DEVELOPING NATIONS. Edited by Roger E. Kanet. Baltimore and London: Johns Hopkins University Press, 1974. 302 p. Illus. Index.

> Contains a chapter on the Middle East by John Campbell.

3728 THE SOVIET UNION AND THE MIDDLE EAST: THE POST-WORLD WAR II ERA. Edited by Ivo J. Lederer and Wayne S. Vucinich. Hoover Institution Publications, 133. Stanford, Calif.: Hoover Institution Press, 1974. xii, 302 p. Bibliog. ref. Map.

> Proceedings of a conference on Russia and the Middle East sponsored by the Hoover Institution in November 1969. Historical, rather than analytical. Contains a country-by-country bibliographical essay on the Soviet Union and the Middle East (Vucinich). Vatikiotis on Egyptian-Soviet relations is particularly insightful.

3729 U.S. Congress. House. Committee on Foreign Affairs. SOVIET INVOLVEMENT IN THE MIDDLE EAST AND THE WESTERN RESPONSE. Joint Hearings before the Subcommittee on Europe and the Subcommittee on the Near East, 92d Cong., 1st sess., October 19-November 3, 1971. 219 p. Apps. Index.

> Primarily nonofficial testimony on the Soviet Union's Middle East policies vis-a-vis NATO. Background articles appended.

3730 THE U.S.S.R. AND THE MIDDLE EAST. Edited by Michael Confino and Shimon Shamir. A Halsted Press book. New York: John Wiley and Sons, 1973. xxii, 441 p. Bibliog. ref.

> Twenty essays--Soviet foreign policy-making, Soviet relations with the Middle East, the Arab-Israeli conflict and Communist party activities in Egypt, the Sudan, Iraq, Syria, and Jordan. Proceedings of a conference on the Soviet Union and the Middle East held at Tel Aviv University in December 1971.

3731 THE USSR AND THE MIDDLE EAST; PROBLEMS OF PEACE AND SECURITY (DOCUMENTS AND OTHER MATERIALS). Moscow: Novosti Press Agency

External Powers in the Middle East

Publishing House, 1972. 265 p.

A book by the official English language publishing house.

3732 USSR AND THE THIRD WORLD: A SURVEY OF SOVIET AND CHINESE RELATIONS WITH AFRICA, ASIA AND LATIN AMERICA. Edited by Peter Howard. London: Central Asian Research Centre (distr. International Publications, New York), 1971- . 8/yr.

3733 Whetten, Lawrence L. THE SOVIET PRESENCE IN THE EASTERN MEDITERRANEAN. Strategy Papers, 10. New York: National Strategy Information Center, 1971. 49 p. Paper. Bibliog.

The Soviet Union's strategic interests and military presence in the region with some historical background. Based upon sources primarily in the English language. Little on the regional states themselves.

3734 Yodfat, Aryeh. ARAB POLITICS IN THE SOVIET MIRROR. The Monograph Series. New York: Halsted Press, 1973. xii, 332 p.

Soviet attitudes toward the Arab states and their domestic politics as gleaned from a sample of serials and speeches. Organized by country. Focuses upon the pre-1967 period.

Historical

3735 Hopwood, Derek. THE RUSSIAN PRESENCE IN SYRIA AND PALESTINE, 1843-1914; CHURCH AND POLITICS IN THE NEAR EAST. Oxford: Clarendon, 1969. 232 p. Bibliog.

Background to Soviet policy in the Middle East.

3736 Kapur, Harish. SOVIET RUSSIA AND ASIA, 1917-1927. New York: Humanities, 1962. 266 p. Bibliog. Index. Map.

Soviet diplomatic strategy in Turkey, Iran, and Afghanistan, in light of security and revolutionary doctrinal concerns. Excellent bibliography, carefully documented.

3737 Kazemzadeh, Firuz. "Russia and the Middle East." In RUSSIAN FOREIGN POLICY, edited by Ivo J. Lederer, pp. 481-530. New Haven, Conn.: Yale University Press, 1962.

Covers Iran, Afghanistan, and Central Asia. Surveys Russian interests and strategies in conflict with regional regimes and Britain over two centuries prior to World War II.

3738 Lenczowski, George. RUSSIA AND THE WEST IN IRAN, 1918-48: A STUDY IN BIG POWER RIVALRY. 1949. Reprint. Westport, Conn.:

External Powers in the Middle East

Greenwood, 1968. xv, 383 p. Bibliog. fnn. Illus. Maps. Ports.

Iran after World War I and its relations with the Soviet Union. Also reviews the development of Communist parties within Iran.

3739 Nollau, Gunther, and Wiehe, Hans Jurgen. RUSSIA'S SOUTH FLANK: SOVIET OPERATIONS IN IRAN, TURKEY AND AFGHANISTAN. Translation by Victor Anderson. Publications in Russian History and World Communism, 126. New York: Praeger, 1963. 171 p. Bibliog.

The responses of the governments of Afghanistan, Iran, and Turkey to Soviet policies, particularly after World War I.

3740 Spector, Ivar. THE SOVIET UNION AND THE MUSLIM WORLD, 1917-1958. Seattle: University of Washington Press, 1959. 328 p.

Soviet policies in the Middle East and toward Communist parties in the region. Extensively documented.

3741 Sumner, Benedict H. TSARDOM AND IMPERIALISM IN THE FAR AND MIDDLE EAST, 1880-1914. Hamden, Conn.: Archon, 1968. 43 p.

Reprint of an essay first published in PROCEEDINGS OF THE BRITISH ACADEMY 27 (London: H. Milford, 1942).

Internal Communism

3742 Agwani, Mohammed Shafi. COMMUNISM IN THE ARAB EAST. New York: Asia Publishing House, 1969. 259 p. Bibliog.

The author examines Communist party activities in the Arab states and concludes that, despite ideological differences, nationalism and Soviet foreign policies are compatible. Includes numerous primary sources.

3743 Harris, George S[ellers]. THE ORIGINS OF COMMUNISM IN TURKEY. Stanford, Calif.: Hoover Institution on War, Revolution and Peace, 1967. 215 p. Apps. Bibliog. Illus. Maps. Ports.

The activities of Turkish Communist politicians during the 1920s and their relations with President Mustafa Kemal's supporters. Several party documents appended. Extensive references.

3744 Laqueur, Walter Z[e'ez]. COMMUNISM AND NATIONALISM IN THE MIDDLE EAST. 2d ed. New York: Praeger, 1957. xi, 375 p. Bibliog. ref.

Communist movements within Middle Eastern countries, except Iran. Focuses upon the groups' evolution and ideological perspectives.

3745 YEARBOOK ON INTERNATIONAL COMMUNIST AFFAIRS 1972. Edited

External Powers in the Middle East

by Richard F. Staar. Stanford, Calif.: Hoover Institution Press, 1972. 708 p. Bibliog. Chron. Index.

> Brief country surveys of internal communist activities. Limited bibliography.

3746 Zabih, Sepehr. THE COMMUNIST MOVEMENT IN IRAN. Berkeley: University of California Press, 1966. 279 p. Bibliog.

> The origins of the Iranian Communist (Tudeh) party as an urban middle-class group which began to participate in politics and to develop a trade union base after 1941.

UNITED STATES FOREIGN POLICY

General

3801 Acheson, Dean G. PRESENT AT THE CREATION; MY YEARS IN THE STATE DEPARTMENT. New York: W.W. Norton, 1969. xiv, 448 p. Bibliog. refs. Index.

> Recollections of the Secretary of State during the Truman Administration, covering the Anglo-Iranian oil negotiations of 1952, and the proposed Middle East Command.

3802 "America and the Middle East." THE ANNALS 401 (May 1972): entire issue.

> This special issue of THE ANNALS was edited by Parker T. Hart and contains articles on contemporary U.S. interests--oil, Israel, and the cold war--and the history of U.S. involvement in the Middle East.

3803 American Assembly. THE UNITED STATES AND THE MIDDLE EAST. Edited by Georgiana Stevens. Englewood Cliffs, N.J.: Prentice-Hall, 1964. 182 p. Maps.

> Background essays prepared for the twenty-fourth American Assembly. One, by Richard H. Nolte, treats U.S. policy in the Middle East specifically. No references or documentation.

3804 American Enterprise Institute for Public Policy Research. UNITED STATES INTERESTS IN THE MIDDLE EAST. Edited by George Lenczowski. Washington, D.C.: 1968. 132 p. Paper. Apps. Bibliog. refs. Illus. Maps.

> Reviews political-strategic, economic, and cultural interests. Prospects for the future in terms of Arab state radicalism, the security of oil, and limitation of Soviet influence. Two official statements appended; numerous references.

External Powers in the Middle East

3805 Badeau, John S. THE AMERICAN APPROACH TO THE ARAB WORLD. New York: Harper & Row for the Council on Foreign Relations, 1968. xi, 209 p.

> Introductory review of U.S. policy by a former ambassador to Egypt. Covers Arab state political forces, U.S. policy instruments and guidelines, the Yemen civil war as a case study. An argument for "tactical non-alignment" (author's).

3806 Bill, James A., and Stookey, Robert W. POLITICS AND PETROLEUM: THE MIDDLE EAST AND THE UNITED STATES. Brunswick, Ohio: King's Court Communications, 1975. Paper. 150 p. App. Bibliog. Illus. Maps.

> Middle Eastern country background, trends in petroleum production relations, and a historical survey of U.S. foreign policy.

3807 Campbell, John Coert. DEFENSE OF THE MIDDLE EAST, PROBLEMS OF AMERICAN POLICY. New York: Harper, for the Council on Foreign Relations, 1958. 392 p. Bibliog. Figures. Maps.

> Events and strategies during the early 1950s; political, military, and economic competition between the United States and the Soviet Union in a cold-war perspective. Short, country bibliographies.

3808 _____. "The Middle East." AGENDA FOR THE NATION; PAPERS ON DOMESTIC AND FOREIGN POLICY ISSUES, edited by Kermit Gordon, pp. 445-74. Washington, D.C.: Brookings Institution, 1968.

> Post-World War II vs. Middle East policy--domestic factors, Soviet relations, and the Arab-Israeli conflict.

3809 Congressional Quarterly. THE MIDDLE EAST: U.S. POLICY, ISRAEL, OIL AND THE ARABS. Edited by Robert A. Diamond. Washington, D.C.: 1974. 100 p. Paper. App. Bibliog. Chron. Maps. Tables.

> Surveys United States interests in the Middle East in the 1970s and provides introductory oil data. Also cited in No. 4024.

3810 Donovan, John, ed. U.S. AND SOVIET POLICY IN THE MIDDLE EAST, 1957-1966. New York: Facts on File, 1974. 282 p. Map.

> A summary record of United States and Soviet actions in the Middle East compiled from Facts on File chronologies [6207].

3811 Ellis, Harry B. CHALLENGE IN THE MIDDLE EAST; COMMUNIST INFLUENCE AND AMERICAN POLICY. New York: Ronald, 1960. 238 p. Bibliog. Illus. Index.

A former Middle East correspondent's observations on U.S. policy, economic and political Soviet competition, and regional politics.

3812 Farrel, Robert H. "United States Policy in the Middle East." In AMERICAN DIPLOMACY IN A NEW ERA, edited by Stephen D. Kertesz, pp. 270-97. International Studies of the Committee on International Relations, University of Notre Dame. Notre Dame, Ind.: University of Notre Dame Press, 1961.

World War II to the late 1950s, especially the establishment of Israel and decision-making in the U.S. government.

3813 Finer, Herman. DULLES OVER SUEZ, THE THEORY AND PRACTICE OF HIS DIPLOMACY. Chicago: Quadrangle, 1964. xi, 538 p. Bibliog. fnn. Index. Ports. Maps.

Diplomatic strategy in the Suez crisis viewed from Washington, and Secretary Dulles' impact upon U.S. policy. Primarily based upon interviews with participants in the decision-making. Useful bibliography. Also cited in No. 4722.

3814 Fisher, Sydney N., ed. NEW HORIZONS FOR THE UNITED STATES IN WORLD AFFAIRS. Columbus: Ohio State University Press, 1966. 162 p.

Includes John S. Badeau's "The Sovereign Middle East: A New Horizon in American Foreign Policy."

3815 Hurewitz, Jacob Coleman. MIDDLE EAST DILEMMAS, THE BACKGROUND OF UNITED STATES POLICY. New York: Harper & Brothers for the Council on Foreign Relations, 1953. Bibliog. notes. Maps.

Country-by-country survey of U.S. policy and summary chapters, from a historical perspective. Based upon papers prepared for council seminars. Little documentation.

3816 Kalb, Marvin, and Kalb, Bernard. KISSINGER. Boston, Mass.: Little, Brown, 1974. xiii, 577 p. Bibliog. ref. Illus.

Discusses the Jordanian civil war of 1970 and the October 1973 war and its aftermath--focuses upon the secretary of state rather than the American political spectrum or the Middle Eastern context.

3817 Mehdi, Mohammad T[aki]. AN ARAB LOOKS AT AMERICA: OF LIONS CHAINED. San Francisco: New World, 1962. 177 p.

An Arab spokesman looks at American Middle East policy and argues that its two basic difficulties are Zionist and Western-European orientations.

3818 THE MIDDLE EAST: QUEST FOR AN AMERICAN POLICY. Edited by Willard A. Beling. Albany: State University of New York Press, 1973. xvi, 347 p. Bibliog. ref. Illus.

Revised and updated papers from a conference entitled "The Middle East in the 1970's," held April 8-10, 1970, at the 47th session of the Institute of World Affairs, sponsored by the University of Southern California. The focus of the papers is upon U.S. policy in the Arab-Israeli conflict. Includes a study of Soviet-American strategic relationships in the Mediterranean (Philip Dadant and Ciro Zoppo); Palestinian, Arab, and Israeli misperceptions of one another's intentions (Malcolm Kerr); the radicalization of the Palestinian movement (George Lenczowski); and newspaper opinion about the Middle East since 1967 (Charles Wagner).

3819 Middle East Institute. A SURVEY OF AMERICAN INTERESTS IN THE MIDDLE EAST. Edited by Francis C. Mattison. Washington, D.C.: 1953. 120 p. Bibliog.

Survey of the range of U.S. governmental and nongovernmental interests in the Middle East.

3820 Murphy, Robert D. DIPLOMAT AMONG WARRIORS. Garden City, N.Y.: Doubleday, 1964. x, 470 p.

Autobiographical, by a former U.S. assistant secretary of state (1958)--includes the 1956 Suez crisis and the 1958 Lebanese invasion, viewed from the perspective of the State Department.

3821 Polk, William R. THE UNITED STATES AND THE ARAB WORLD. Rev. ed. The American Foreign Policy Library. Cambridge, Mass.: Harvard University Press, 1969. xix, 377 p. Bibliog. Maps.

Introduction to American-Arab relations by a former member of the Policy Planning Council of the Department of State. General background and pre-World War II history of the area.

3822 Pranger, Robert J. AMERICAN POLICY FOR PEACE IN THE MIDDLE EAST 1969-1971: PROBLEMS OF PRINCIPLE, MANEUVER AND TIME. Foreign Affairs Study, 1. Washington, D.C.: American Enterprise Institute for Public Policy Research, 1971. 69 p. Paper. Bibliog. refs.

Analyzes Secretary of State Rogers's proposals in the context of U.S. and Soviet involvement in the Arab-Israeli conflict and makes suggestions for U.S. initiatives.

3823 Quandt, William B. UNITED STATES POLICY IN THE MIDDLE EAST: CONSTRAINTS AND CHOICES. RM-5980-FF. Santa Monica, Calif.: Rand Corporation, 1970. 86 p.

Republished in POLITICAL DYNAMICS IN THE MIDDLE EAST [1010]. Surveys U.S. interests in the Middle East and examines future priorities.

3824 Reitzel, William. THE MEDITERRANEAN, ITS ROLE IN AMERICA'S FOREIGN POLICY. New York: Harcourt, Brace, 1948. 195 p. Bibliog. refs.

Issued by the Yale Institute of International Studies. Considers the Mediterranean as a region in U.S. post-World War II policy-- the Truman Doctrine, the Middle East Supply Center, Turkey. Few references.

3825 Rostov, R. THE UNITED STATES AND ITS ROLE IN THE MIDDLE EAST CONFLICT. Moscow: Novosti, 1973. 72 p.

3826 Spielman, William Carl. THE UNITED STATES IN THE MIDDLE EAST: A STUDY OF AMERICAN FOREIGN POLICY. New York: Pageant, 1959. 63 p.

Survey of military and economic relations.

3827 Thomas, Lewis Victor, and Frye, Richard Nelson. THE UNITED STATES, TURKEY, AND IRAN. Cambridge, Mass.: Harvard University Press, 1951. xii, 291 p. Apps. Bibliog. Maps.

Primarily an interpretation of internal economic and political conditions in Turkey and Iran with brief separate chapters on the two countries' positions in the United States's strategic framework.

3828 Truman, Harry S. MEMOIRS. 2 vols. 1955-56. Reprint. New York: New American Library, 1965. Index.

Numerous references to U.S. policy toward the establishment of Israel and toward specific Middle East countries which the index makes readily accessible.

3829 U.S. Congress. House. Committee on Foreign Affairs. U.S. FOREIGN POLICY AND THE EXPORT OF NUCLEAR TECHNOLOGY TO THE MIDDLE EAST. Hearings before the Subcommittees on International Organizations and Movements and on the Near East and South Asia, 93d cong., 2d sess., June-September, 1974. Washington, D.C.: Government Printing Office, 1974. 333 p. Apps. Illus.

Technical and political issues raised in discussions. Extensive appended materials.

3830 _____. U.S. INTERESTS IN AND POLICY TOWARD THE PERSIAN GULF. Hearings before the Subcommittee on the Near East, 92d Cong.,

2d sess., February 2-August 15, 1972. Washington, D.C.: Government Printing Office, 1972. 212 p. App. Maps.

> Official testimony. Statements of official policy are appended with background articles.

3831 U.S. Congress. Senate. Committee on Foreign Relations. ARMS SALES TO THE NEAR EAST AND SOUTH ASIA. Hearings before the Subcommittee on the Near East and South Asia, 89th Cong., 1st sess., March 14-June 22, 1967. Washington, D.C.: Government Printing Office, 1967. 120 p.

> Official testimony on executive policies on arms sales to the region prior to passage of restrictive legislation in which the question of relative priorities to Israel and the Arab states is discussed.

3832 THE UNITED STATES IN WORLD AFFAIRS. Compiled by Richard P. Stebbins. New York: Harper for the Council on Foreign Relations, 1931-67. Annual (except 1941-44).

> Summary of American policy in various regions of the world designed to serve as companion volume to DOCUMENTS ON AMERICAN FOREIGN RELATIONS. Both were absorbed into AMERICAN FOREIGN RELATIONS [3864] in 1976.

3833 Utley, Freda. WILL THE MIDDLE EAST GO WEST? Chicago: Henry Regnery, 1957. 198 p.

> Develops the theme that U.S. foreign policy discourages a pro-Western position among the Arab states.

Iran

3834 Cottam, Richard W. COMPETITIVE INTERFERENCE AND TWENTIETH CENTURY DIPLOMACY. Pittsburgh, Pa.: University of Pittsburgh Press, 1973. 243 p. Bibliog. fnn.

> A case study of U.S. policy in Iran. Internal Iranian politics as affected by external influence on the monarchy.

3835 Millspaugh, Arthur Chester. AMERICANS IN PERSIA. Washington, D.C.: Brookings Institution, 1946. 292 p. Apps. Index.

> By an American who served as financial advisor to the government of Iran (1922-27; 1943-45). Devotes considerable attention to Iran's internal politics and culture and to Soviet, British, and American competition in Iran.

3836 Sheehan, Michael Karl. IRAN: THE IMPACT OF UNITED STATES INTERESTS AND POLICIES, 1941-54. Brooklyn, N.Y.: Theo. Gaus' Sons,

1968. xiv, 88 p. Bibliog. Illus. Ports.

> A revision of the author's doctoral thesis, American University. Considers United States's involvement in the 1953 overthrow of Prime Minister Mossadegh and the pre-Mossadegh period during which the United States pressured the Shah to introduce land and political reforms. The author argues that the major U.S. interest was participation in Iranian oil production.

3837 Yeselson, Abraham. UNITED STATES-PERSIAN DIPLOMATIC RELATIONS, 1883-1921. New Brunswick, N.J.: Rutgers University Press, 1956. 252 p. Apps. Bibliog.

> The beginnings of official U.S. contacts with Iran during which period the main contest for influence was between Britain and Russia. Some documentation; a background survey.

Israel/Palestine

3838 Arakie, Margaret. THE BROKEN SWORD OF JUSTICE: AMERICA, ISRAEL AND THE PALESTINIAN TRAGEDY. Midway edition. London: Quartet Books, 1973. 105 p. Sel. bibliog.

> The author condemns the United States and Britain for their responsibility for the establishment of Israel and the "injustice to the Palestinian Arabs." Based upon personal experience, the account includes the Mandate and continues through 1972.

3839 Berger, Elmer. LETTERS AND NON-LETTERS; THE WHITE HOUSE, ZIONISM, AND ISRAEL. Monograph Series, 31. Beirut: Institute for Palestine Studies, 1972. 55 p.

> U.S. policy toward Israel and domestic political pressures on the president.

3840 Feis, Herbert. THE BIRTH OF ISRAEL: THE TOUSLED DIPLOMATIC BED. New York: W.W. Norton, 1969. 90 p. Bibliog. refs. Maps.

> The international political background of the establishment of Israel, focusing upon American diplomatic involvement.

3841 Fink, Reuben. AMERICA AND PALESTINE; THE ATTITUDE OF OFFICIAL AMERICA AND OF THE AMERICA PEOPLE TOWARD THE REBUILDING OF PALESTINE AS A FREE AND DEMOCRATIC JEWISH COMMONWEALTH. 2d rev. ed. New York: Herald Square, 1945. 538 p. Illus. Map.

> Collection of the statements of U.S. political leaders, congressional resolutions, and U.S. diplomatic correspondence illustrating American support for Israel.

3842 Friedrich, Carl J. AMERICAN POLICY TOWARD PALESTINE. Washington, D.C.: Public Affairs Press, 1944. 106 p.

> Published under the auspices of the American Council on Public Affairs. A legal essay with a pro-Zionist perspective on public affairs.

3843 Jansen, Michael E. THE UNITED STATES AND THE PALESTINIAN PEOPLE. Monograph Series, 23. Beirut: Institute for Palestine Studies, 1970. 215 p. Paper. Bibliog. Index. Maps.

> The U.S. Palestinian refugee policies as they relate to American support for Israel, with some historical background and sympathy for the Palestinians' situation. Extensive use of U.S. government documents.

3844 McDonald, James Grover. MY MISSION IN ISRAEL--1948-1951. New York: Simon and Schuster, 1951. xiv, 303 p. Index.

> Journals of the first official American representative to Israel after the latter's independence, covering U.S. policies toward Israel, negotiating processes, and Israeli negotiating positions.

3845 Manuel, Frank E. THE REALITIES OF AMERICAN-PALESTINE RELATIONS. Washington, D.C.: Public Affairs Press, 1950. 378 p. Bibliog. refs.

> United States policy toward Palestine, especially the Palestine Jewish community from the mid-nineteenth century through the recognition of Israel. Little documentation or discussion of U.S. strategic interests other than commercial involvement in Turkey.

3846 Reich, Bernard. ISRAELI-AMERICAN RELATIONS. Shiloh Monograph Series. Jerusalem: Israel Universities Press, n.d.

3847 Robertson, Wilmot. THE DISPOSSESSED MAJORITY. Rev. ed. Cape Kennedy, Fla.: Howard Allen, 1973. xii, 586 p. Bibliog. refs.

> U.S. politics and foreign policy with a chapter on American Zionist imperialism (author's view) in the Middle East.

3848 Safran, Nadav. THE UNITED STATES AND ISRAEL. The American Foreign Policy Library. Cambridge, Mass.: Harvard University Press, 1963. xvii, 341 p. Bibliog. Maps. Tables.

> A general background to the Arab-Israeli conflict and the position of Israel in the Middle East. Discusses the disparity between U.S. cold war concerns and involvement with Israel. Little documentation.

3849 Schechtman, Joseph B. THE UNITED STATES AND THE JEWISH STATE MOVEMENT. New York: Herzl, 1966. 474 p. Bibliog. Index.

> U.S. relations with the Zionist movement during final decade of the mandate and President Roosevelt's relations with King Saud. Analyzes the American Jewish community as a political interest group.

3850 Silverberg, Robert. IF I FORGET THEE, O JERUSALEM: AMERICAN JEWS AND THE STATE OF ISRAEL. New York: Morrow, 1970. xii, 620 p. Bibliog. Illus. Index. Notes.

> American Jews and U.S. policies on Palestine/Israel since World War I, including interpretations of U.S. presidents' attitudes toward the conflict. Little historical criticism.

3851 Snetsinger, John. TRUMAN, THE JEWISH VOTE AND THE CREATION OF ISRAEL. Hoover Institution Studies, 39. Stanford, Calif.: Hoover Institution Press, 1974. xv, 208 p. Bibliog. Index.

> Analysis of numerous government documents and memoirs. Truman is seen by the author as a reluctant supporter of Israel.

3852 Stevens, Richard P. AMERICAN ZIONISM AND UNITED STATES FOREIGN POLICY, 1942-1947. New York: Pageant, 1962. xxi, 227 p. Bibliog.

3853 Welles, Sumner. WE NEED NOT FAIL. Boston: Houghton Mifflin, 1948. xiv, 143 p.

> An American diplomat and journalist asks for a consistent U.S. foreign policy toward Palestine.

Morocco

3854 Blair, Leon Borden. WESTERN WINDOW IN THE ARAB WORLD. Austin: University of Texas Press, 1970. xiv, 328 p. Bibliog. Illus. Maps. Ports.

> Diplomatic contacts among the United States, France, and Morocco during and after the Second World War. Good bibliography.

3855 Hall, Luella. THE UNITED STATES AND MOROCCO, 1776-1956. Metuchen, N.J.: Scarecrow Press, 1971. 1,114 p. Bibliog. ref. Map.

> U.S.-Moroccan diplomatic relations from 1776 to 1956. No bibliography, and inconsistent coverage of historical periods.

Turkey

3856 Evans, Laurence. UNITED STATES POLICY AND THE PARTITION OF TURKEY, 1914-1924. Baltimore: Johns Hopkins Press, 1965. 417 p. Bibliog. Index.

> Wilson's diplomacy during the Paris Peace Conference and Congress's subsequent retraction from a positive role to a more limited protection of American cultural and economic interests. Uses primary and secondary sources.

3857 Gordon, Leland James. AMERICAN RELATIONS WITH TURKEY 1830-1930: AN ECONOMIC INTERPRETATION. Philadelphia: University of Pennsylvania Press, 1932. 402 p. Apps. Bibliog.

> Revised doctoral dissertation. Potential and actual commercial and capital relations. Full bibliography and chronology.

3858 Howard, Harry N. TURKEY, THE STRAITS, AND UNITED STATES POLICY. Baltimore: Johns Hopkins University Press, 1974. xii, 337 p. Map.

> American diplomacy in the Turkish straits from 1830 to present.

3859 Trask, Roger R. THE UNITED STATES RESPONSE TO TURKISH NATIONALISM AND REFORM 1914-1939. Minneapolis: University of Minnesota Press, 1971. 247 p. Bibliog. Index.

> Survey of U.S.-Turkish relations during Turkey's transition from imperial to small state international politics. The author omits Turkish sources and has integrated several already-published articles into the volume.

Historical

3860 De Novo, John A. AMERICAN INTERESTS AND POLICIES IN THE MIDDLE EAST, 1900-1939. Minneapolis: University of Minnesota Press, 1963. xii, 447 p. Bibliog. Index. Maps.

> Political, religious, and cultural contacts between the United States and the Middle East. Develops theme that the principal goal of the United States was to avoid political entanglements while enhancing cultural and economic ties. Extensive bibliography. Uses diplomatic correspondence.

3861 Field, James A., Jr. AMERICA AND THE MEDITERRANEAN WORLD 1776-1882. Princeton, N.J.: Princeton University Press, 1969. 485 p. Bibliog. notes. Index.

> Missionary and diplomatic contacts with the Near East and North Africa (rather than the European littoral states). Develops the theme that the U.S. goal was largely to stem influence of European monarchical regimes. Extensively documented.

3862 Grabill, Joseph L. PROTESTANT DIPLOMACY AND THE NEAR EAST: MISSIONARY INFLUENCE ON AMERICAN POLICY, 1810-1927. Minneapolis: University of Minnesota Press, 1971. x, 395 p. Bibliog. Illus. Maps. Ports.

"Near East" refers to the Balkan and Caucasus areas, Persia, and the Ottoman Empire. Focuses upon the period from 1900-1927, especially missionaries and Wilsonian diplomacy. Source materials include records of the American Board of Commissioners for Foreign Missions and the Department of State. Argues that the missionary movement involved the United States in the affairs of the Ottoman Empire, and established a tradition for Point Four, NATO, and the Peace Corps. Bibliographic essay.

3863 Speiser, Ephrem Avigdor. THE UNITED STATES AND THE NEAR EAST. Rev. ed. The American Foreign Policy Library. Cambridge, Mass.: Harvard University Press, 1947. xvi, 263 p. Bibliog. Index. Maps.

Diplomatic and cultural history of the Middle East, considers regional politics and the European powers. Little on U.S. policy. Undocumented.

Documents

3864 AMERICAN FOREIGN RELATIONS. New York: New York University Press for the Council on Foreign Relations, 1976- . Annual.

Combines the annual DOCUMENTS ON AMERICAN FOREIGN RELATIONS (New York: Harper, 1939- .) and THE UNITED STATES IN WORLD AFFAIRS [3832]. The 1976 volume provides documents and events for 1971.

3865 Branyan, Robert L., and Larsen, Lawrence H., comps. THE EISENHOWER ADMINISTRATION 1953-1961: A DOCUMENTARY HISTORY. 2 vols. New York: Random House, 1971. 1,414 p. Apps. Index. Bibliog. essay.

Two chapters on the Middle East--the U.S. role in the Suez crisis and the Eisenhower Doctrine.

3866 DEPARTMENT OF STATE BULLETIN. Washington, D.C.: Superintendent of Documents. Weekly.

Indexed selected documents and official statements. Official weekly record.

3867 Magnus, Ralph H., comp. DOCUMENTS ON THE MIDDLE EAST. Washington, D.C.: American Enterprise Institute for Public Policy Research, 1969. Paper. 232 p. Bibliog.

The documents collected predominantly relate to U.S. policy

toward specific states in the Middle East, regional security arrangements, and the Arab-Israeli conflict. Statements and written documents focus on the post-World War II period.

3868 Schlesinger, Arthur M., Jr., ed. DYNAMICS OF WORLD POWER; DOCUMENTARY HISTORY OF U.S. FOREIGN POLICY, 1945-1973. 5 vols. New York: Chelsea House and McGraw-Hill, 1973- .

The fifth volume contains materials pertinent to the Middle East within the section on the U.N. The series includes Western Europe, USSR, Latin America, the Far East, and Africa.

3869 U.S. Congress. Senate. Committee on Foreign Relations. A DECADE OF AMERICAN FOREIGN POLICY: BASIC DOCUMENTS, 1941-49. 1950. Reprint. Grosse Pointe, Mich.: Scholarly Press, 1968. xiv, 1,381 p. Maps.

Prepared at the request of the Senate Committee on Foreign Relations by the committee staff and the Department of State.

3870 U.S. Department of State. UNITED STATES FOREIGN POLICY 1972, A REPORT OF THE SECRETARY OF STATE. General Foreign Policy Series, 254. Washington, D.C.: 1972. Illus. Index. [S1.71].

The secretary's report to congress. Follows similar reports published from 1969 on. Indexed by topic and region.

3871 _____. UNITED STATES POLICY IN THE MIDDLE EAST, SEPT. 1956-JUNE 1957 DOCUMENTS. Publication 6505. Washington, D.C.: Government Printing Office, 1957. Reprint. New York: Greenwood Press, 1968. xiv, 425 p. Bibliog. fnn.

Over 100 documents arranged thematically and chronologically, encompassing the 1956 war and its aftermath. Also includes several documents relating to the Palestinian refugee problem and the formation of the Baghdad Pact.

3872 U.S. Department of State. Bureau of Public Affairs. Office of Media Services. NEAR EAST AND SOUTH ASIA SERIES. Washington, D.C.: 1948- . Irregular. [S1.86].

Series has been printed under different titles. Includes selected documents including special topic collections reprinted from the Department of State BULLETIN and irregular pamphlets appearing under the title CURRENT FOREIGN POLICY.

3873 U.S. Department of State. Historical Office. AMERICAN FOREIGN POLICY: BASIC DOCUMENTS, 1950-55. 2 vols. Publication 6446. General Foreign Policy Series, 117. 1957. Reprint. New York: Arno, 1971. lix, 3244, xxv p. Bibliog refs. Illus. Maps.

3874 _____. AMERICAN FOREIGN POLICY; CURRENT DOCUMENTS. Washington, D.C.: 1956- . Reprints. New York: Arno, 1971- . [S1.71.2].

Documents classified by region.

3875 _____. THE FOREIGN RELATIONS OF THE UNITED STATES: DIPLOMATIC PAPERS. Washington, D.C.: Government Printing Office, 1861- . Annual.

Recent volumes which review the Middle East in detail include 8 (1946) and 5 (1947), published in 1969 and 1971 respectively, which cover Greece, Turkey, the Arab States, and Palestine. Various numbers of volumes are published each year.

3876 U.S. FOREIGN POLICY FOR THE 1970'S, SHAPING A DURABLE PEACE. A Report to the Congress by Richard Nixon, President of the United States, May 3, 1973. Washington, D.C.: Government Printing Office, 1973. 234 p.

The fourth foreign policy review. Divided by region and topic.

Chapter 5

THE ARAB-ISRAELI CONFLICT

The Arab-Israeli conflict is the most written-about international issue in the Middle East but in many ways the least comprehensively analyzed. The literature includes journalists' reports (Collins [4707]); chronological summaries of events (Laqueur [4761]); readers which survey the range of issues--the Palestinians, external powers, Israeli and Arab state objectives, and, recently, the impact of petroleum on the conflict; pleas for "reason"; and legal arguments over the "Palestine Question."

Only four studies of international politics cover the conflict as whole (Bose [4016], Evron [4028], Khouri [4049], and Safran [4061]). All four overviews are careful and relatively current; each has a place in a basic collection of materials. Safran includes more diplomatic detail. Evron has made more of an effort to be analytical. Khouri in THE ARAB-ISRAELI DILEMMA [4049] writes about the Palestinian issue as a refugee problem rather than one of national loyalties and emphasizes long-range solutions through resettlement and development. THE SUPERPOWERS AND THE MIDDLE EAST [4016] is a chronological account of the conflict since Israel's independence which, as its title suggests, attributes the prolonged conflict to external intervention--a view often taken by the immediate adversaries.

Readers or collections of essays also include numerous aspects of the conflict. The most inclusive, Gendzier's A MIDDLE EAST READER [4031], is made up of previously published articles but presents both Israeli and Palestinian views. One reader includes original essays on the Mandate period and the contemporary international political scene (Abu-Lughod, THE TRANSFORMATION OF PALESTINE [4069]). Laqueur's volume [4052] spans the Second World War but it is too short to adequately cover the subject matter and the essays are available elsewhere.

In addition to these general books, a basic collection can be built upon one or two volumes from each of several topics: the historical background of the conflict prior to the creation of Israel as a state, the emergence of Palestinian nationalism, military conflicts and efforts to end those conflicts and negotiate a settlement. Collections of documents are available in separate volumes or, in many cases, in appendixes of secondary studies.

Arab-Israeli Conflict

HISTORICAL BACKGROUND

Studies of Britain's Palestine Mandate continue to appear thirty years after its dissolution. However, the most extensive and thoroughly documented study of the Mandate period and the background to the Palestinian-Israeli dilemma is still Hurewitz's THE STRUGGLE FOR PALESTINE [4124]. Hurewitz draws upon Arabic, Hebrew, and English language sources and lists them in his extensive bibliography.

Hurewitz is less concerned with Arab politics than with Zionist and British activities. This is also true of a more recent, and provocative, study of mandated Palestine by Christopher Sykes (CROSSROADS TO ISRAEL [4161]). Sykes, though sensitive to the failure of the Mandate administration to consult with Arab Palestinian leaders at various junctures, spends little time describing the Arab Palestinian community during that period.

Another volume which, like Hurewitz's, contains a voluminous quantity of information is the Esco Foundation for Palestine's PALESTINE: A STUDY OF JEWISH, ARAB, AND BRITISH POLICIES [4113]. The foundation's collection of essays presents a variety of perspectives, a wide selection of source material, and focuses upon the growth of Zionism, the Mandate administration, and international diplomacy.

The World War I period is a turning point in the fortunes of Zionism and the disposition of Palestine. A major debate in the historical literature concerns the motivation behind the British government's (1917) Balfour Declaration--the first official sanction of a "Jewish National Home." Sykes points to several contributory events--Foreign Secretary Balfour's personal politics, domestic British issues, and careless naivete. Isaiah Friedman's THE QUESTION OF PALESTINE, 1914-1918 [4114] contends that the chief consideration was the international political strategy, namely, British fears of a Turkish-German protectorate in the Palestine region. The most detailed study of the declaration is Leonard Stein's [4158]; his explanation is an amalgam of the others.

Most of the extensively documented analyses of the Mandate and Zionist history approach their topics from the standpoint of diplomacy and politics. These books can be supplemented further by general surveys of British Middle-East policy and the Mandate system (see entries under "Nationalism and the Colonial Experience."

Another vein in the conflict literature is the cultural or religious theme. In the literature on the contemporary period, the common Semitic heritage of the Arabs and Israelis is occasionally developed as a potential unifying force (Chouraqui, LETTER TO AN ARAB FRIEND [4023]). Goitein's JEWS AND ARABS [4117] is a counterpoint which disputes that common background after tracing Jewish and Arab traditions since Islam. A more inclusive survey of the religious background is RELIGION IN THE MIDDLE EAST, edited by Arthur Arberry [4105], which considers the three major religions in the region.

Arab-Israeli Conflict

Several authors point to errors in policy during the Mandate period in order to explain the persistence of the post-World War II conflict. Robert John and Sami Hadawi are among those who are critical of British vacillation over whether or not to back a Jewish national home [4129]. A variety of historical views are raised in BACKDROP TO TRAGEDY [4145], a documented introduction to the Mandate from the perspectives of an American, a British Zionist, and a Palestinian. Any of the historical critiques can be juxtaposed to the firsthand accounts of various participant-observers who also made recommendations on Mandate policy. Among these accounts are Bentwich and Bentwich [4108], Crossman [4111], Crum [4112], Kirkbride [4134], and Meinertzhagen [4142].

Like Sakran, many of the authors have written as participant-observers. Former Palestine Governor Storrs' memoirs [4159] are extensive. For a balance of firsthand accounts, American, Arab, British, and Zionist observations are all available in English. However, these works tend not to provide the variety of perspective and the overview of resource material that is available in the later, secondary analyses.

DOCUMENTS

In addition to his own record of the Mandate period, Hurewitz has compiled two volumes of documents which, starting from the Middle Ages, extend through and stress the interwar period (1918-38). Ingrams's PALESTINE PAPERS [4206] supplements Hurewitz, but is not complete enough to make a strong case for its addition in a basic collection.

Few collections of documents are available which focus upon the policies of the immediate participants in the conflict. Chronologically incomplete collections of both Israeli and Arab state documents are available for the 1950s and 1960s, where Hurewitz leaves off (see Israel, Ministry of Foreign Affairs [4208] and Jabber [4207]). In lieu of more thorough coverage of governmental and intergovernmental communications, chronologies which publish documents as they appear are especially useful (see ORIENTE MODERNO [6215]).

The most complete collections of documents are those of UN proceedings and, for specific periods, of U.S. policies. Special collections of UN documents have been compiled which are helpful shortcuts to peacekeeping activities. UNITED NATIONS PEACEKEEPING (Higgins [4203]) is the most useful. It describes the several organizations that have been set up to deal with the Arab-Israeli conflict. The papers of secretaries-general give a different perspective on U.N. operations (Cordier and Foote [4201]).

PEACEKEEPING AND NEGOTIATIONS

For less specialized collections, secondary analyses of the peacekeeping and negotiating functions of the U.N. may be most useful. Firsthand observers' comments on peacekeeping are abundant. The first fifteen years after 1948 on both

Arab-Israeli Conflict

the Egyptian and Syrian fronts could be covered with a combination of Burns (BETWEEN ARAB AND ISRAELI [4511]) and Bar-Yaccov (THE ISRAEL-SYRIAN ARMISTICE [4503]).

Bar-Yaccov compares the demilitarized zone on Syria's Israeli frontier with similar zones outside the Middle East. Other useful comparisons with various United Nations peacekeeping operations are made in UNITED NATIONS PEACE-KEEPING, (Boyd [4508]). Boyd suggests improvements in the organization of peacekeeping for the future.

Several analyses of U.N. intervention in peacekeeping and negotiations are available, although few place the intervention within the context of international politics. Two exceptions appeared in the early 1970s--Elkordy (CRISIS OF DIPLOMACY [4512]) and Forsythe (UNITED NATIONS PEACEMAKING [4514]). Elkordy's description of the post-1967 war period as "the diplomacy of peacemaking" needs updating. However, the flurry of diplomatic activity between 1967 and 1973 misled many writers into believing a lasting peace had been secured.

Beyond peacekeeping forces are negotiations and the accommodation of conflicting interests. The widest range of proposals for negotiation, from the West and Israel, is published in APPROACHES TO PEACE IN THE MIDDLE EAST (U.S., Congress [4531]). Fisher (DEAR ISRAELIS, DEAR ARABS [4513]) and Reisman (THE ART OF THE POSSIBLE [4526]) supplement but do not duplicate the congressional collection. Fisher maintains that solutions to conflicts must be created, and he attempts to set out a detailed model for negotiating. Reisman develops long-range schemes such as a multinational administration for the Sinai peninsula. The post-1974 negotiations with their detailed nuances suggest Reisman's approach to be of lower priority.

A third type of book on peacekeeping and negotiations records actual negotiations. Ben-Gurion's MY TALKS WITH ARAB LEADERS [4504] includes the pre-independence years as well as his term as prime minister. The talks include one-way correspondence. Earlier, NEGOTIATIONS WITH NASSER [4505] recorded "secret" Nasser-Ben Gurion negotiations. A secondary analysis of these talks, like that by Merlin on Bourguiba (THE SEARCH FOR PEACE IN THE MIDDLE EAST [4523]) will be welcome.

PALESTINIAN NATIONALISM

The most comprehensive and thorough study of the contemporary Palestinian movement is Quandt's THE POLITICS OF PALESTINIAN NATIONALISM [4627]. The three contributing authors review the movement's history, organization, and relations with Arab states. The other major study of the organization of the Palestine national movement is Sharabi's PALESTINE GUERRILLAS [4632].

Several accounts of Palestinian ideology and the Palestinian experience are available. Two unique French-language publications have been included in this bibliography--Carre's L'IDEOLOGIE PALESTINIENNE DE RESISTANCE [4607] and Fath's LA REVOLUTION PALESTINIENNE ET LES JUIFS [4612]. The study available in English which comes closest to Carre in presenting the ideological perspectives of the various Palestinian groups and the dynamic of the movement is Chaliand (THE PALESTINIAN RESISTANCE MOVEMENT [4608], a translation from the French. A Palestinian writer, Sami Hadawi, discusses the Palestinian experience, focusing on the Mandate period (BITTER HARVEST [4614]). Hadawi gives a documented and firsthand statement which ends just as the movement was developing more coherent organization. A less evenly documented firsthand historical account is Furlonge's PALESTINE IS MY COUNTRY [4613].

One other book warrants particular mention because it deals with the motivations of the Palestinians who left the occupied territories in 1967. Dodd and Barakat in RIVER WITHOUT BRIDGES [4611] attempt to sort systematically through the images which the refugees had of their land versus those of their refugee status. In some respects, this study bridges the transition from the earlier concern with the physical well-being of the refugees (Peretz [4623]) to the stronger contemporary interest in the national aspirations of the Palestinians.

MILITARY CONFLICTS

Each of the four major conflicts which has grown out of the Palestinian dispute has been unique both in how it has been fought and in the participants and their objectives. The 1948 war was fought by armed civilians as much as it was by organized military units. By contrast, post-1975 borders were to be ensured by electronic instruments designed to detect troop and weapons movements. The nature of warfare either condemns or recommends itself as a tool for international influence.

The books listed under this section can be divided into those which show why nations went to war and those which show how nations fought. Few authors have tried to do both. The Kimches' war books come the closest but do not include detailed information on weapons and troop strength. Whetten, in THE CANAL WAR [4705], provides an extensive military and diplomatic analysis of the "war of attrition" waged across the Suez during the years between the 1967 and 1973 wars. Edgar O'Ballance and Walter Laqueur have each written several war studies from, respectively, a military and a diplomatic perspective.

Any of these researched studies could be combined with the firsthand recollections that are available. Garcia-Granados was a UN representative on the scene in 1947. General Beaufre led the French forces in the invasion of the Suez in 1956. Roderick MacLeish was in Cairo and Tel Aviv during the 1967 war; Eric Rouleau, in Cairo.

The MacLeish and Rouleau books are unusual; few of the primary or secondary works on the four wars develop Arab sources to the same extent. D.K. Palit (RETURN TO SINAI [4762]) does describe the Egyptian's 1973 canal crossing

Arab-Israeli Conflict

but does so only in such laudatory terms that his book is of little use as a critical history. The relationship between the Middle East wars and the U.S.-Soviet military capacities is also a relatively undeveloped topic. Laqueur devotes much attention to U.S. diplomatic perspectives. For the 1956 war, Kennett Love's SUEZ [4724] also covers American policies and is one of the most comprehensive accounts available.

RELATED REFERENCES

In addition to sections already cross-referenced in the essay, various aspects of the Arab-Israeli conflict also are discussed extensively in periodical articles. Periodical literature is the major source for information and analysis of military strategy in particular. The most useful guide to this literature is the AIR UNIVERSITY INDEX TO MILITARY PERIODICALS [7201] which references military and international politics serials. In addition, several of the irregular serials cover military issues.

For more general analyses of the conflict and negotiating positions, readers should consult the international politics journals listed, as well as three of the Middle East area serials—THE JOURNAL OF PALESTINE STUDIES, NEW OUTLOOK, PRESENT TENSE.

Beyond the periodical literature, books and monographs which are directly pertinent to the Arab-Israeli conflict are also listed under specific countries' foreign policy studies. The two most fruitful sections among these are Israel and Jordan.

GENERAL WORKS

4001 Abboushi, W. F. THE ANGRY ARABS. Leiden: E.J. Brill; Philadelphia: Westminster Press, 1974. 288 p. Maps.

> This volume is devoted to Arab history and European images of that history; the second half discusses the Palestinian position in the Arab-Israeli conflict, with documentation.

4002 Alexander, Yonah. THE ROLE OF COMMUNICATIONS IN THE MIDDLE EAST CONFLICT. New York, N.Y.: Praeger, 1974 [c1973]. 287 p. Bibliog.

> A collection of Arab leaders' most vitriolic anti-Zionist statements and the "defensive" responses of Israeli spokesmen. Illustrates the emotionality of the conflict; this is lively reading.

4003 Alexander, Yonah, and Kittrie, Nicholas N., eds. CRESCENT AND STAR: ARAB-ISRAELI PERSPECTIVES ON THE MIDDLE EAST CONFLICT.

Arab-Israeli Conflict

New York: A M S Press, 1973. 486 p. Apps. Bibliog. Maps.

> Palestinian, other Arab, and Israeli statements--some official--on the issues that divide them. The most polarized opinions are presented.

4004 Alroy, Gil Carl. BEHIND THE MIDDLE-EAST CONFLICT: THE REAL IMPASSE BETWEEN ARAB AND JEW. New York: G.P. Putnam's, 1975. 317 p. Bibliog. Index.

> Develops the theme that the conflict results from the clash of nationalisms which cannot be defused by external diplomatic invervention.

4005 American Academic Association for Peace in the Middle East. ANATOMY OF PEACE. New York: 1969. 114 p.

> Proceedings of a 1969 conference sponsored by the association. Largely concerned with responses to the 1967 war.

4006 _____. ATTITUDES TOWARD JEWISH STATEHOOD IN THE ARAB WORLD. Edited by Gil Carl Alroy. Middle East Area Studies Series, 4. New York: 1971. 187 p. Bibliog. refs.

> Six essays concerning Palestinian attitudes toward Israel, the communication of hostility toward Israel by Arab state leaders, and the varieties of Arab nationalism.

4007 _____. PEOPLE AND POLITICS IN THE MIDDLE EAST. Edited by Michael Curtis. New Brunswick, N.J.: Transaction, 1971. 325 p. Paper. Index.

> Seventeen essays on topics ranging from Israeli and Palestinian nationalism to the economic implications of the Arab-Israeli conflict and great power involvement in the conflict, published as the proceedings of the third annual conference of the American Academic Association for Peace in the Middle East (1970). The authors are experienced scholars in their fields and the collection is balanced.

4008 American Friends Service Committee. SEARCH FOR PEACE IN THE MIDDLE EAST. New York: Hill and Wang, 1971. 126 p.

> A discussion guide to the background of, and various positions in, the Arab-Israeli conflict. It has received wide notice for its clarity and balance.

4009 ARABS AND ISRAELIS: A DIALOGUE WITH MAHMOUD HUSSEIN AND SAUL FRIEDLANDER. New York: Holmes and Meier, 1975. 240 p. Maps.

Arab-Israeli Conflict

Dialogue among two Arab activists (using the pseudonym of Mahmoud Hussein) and an Israeli writer. Originally published in French.

4010 Avineri, Shlomo, comp. ISRAEL AND THE PALESTINIANS: REFLECTIONS ON THE CLASH OF TWO NATIONAL MOVEMENTS. New York: St. Martins, 1971. xxiv, 168 p. Bibliog. refs.

Previously published essays by Israeli Jews and a West Bank Palestinian leader. Despite the volume's polarized opinions, the editor concludes that accommodation will grow from a mutual recognition of the Palestinians and Zionists.

4011 Azar, Edward E. PROBE FOR PEACE: SMALL STATE HOSTILITIES. Minneapolis, Minn.: Burgess, 1973. 89 p.

Data on the incidence of conflict involving small states, a survey of causes of war theories and a case study of the Arab-Israeli conflict (1948-72). Uses event data and strategic perspectives to plot alternative futures from current policies. Introduction to peace research.

4012 Becker, Abraham S.; Hansen, Bent; and Kerr, Malcolm H. THE ECONOMICS AND POLITICS OF THE MIDDLE EAST. New York: American Elsevier, 1975. 142 p.

Three essays in which (1) Hansen examines the economic development prospects for the Middle East, (2) Kerr describes the local political outlook, and (3) Becker analyzes the role of the superpowers in the Arab-Israeli conflict through the 1973 war. Concluding volume of a survey by the Rand Corporation and Resources for the Future. The Becker and Kerr essays merely update material in the earlier volume, POLITICAL DYNAMICS IN THE MIDDLE EAST [1010].

4013 Bentwich, Norman. ISRAEL: TWO FATEFUL YEARS, 1967-1969. London: Elek, 1970. 115 p. Bibliog.

Israeli-Arab relations and an ethical proposal for accomodation. By a former attorney general in the Palestine Mandate.

4014 Berger, Earl. THE COVENANT AND THE SWORD: ARAB-ISRAELI RELATIONS, 1948-56. Toronto: University of Toronto Press, 1965. x, 245 p. App. Bibliog. Index. Maps.

A little-documented but well-written essay in which the author maintains that without great power intervention, peace could have been attained in 1949. Chronological introduction to the pre-Suez period with the (1949) Israel-Lebanon Armistice Agreement appended.

Arab-Israeli Conflict

4015 Berger, Elmer. WHO KNOWS BETTER MUST SAY SO. Reprint Series, 6. Beirut: Institute for Palestine Studies, 1970; New York: American Council for Judaism, 1955. xvi, 113 p. Illus. Index.

> Personal letters from the author written during a 1955 tour of the Arab states and Israel to the chairman of the board of the American Council for Judaism. Interviews with Arab and Jewish leaders emphasized the national, rather than religious, character of the conflict.

4016 Bose, Tarun Chandra. THE SUPERPOWERS AND THE MIDDLE EAST. New York: Asia Publishing House, 1972. x, 208 p. Apps. Bibliog. Index. Maps. Ref.

> Chronological analysis of the Arab-Israeli conflict from 1945-70. Using Western sources, the author concludes that superpower intervention has prevented the immediate adversaries from reaching an accommodation.

4017 Brown, Neville, et al. HAS ISRAEL REALLY WON? Tract 376. London: Fabian Society, 1967. 20 p. Paper.

> Arab state politics, Israeli negotiating positions, the United Nations, and, minimally, the Palestinian situation. A balanced introduction from a pacifist perspective.

4018 Bullock, John. THE MAKING OF A WAR: THE MIDDLE EAST FROM 1967 TO 1973. London: Longman, 1975. xix, 220 p. Maps.

4019 Cattan, Henry. PALESTINE AND INTERNATIONAL LAW: THE LEGAL ASPECTS OF THE ARAB-ISRAELI CONFLICT. New York: Longman, 1973. 242 p. Apps. Index.

> An analysis of major international documents and communications concerning Palestine with respect to their compatibility with international legal precepts. Begins with the Balfour Declaration and ends with the 1972 U.N. General Assembly resolutions on Palestinian rights and the occupied territories. The appendices include twenty-three entries; twenty-one are U.N. resolutions.

4020 _____. PALESTINE, THE ARABS, AND ISRAEL. London: Longman, 1969. 281 p. Bibliog. Maps.

> Presents the Palestinian Arab case that the original U.N. partition was illegal. A review of the history of the conflict and examination of possible future solutions. The author is a lawyer who represented the Arab League to U.N. mediator Count Bernadotte. Well documented.

4021 _____. PALESTINE, THE ROAD TO PEACE. London: Longman, 1970.

Arab-Israeli Conflict

75 p. Paper. Apps. Maps.

A monograph based upon the author's 1969 book which presents population and landowning data for Arabs and Jews at the time of the U.N. partition. This volume was written to balance excessive publicity for the Zionist position. No bibliography, but useful documentation of early U.N. references.

4022 Chomsky, Noam. PEACE IN THE MIDDLE EAST: REFLECTIONS ON JUSTICE AND NATIONHOOD. New York: Vantage, 1974. xlviii, 198 p. Bibliog. refs.

A collection of essays on the Arab-Israeli conflict through the 1973 war. The author advocates socialist binationalism in Palestine. One essay discusses attitudes of persons within the peace movement toward Israel.

4023 Chouraqui, Andre. LETTER TO AN ARAB FRIEND. Translated by William Gugli. Amherst: University of Massachusetts Press, 1972. 271 p. Illus.

Born in Algeria, Chouraqui is Arabic-speaking and became deputy mayor of Jerusalem in 1965. His "letters" serve as a vehicle for illustrating the shared history of Arabs and Jews in Palestine. Includes imaginative proposals for accommodation based upon the author's conviction that this shared history must continue.

4024 Congressional Quarterly. THE MIDDLE EAST: U.S. POLICY, ISRAEL, OIL, AND THE ARABS. Edited by Robert A. Diamond. Washington, D.C.: 1974. 100 p. Paper. App. Bibliog. Chron. Maps. Tables.

Essays on the post-1973 outlook for accommodation. Considers U.S. policy and petroleum politics. Not well-documented. The bibliography contains a short list of recent U.S. congressional reports on oil and the Arab-Israeli conflict. Also cited in No. 3809.

4025 Davis, John H. THE EVASIVE PEACE: A STUDY OF THE ZIONIST-ARAB PROBLEM. New York: New World, 1970. x, 136 p. Bibliog. Illus. Maps.

A personal statement calling for the "de-Zionization" of Israel and the establishment of an Arab territory within Palestine. By a former Commissioner-General of UNRWA.

4026 Ellis, Harry B. ISRAEL AND THE MIDDLE EAST. New York: Ronald Press, 1957. 260 p. Bibliog. Index. Map.

Popularly written background to the Arab-Israeli conflict, with surveys of Arab state internal politics. Written by a former correspondent for the CHRISTIAN SCIENCE MONITOR.

Arab-Israeli Conflict

4027 Elon, Amos, and Hassan, Sana. BETWEEN ENEMIES; A COMPASSIONATE DIALOGUE BETWEEN AN ISRAELI AND AN ARAB. New York: Random House, 1974. 151 p.

> An informal dialogue between an Israeli and an Egyptian. Raises questions of historical perspective and moral issues, concluding with shared expectations of long-term accommodation.

4028 Evron, Yair. THE MIDDLE EAST: NATIONS, SUPERPOWERS AND WARS. New York: Praeger, 1973. 247 p. Bibliog. Index.

> A study of international politics in the Arab-Israeli conflict that is both: (1) an interpretive review of the development of the conflict since 1948; and (2) an analysis of international behavior at the local, local-superpower, and superpower levels. The author, an Israeli political scientist, has attempted to develop a rigorous conceptual framework. Based primarily on secondary sources.

4029 Feinberg, Nathan. THE ARAB-ISRAELI CONFLICT IN INTERNATIONAL LAW. Jerusalem: Magnes, 1970. 120 p.

> A point-by-point response to the conclusions of a meeting of Arab jurists in 1967, which has been translated and published in SEMINAR OF ARAB JURISTS ON PALESTINE; ALGIERS, 22-27 JULY 1967--THE PALESTINE QUESTION. Extensive documentation on topics ranging from the Palestine Mandate to the Jordan River controversy.

4030 Forrest, Alfred C. THE UNHOLY LAND. Old Greenwich, Conn.: Devin-Adair, 1972. xiii, 178 p. Bibliog. Illus. Map.

> An account of the author's firsthand observations of the situation of the Palestinian refugees in the post-1967 period, reflecting both sides of the question (author's judgment)--justice for the refugees and the legitimate rights of the Israelis.

4031 Gendzier, Irene L., comp. A MIDDLE EAST READER. New York: Pegasus, 1969. xi, 477 p. Bibliog. Map.

> Twenty-nine previously published articles about the Arab-Israeli conflict, inter-Arab politics, and domestic politics. An unusual collection which includes contributions by Palestinians and Israelis, scholars and journalists. The bibliography is useful and organized. A well-rounded introductory reader also of interest to specialists.

4032 Glubb, Sir John Bagot. THE MIDDLE EAST CRISIS: PERSONAL INTERPRETATION. London: Hodder & Stoughton, 1969 (c1967). 63 p. Maps.

Arab-Israeli Conflict

A plea for the recognition of Palestinian grievances and Israeli strengths. More evenhandedness toward the Arab states would support the West's anti-Soviet strategic interests.

4033 Hadawi, Sami. PALESTINE IN FOCUS. Edited by Yusif A. Sayigh. Palestine Essays, 7. Beirut: Palestine Research Center, 1968. 122 p. Bibliog.

4034 Harkabi, Yehoshafat. ARAB ATTITUDES TOWARD ISRAEL. New York: Hart, 1972. xxiii, 476 p. Bibliog. Index.

Extreme statements of Arab leaders are presented to illustrate the author's premise that "liquidation of Israel" is the official Arab community viewpoint. The author, former chief of intelligence for the Israeli army, concentrates on pre-1967 statements.

4035 Hauer, Christian E., Jr. CRISIS AND CONSCIENCE IN THE MIDDLE EAST. Chicago: Quadrangle, 1970. 159 p. Paper. Apps. Illus. Maps.

The author presents his case for Israeli claims to sovereignty in Palestine. Little documentation or new material.

4036 Heradstveit, Daniel. ARAB AND ISRAELI ELITE PERCEPTIONS. New York: Humanities Press, 1974. 148 p. Apps.

Interviews with thirty-five Israelis and fifty-six Arabs, including Palestinians. Not a scientific sampling procedure. The views expressed to the author were polarized and unreceptive to negotiations.

4037 Hobeychi, General Abdullah. THE PALESTINE PROBLEM. Damascus: al-Tawjih Press, 1971. 85 p. Bibliog.

Theme of author's study at Paris, Superior Military School.

4038 Howe, Irving, and Gershman, Carl, comps. ISRAEL, THE ARABS AND THE MIDDLE EAST. New York: Quadrangle, 1972. 440 p. Bibliog. ref.

A collection of essays published previously in accessible sources. The collection covers Israeli society, Palestinian nationalism, and the international dimensions of the conflict--from an Israeli perspective.

4039 Indian Society of International Law. THE ARAB-ISRAELI CONFLICT: DOCUMENTS AND COMMENTS. New Delhi: Scandia House, 1967. 306 p. Apps. Bibliog.

See No. 4205.

4040 Institute for Strategic Studies. SOURCES OF CONFLICT IN THE MIDDLE EAST. Adelphi Papers, 26. London: 1966. 44 p.

A survey, by the staff.

4041 Jacobs, Paul. BETWEEN THE ROCK AND THE HARD PLACE. New York: Random House, 1970. 155 p.

A popular account of the author's attempt to set up a conference between Arab and Israeli scholars on behalf of the Center for the Study of Democratic Institutions in Santa Barbara, California, in 1969.

4042 Japeth, Maurice David, and Rajiv, P. K. THE ARAB ISRAEL CONFLICT, AN INDIAN VIEWPOINT. Bombay: Pearl Publications (Distr. New York: Indian Book House), 1967. 107 p. Paper. Illus. Ports.

A summary of the conflict sympathetic to Israel and critical of India's support for the Arab states. Undocumented opinion.

4043 JERUSALEM PAPERS ON PEACE PROBLEMS. Jerusalem: Hebrew University of Jerusalem, Leonard Davis Institute for International Relations, 1974. Var. pag.

Five papers to date: (1) "Peace Conferences" (R. Cohen and S. Cohen); (2) "The Juridical Status of Jerusalem" (Y. Z. Blum); (3) "The Role of Great Power Guarantees in International Peace Agreements" (A. Dowty); (4) "Soviet and Chinese Relations with the Palestinian Guerilla Organizations" (M. Ma'oz); and, (5) "Sharm al-Sheikh-Bab al-Mandeb: the Strategic Balance and Israel's Southern Approaches" (M. Abir).

4044 A JUST PEACE IN THE MIDEAST: HOW CAN IT BE ACHIEVED? By I. L. Kenen, et al. Washington, D.C.: American Enterprise Institute, 1971. 167 p. Notes.

A record of debates among four discussants on the opposing claims of the various protagonists in the Arab-Israeli conflict. The participants' comments in the Arab-Israeli conflict reflect their divergent perspectives toward the Palestinian-Zionist dilemma and, as such, form an interesting introduction to the conflict. Little reference material included.

4045 Kantor, David Mark. THE MIDDLE EAST; CAULDRON OF INTERNATIONAL POLITICS: THE ARAB-ISRAELI CONFLICT AND THE INTERNATIONAL STRUGGLE FOR POWER IN THE MIDDLE EAST UNTIL 1958.

Arab-Israeli Conflict

Vol. II. Potchesfstroom, South Africa: Potchesfstroom University for Christian High Education, Center for International Politics, 1973. 187 p. Bibliog.

4046 Kerr, Malcolm H. THE MIDDLE EAST CONFLICT. Headline Series, 191. New York: Foreign Policy Association, 1968. 63 p. Bibliog. Illus. Map.

> An excellent summary of the Arab-Israeli conflict which points up the increasing Palestinian involvement in the year following the 1967 war.

4047 _____. REGIONAL ARAB POLITICS AND CONFLICT WITH ISRAEL. RM-5966-FF. Santa Monica, Calif.: Rand Corporation, 1969. 50 p.

> The section on Arab state relations with Israel describes, according to the author's views, the Arab states' lack of initiative in either military preparedness or in diplomacy. Also cited in No. 1210.

4048 Khadduri, Majdia D., ed. THE ARAB-ISRAELI IMPASSE. Washington, D.C.: Robert R. Luce, 1968. 223 p. Bibliog. Map.

> Most of the essays included have been published previously, but are by experienced analysts of Middle East politics--John Badeau, Harry Howard, Jean Lacouture, and Albert Hourani, among others. Topics are recent history rather than strategy or diplomacy. A unique article on the refugee policies of Syria, Jordan, and Lebanon. The Arab state and Palestinian positions are developed well.

4049 Khouri, Fred J. THE ARAB-ISRAELI DILEMMA. Syracuse, N.Y.: Syracuse University Press, 1968. x, 436 p. Apps. Bibliog. Illus. Index. Maps.

> A history of the Arab-Israeli conflict, with particular attention to military policy, the role of the U.N., and the refugee problem. The author seeks solutions in resettlement, the economic development of occupied areas, and more equitable treatment of Israeli Arabs. States the Palestinian positions more clearly than the Israeli. Extensive bibliography including many Arab publications not elsewhere cited.

4050 Kimche, Jon. THERE COULD HAVE BEEN PEACE. New York: Dial, 1973. PALESTINE OR ISRAEL. London: Secker and Warburg, 1973. xx, 359 p. Apps. Bibliog. Index. Maps.

> Mandate history and the aftermath of the Six Day War. Develops the theme that "The real trouble about Palestine--was that it had nothing to do with the Jews and Arabs." Based on interviews with Arab and Israeli leaders and numerous secondary sources.

Arab-Israeli Conflict

4051 el-Kodsy, Ahmad, and Lobel, Eli. THE ARAB WORLD AND ISRAEL. Translated by Brian Pearce and Alfred Ehrenfield. Monthly Review Press, 1970. 137 p. Bibliog. ref.

> Two essays, basically Marxist, and originally in French, in which the Palestinian problem is attributed to the Arab states, the Soviet Union, the United States, and Israel. Recommended for special collections.

4052 Laqueur, Walter [Ze'ez], ed. THE ISRAELI-ARAB READER. A DOCUMENTARY HISTORY OF THE MIDDLE EAST CONFLICT. Rev. ed. New York: Bantam, 1969. 371 p. Bibliog. Map.

> Documents and official policy statements regarding the development of the Arab-Israeli conflict from the 1919 King-Crane Report to 1967. The editor also includes a number of previously published, outstanding articles on contemporary aspects of the conflict. Well-edited, solid background material.

4053 Lilenthal, Alfred M. THE OTHER SIDE OF THE COIN: AN AMERICAN PERSPECTIVE OF THE ARAB-ISRAELI CONFLICT. New York: Devin-Adair, 1965. xii, 420 p. Map. ref.

> The perspective of an American Jewish lawyer rather than of official American policy. The author has argued several times in print that Israel must transform itself into a secular, Middle Eastern state and repatriate refugee Palestinians if there is to be peace in the area.

4054 Mason, Herbert, ed. REFLECTIONS ON THE MIDDLE EAST CRISIS. New Babylon, Studies in the Behavioral Sciences, 7. The Hague: Mouton, 1970. 236 p.

> A symposium of essays on topics ranging from the experience of Jews in Arab lands, to the Palestinians as a political entity and the editor's conclusion that Israel must develop a less exclusive identity.

4055 Mehdi, Mohammed Taki. PEACE IN THE MIDDLE EAST. New York: World, 1967. 109 p.

> A statement of the author's case for the restoration of Arab sovereignty in Palestine. By a spokesman for the Palestinian position in the United States.

4056 Merlin, Samuel, ed. COLLOQUIUM ON THE BIG POWERS AND THE PRESENT CRISIS IN THE MIDDLE EAST. Cranbury, N.J.: Associated University Presses, 1968. 201 p. Apps.

> Papers presented at a colloquium jointly sponsored by the Institute for Mediterranean Affairs and Fairleigh Dickinson University, December 6, 1967. Participation extended to

diplomats, military leaders, and academicians. The volume includes ten papers, with comments, covering the Arab world and the major powers with respect to peacekeeping, international development, and the origins of the Arab-Israeli conflict. Documents appendixed include: the Eisenhower Doctrine, the Baghdad Pact, and the U.N. Security Council Resolution of 1967.

4057 THE MIDDLE EAST: SOME BASIC ISSUES AND ALTERNATIVES. Edited by Walter Isard and Julian Wolpert. Cambridge, Mass.: Schenkman Publishing Co. and Peace Research Society (International), 1972. 167 p. Paper.

Seven papers which were presented at the June 1970 conference on the Middle East of the Peace Research Society (International), published as a volume (15) of the Society's PAPERS. The papers are original and extensively documented. They focus primarily on the dynamics of conflict rather than background. New methodological approaches used.

4058 THE MIDDLE EAST CRISIS: TEST OF INTERNATIONAL LAW. Edited by John W. Halderman. Dobbs Ferry, N.Y.: Oceana, 1969. 193 p. Bibliog. fnn.

A collection of essays on the Arab-Israeli conflict from both political and legal viewpoints by Arab and Israeli scholar-diplomats and American jurists.

4059 Moore, John Norton, ed. THE ARAB-ISRAELI CONFLICT. 3 vols. Leiden: E.J. Brill and the American Society for International Law, 1964. 2,700 p. Bibliog.

Reprinted journal articles and excerpts from books and magazines, with a topically organized bibliography (volume 3). Volume 1 surveys the Arab-Israeli conflict from the standpoint of international law, particularly conflicting nationalism and navigational issues. Volume 2 covers the post-1967 period and the United Nations. Volume 3 includes relevant documents. Reviews various peace proposals.

4060 Rodinson, Maxime. ISRAEL AND THE ARABS. Translated by Michael Perl. New York: Pantheon Books; Harmondsworth, Eng.: Penguin, 1968. 239 p. Bibliog. fnn.

Background to the conflict from the Arab perspective--U.S. policy, peace initiatives, the Arab states. Little documentation.

4061 Safran, Nadav. FROM WAR TO WAR: THE ARAB-ISRAELI CONFRONTATION, 1948-1967. New York: Pegasus, 1969. 464 p. Illus. Maps.

The U.S.-USSR cold war and inter-Arab politics as they relate

to the conflict. Primarily valuable for its analysis of the
military and related economic capacities of the Arab states
and Israel, and their use of those capacities in three wars
(1948, 1956, 1967). The author has written extensively on
the conflict and uses Arabic as well as English and Hebrew
language sources. Little documentation.

4062 Schleifer, Abdullah. THE FALL OF JERUSALEM. New York: Monthly
Review Press, 1972. 247 p. Bibliog. Maps. Ref.

Standard account of the historical background and political
context of the Arab-Israeli conflict from the Arab perspective.
A historical review of al-Fatah. Some personal recollections.

4063 Schmidt, Dana Adams. ARMAGEDDON IN THE MIDDLE EAST. New
York: John Day for the New York Times Co., 1974. 269 p. Bibliog.
Index.

The Arab-Israeli conflict, the Palestinians, and the great
powers. A Middle East correspondent for the NEW YORK
TIMES writes that accommodation depends upon Soviet-U.S.
detente and arms export limitations, U.S. self-sufficiency
in petroleum, and the creation of a Palestinian state. An
introductory text.

4064 Segal, Ronald. WHOSE JERUSALEM? THE CONFLICTS OF ISRAEL.
London: Jonathan Cape, 1973. 284 p. Apps. Bibliog. Index.

Political conflicts within the states which are adversaries in
the Arab-Israeli conflict, excepting Syria. The title is mis-
leading. The author compares the Palestinian demands for self-
determination with South Africa and Vietnam, but otherwise devotes most of his attention to what he concludes are elitist politics
in Israel and Egypt. Introductory material; somewhat unfocused.

4065 Seminar of Arab Jurists on Palestine. THE PALESTINE QUESTION.
Beirut: Institute for Palestine Studies, 1968. 203 p.

Proceedings of a 1967 seminar of Arab jurists in Algiers.
Challenges Israel's historical rights.

4066 SETTLER REGIMES IN AFRICA AND THE ARAB WORLD. Edited by Ibrahim
Abu-Lughod and Baha Abu-Laban. Arab-American University Graduates
Monograph Series, 4. Wilmette, Ill.: Medina University Press, 1974.
255 p. Index.

Essays on mandated Palestine, Zionist ideas, Arab communities
in the United States, and the alienation of Palestinians in the
Arab world.

Arab-Israeli Conflict

4067 Sharabi, Hisham. PALESTINE AND ISRAEL: THE LETHAL DILEMMA. New York: Pegasus, 1969. 224 p. Bibliog. fnn. Illus.

> A short and readable account of U.S. policy toward the Arab-Israeli conflict (which the author sees as having conditioned American relations with the Arab world in general) and of the issues in that confrontation. Sharabi shows the protagonists' positions at their most extreme.

4068 Taylor, Alan R., and Tetlie, Richard N., eds. PALESTINE: A SEARCH FOR TRUTH. Washington, D.C.: Public Affairs Press, 1970. 284 p. Bibliog.

> A collection of twenty-four previously published articles and speeches primarily by academics specializing in either Jewish or Arab studies. Little attention is devoted to the Palestinians as a separate entity, much to the potential opportunities which Israeli statesmen could exploit to declare their peaceful intentions to their opponents. The biographies of the authors are useful guides to further reading as well as to the backgrounds of prominent writers on the Arab-Israeli conflict. Little documentation.

4069 THE TRANSFORMATION OF PALESTINE: ESSAYS ON THE ORIGIN AND DEVELOPMENT OF THE ARAB-ISRAELI CONFLICT. Edited by Ibrahim Abu-Lughod. Evanston, Ill.: Northwestern University Press, 1971. xv, 522 p. Bibliog. Maps.

> Sixteen articles cover the development of Zionism and Palestinian nationalism under the British mandate, the refugee problem, the role of the Arab states in the conflict, and the reaction of states outside the Middle East to the conflict. The last category includes an essay on Asian state perspectives on Palestine, a topic rarely discussed in the literature. The essays are original and nonpolemical, analytical and current. A well-organized and balanced bibliography.

4070 Tuma, Elias H. PEACEMAKING AND THE IMMORAL WAR: ARABS AND JEWS IN THE MIDDLE EAST. New York: Harper Torchbooks, 1972. 126 p. Paper. Index.

> The claims advanced by Israel, the Arab states, and the Palestinians, placed in the context of international politics and peacemaking. The conflict is seen as territorial, not religious. Little documentation.

4071 U.S. Congress. House. Committee on Foreign Affairs. THE MIDDLE EAST, 1971: THE NEED TO STRENGTHEN THE PEACE. Hearings before the Subcommittee on the Near East. 92d Cong., 1st sess., July-October, 1971. Washington, D.C.: Government Printing Office, 1971. 369 p. Apps. Illus. Index. Maps.

Arab-Israeli Conflict

Survey of international regional issues--the Suez Canal, the Palestine movement, the Persian Gulf, and Arab-Israeli conflict settlement potential. Four articles on related issues appended; fourteen statements by scholars of the Middle East.

4072 Vatikiotis, Panayiotis J. CONFLICT IN THE MIDDLE EAST. London: Allen and Unwin, 1971. xvi, 224 p. Bibliog. Index. Map.

The Arab-Israeli conflict, the Palestinian Fedayeen, and the post-1967 period. Reviews Arab state politics and argues that a set of tensions lies behind the Arab-Israeli conflict, not one issue. A conventional treatment by an experienced scholar.

4073 Warburg, James P. CROSSCURRENTS IN THE MIDDLE EAST. New York: Atheneum, 1968. 244 p. Bibliog. Maps.

A balanced introduction to the Arab-Israeli conflict. The author is especially critical of the United States's role.

HISTORICAL BACKGROUND

4101 Allen, Sir Richard H.S. IMPERIALISM AND NATIONALISM IN THE FERTILE CRESCENT: SOURCES AND PROSPECTS OF THE ARAB-ISRAELI CONFLICT. New York: Oxford University Press, 1974. x, 686 p. App. Bibliog. Maps.

A historical view of the Arab-Israeli conflict by a retired British diplomat who describes Palestine as a center of religious and imperial conflict since the time of Judaism. The author argues that accommodation must involve rectifying the status of the Palestinian Arabs and ending Israel's dependence upon foreign assistance. A good bibliography.

4102 Andrews, Fannie Fern. THE HOLY LAND UNDER THE MANDATE. 2 vols. 1931. Reprint. Westport, Conn.: Hyperion, 1975. 361 and 436 p.

The background of the League Mandate system, Arab claims to Palestine and Zionism. Firsthand experience and research.

4103 Anglo-American Committee of Inquiry on Jewish Problems in Palestine and Europe. REPORT TO THE UNITED STATES GOVERNMENT AND HIS MAJESTY'S GOVERNMENT IN THE UNITED KINGDOM. LAUSANNE, SWITZERLAND, APRIL 20, 1946. U.S. Department of State Publication, no. 2536, Near Eastern Series, 2. Washington, D.C.: Government Printing Office, U.S. Department of State, 1946. 92 p.

Jews and Arabs in post-World-War-II Palestine and Europe. Does not discuss policies of the major powers.

Arab-Israeli Conflict

4104 Arab Office (London). THE FUTURE OF PALESTINE. 1947. Reprint. Westport, Conn.: Hyperion, 1975. 166 p.

> An Arab viewpoint on the historical background of the conflict which traces it to the Balfour Declaration.

4105 Arberry, Arthur John, ed. RELIGION IN THE MIDDLE EAST: THREE RELIGIONS IN CONCORD AND CONFLICT. Vol. 1: JUDAISM AND CHRISTIANITY; vol. 2: ISLAM. London: Cambridge University Press, 1969. xii, 596 and xii, 750 p. Illus. Maps.

> A collection of essays dealing with Judaism, Islam, and Christianity in the Middle East in the nineteenth and twentieth centuries.

4106 Barbour, Nevill. NISI DOMINUS. London: Harrap, 1946. PALESTINE: STAR OR CRESCENT? New York: Odyssey Press, 1947. x, 310 p. Bibliog. fnn. Diagr. Illus.

> The Arab viewpoint regarding partition, the establishment of a separate Jewish state, and the mandate system. Written immediately prior to the Anglo-American Commission REPORT (4103). Based upon firsthand experience and published sources.

4107 Bauer, Yehuda. FROM DIPLOMACY TO RESISTANCE: A HISTORY OF JEWISH PALESTINE, 1939-1945. Translated by Alton M. Winters. Philadelphia: Jewish Publication Society of America, 1970. 432 p. Bibliog. Index.

> The Zionist resistance as it reacted to international diplomatic events. No documentation.

4108 Bentwich, Norman and Bentwich, Helen. MANDATE MEMORIES, 1918-1948. London: Hogarth, 1965. 231 p.

> The firsthand recollections of a Palestine attorney general (under High Commissioner Plumer). Takes the form of contemporary letters from Helen Bentwich. Focus upon the first decade of the Mandate. Little on the Arab position.

4109 Berger, Elmer. THE JEWISH DILEMMA. New York: Devin-Adair, 1945. 257 p.

> Focuses upon the Balfour Declaration, the Sykes-Picot agreement and the 1939 White Paper. Criticizes the combination of national and religious identity in Zionism.

4110 Cohen, Israel. THE ZIONIST MOVEMENT. New York: Zionist Organization of America, 1946. 400 p. Bibliog.

> A favorable history of Zionism and the Palestine Mandate. First published in 1945 in Great Britain. Edited and revised,

with supplementary chapter on Zionism in the United States by Bernard G. Richards.

4111 Crossman, Richard. PALESTINE MISSION: A PERSONAL RECORD. New York and London: Harper, 1947. 210 p. Maps.

> A member of the 1946 Anglo-American Commission of Inquiry on Palestine, critical of Zionism and of U.S. policy in Palestine, argues for partition and an end to external involvement in the area.

4112 Crum, Bartley C. BEHIND THE SILKEN CURTAIN: A PERSONAL ACCOUNT OF ANGLO-AMERICAN DIPLOMACY IN PALESTINE AND THE MIDDLE EAST. New York: Simon and Schuster, 1947. xiv, 297 p. Map.

> An American member of the 1946 Anglo-American Commission of Inquiry on Palestine cites documents illustrating the "duplicity" of U.S. policy toward Arabs and Jews. A sometimes careless pro-Zionist interpretation.

4113 Esco Foundation for Palestine. PALESTINE: A STUDY OF JEWISH, ARAB, AND BRITISH POLICIES. 2 vols. 1947. Reprint. New York: Kraus Reprint, 1970. 1,380 p. Bibliog. Index. Maps.

> Essays by Jewish scholars on the growth of Zionism, British mandate policy, and international diplomacy between the two world wars. The bibliography is extensive and covers public documents, monographs, journal articles, and periodicals. Much detail, less objectivity; contains a wealth of information.

4114 Friedman, Isaiah. THE QUESTION OF PALESTINE, 1914-1918: BRITISH-JEWISH-ARAB RELATIONS. London: Routledge & Kegan Paul; New York: Schocken, 1973. xiii, 433 p. Bibliog.

> Attempts to document the theory that the Balfour Declaration was a deliberate response to a possible Turco-German protectorate in the area.

4115 Gabbay, Rony E. A POLITICAL STUDY OF THE ARAB-JEWISH CONFLICT. Etudes d'Histoire Economique, Politique, et Sociale, 29. Paris: Libraire Minard; New York: Gregory Lounz, 1959. xvii, 611 p. Bibliog. Maps.

> Bibliography of League of Nations, U.N. and Arab League documents, official state papers, and secondary sources in Arabic, Hebrew, English, and French. Covers the Mandate period, the refugee issue, and the aftermath of the 1956 war.

4116 Gervasi, Frank H. TO WHOM PALESTINE? New York and London: D. Appleton-Century, 1946. 213 p.

Arab-Israeli Conflict

Zionist sovereignty over Palestine justified by lack of Palestinian Arabs' historical or political counterclaims (author's assessment).

4117 Goitein, Solomon D. JEWS AND ARABS: THEIR CONTACTS THROUGH THE AGES. 3d rev. ed. New York: Schocken Books, 1974. 263 p. Bibliog. Chron. Index.

Jews and Arabs in the Middle East since Islam--their varying economic, social, and legal traditions, challenging the notion of common Semitic backgrounds. Written by an Israeli scholar. Limited bibliography.

4118 Great Britain. Palestine Royal Commission. REPORT PRESENTED BY THE SECRETARY OF STATE FOR THE COLONIES TO PARLIMENT BY COMMAND OF HIS MAJESTY, JULY, 1937. Parliament. Papers by Command. Command 5479. London: H.M. Stationery Office, 1937. xii, 404 p. Illus. Maps.

Known as the Peel Report, this entry documents the development of the Arab and Jewish communities in Palestine and the British Mandate administration. Recommends partition.

4119 Hattis, Susan Lee. THE BI-NATIONAL IDEA IN PALESTINE DURING MANDATORY TIMES. Haifa: Shikmona, 1970. 355 p. Bibliog. Index.

The author's doctoral thesis for the University of Geneva which examines the support for binationalism within the Jewish community and in British policy during the Mandate period. Based upon extensive review of Israeli archives, as well as other primary and secondary sources.

4120 Herzl, Theodor. COMPLETE DIARIES. Edited by Raphael Patal. Translated by Harry Zohn. 5 vols. New York: Herzl Press, 1960. 1,961 p. Ports.

The first complete publication of the diaries kept by the founder of political Zionism covering the period 1895 to 1904 as Herzl developed his conception of the Jewish state and support for it among European political leaders. The fifth volume contains explanatory references to names and terms found in the diaries and an index.

4121 Holmes, John Haynes. PALESTINE TO-DAY AND TOMORROW: A GENTILE'S SURVEY OF ZIONISM. London: George Allen and Unwin, 1930 [c1929]. 271 p.

A journalist's account of Zionists in Palestine, focusing upon the 1929 violence, and the political basis of Arab Palestinians' opposition to Zionism.

Arab-Israeli Conflict

4122 Horowitz, David. STATE IN THE MAKING. Translated by Julian [L.] Meltzer. New York: Alfred A. Knopf, 1953. 349 p.

    British and Arab State policy vis-a-vis the Palestinian issue after World War II.

4123 Howard, Harry N. THE KING-CRANE COMMISSION: AN AMERICAN INQUIRY IN THE MIDDLE EAST. Beirut: Khayats, 1963. xiv, 369 p. Apps. Bibliog. Maps.

    Describes the commission's investigations and concludes that its work made a "challenging contribution to the technique of peacemaking." Lengthy bibliography of primary and secondary sources, with comment.

4124 Hurewitz, Jacob C[oleman]. THE STRUGGLE FOR PALESTINE. New York: Norton, 1950. 404 p. Bibliog. Index. Map.

    Issued also as a thesis, Columbia University, entitled: "The Road to Partition." History of the Palestine Mandate, the war years, and the partition arrangement. Less critical of the Zionist position than of the Palestinian Arabs. Extensive bibliography drawing upon Arabic, Hebrew, and English language sources.

4125 Hyamson, Albert M[ontefiore]. PALESTINE: A POLICY. London: Methuen, 1942. xiv, 214 p. Index.

    Background on Zionism in religious thought, the diaspora, and Palestine under the Mandate. No notes. The author describes himself as a spiritual, not a political, Zionist.

4126 _____. PALESTINE UNDER THE MANDATE; 1920-1948. London: Methuen, 1950; New York: British Book Centre, 1951. 210 p. Index.

    Includes much detail, some firsthand, particularly for the 1920s. A positive evaluation of the British Mandate from the standpoint of "orderly administration" and the fulfillment of the Balfour Declaration on behalf of a Jewish National Home.

4127 ISRAEL AND THE ARABS: PRELUDE TO THE JEWISH STATE. Edited by Anne Sinai and I. Robert Sinai. New York: Facts on File, 1972. 248 p. Paper. Index.

    The diplomatic record from World War II and the Anglo-American Committee of Inquiry to the U.N. Partition Resolution. No documentation or analysis.

4128 Jeffries, Joseph M. N. PALESTINE THE REALITY. London: Longmans, Green, 1939. xxiii, 728 p. Bibliog. Maps.

Arab-Israeli Conflict

      Originally appeared as one of several DAILY MAIL books on the Middle East entitled THE PALESTINE DECEPTION (1922, 1937). An anti-Zionist, journalist's view of the British Mandate and the Jewish population in Palestine. The author was the first (1922) to publish the Hussein-McMahon correspondence in Britain.

4129 John, Robert, and Hadawi, Sami. THE PALESTINE DIARY. 2 vols. New York: New World Press, 1970. 851 p. App. Bibliog. ref. Index. Maps.

      British Mandate policy, the Zionist movement, and Arab rebellions (volume 1, 1914-45) and the United States and the United Nations (volume 2, 1945-48). Based upon public documents, which are referenced. Condemns British vacillations over the Jewish National Home. Complements Hurewitz's work on the same period [4124].

4130 Joseph, Bernard. BRITISH RULE IN PALESTINE. Washington, D.C.: Public Affairs Press, 1948. 279 p. Bibliog. fnn.

      Zionist demands for sovereignty favorably reviewed through a legal framework.

4131 Katznelson, Siegmund. THE PALESTINE PROBLEM AND ITS SOLUTION: A NEW SCHEME. Jerusalem: Jewish Publishing House, 1946. 117 p. Bibliog. fnn.

      The mandate period and recommended solutions from a pro-Zionist viewpoint.

4132 el-Khalidi, Walid, comp. FROM HAVEN TO CONQUEST: READINGS IN ZIONISM AND THE PALESTINE PROBLEM UNTIL 1948. Beirut: Institute for Palestine Studies, 1971. lxxxiii, 914 p.

      Most of the eighty readings selected are from non-Arab sources, and many have not appeared in earlier compilations. Develops the conflict from the point of view of the "Palestine Tragedy." Appendices include military, economic, and demographic data. The compiler is a Palestinian scholar and spokesman.

4133 Kimche, Jon. SEVEN FALLEN PILLARS: THE MIDDLE EAST, 1915-1950. London: Secker and Warburg, 1950. xxi, 326 p. Maps. Ports.

      Arab nationalism and the unperceptive and outdated British approach to it which was made evident by the organized Zionist movement (author). Focuses on the period 1944-48.

4134 Kirkbride, Alec. A CRACKLE OF THORNS. London: John Murray, 1956. 201 p. Index. Ports.

Arab-Israeli Conflict

Personal recollections of a British soldier in the Middle East, Palestine administrator, and first British Minister in Jordan.

4135 Kisch, Frederick H. PALESTINE DIARY. London: Victor Gollancz, 1938. 478 p. Front. Illus. Plates. Ports.

Favorable picture of Zionist leaders' attempts to improve Jewish-Arab relations in Palestine during the early years of the Mandate. Also cited in No. 2634.

4136 Koestler, Arthur. PROMISE AND FULFILLMENT: PALESTINE 1917-1949. New York: Macmillan, 1949. xv, 335 p. Map.

Popular account of the background to the establishment of the state of Israel, focusing on the post-World-War-II period. Pro-Zionist.

4137 Levin, Norman Gordon, comp. THE ZIONIST MOVEMENT IN PALESTINE AND WORLD POLITICS, 1880-1918. Lexington, Mass.: D.C. Heath, 1974. xx, 258 p. Bibliog. refs.

Addresses, essays, and lectures on the history of Zionism.

4138 Litvinoff, Barnet. TO THE HOUSE OF THEIR FATHERS. New York: Praeger, 1965. ROAD TO JERUSALEM: ZIONISM'S IMPRINT ON HISTORY. London: Weidenfeld & Nicolson, 1966. 311 p. Bibliog. Maps. Plates.

Describes the Zionist experience in creating a Jewish state-- from Moses Hess to Ben Gurion. An intellectual and political history. No references.

4139 Lowdermilk, Walter Clay. PALESTINE: LAND OF PROMISE. Rev. ed. New York: Harper, 1949. 244 p. Map. Plates.

Zionist demands for national sovereignty in Palestine justified from the standpoint of Jewish development projects.

4140 Marlowe, John. REBELLION IN PALESTINE. London: Cresset, 1946. 279 p. Bibliog. Ref. Illus.

A former British resident of Palestine presents largely undocumented personal interpretive material with recommendations for a solution.

4141 _____. THE SEAT OF PILATE: AN ACCOUNT OF THE PALESTINE MANDATE. London: Cresset, 1959. 289 p. Bibliog. Illus.

The Mandate years with emphasis upon the Palestine administration and views of the Arab community under Haj Amin Husseini's leadership. The author has made use of hitherto unpublished recollections of participants. Brief bibliography, including colonial records. Mandate instrument appended.

4142 Meinertzhagen, Richard. MIDDLE EAST DIARY, 1917-1956. London: Cresset, 1959; New York: Thomas Yoseloff, 1960. 376 p. Chron. Index. Map.

Diaries of a British diplomat who was chief political officer in Palestine and Cairo and who was dedicated to the establishment of an Israeli state. Includes frequent quotations from official correspondence.

4143 Parkes, James W. A HISTORY OF PALESTINE FROM 135 A. D. TO MODERN TIMES. New York: Oxford University Press, 1949. 391 p. Bibliog. Index. Maps.

One-third of the book is addressed to Palestine in the twentieth century, during which the Palestinian Arabs are portrayed as religious fanatics and the Jews as binationalists. The bibliography is introductory, and there are no footnotes.

4144 ———. WHOSE LAND? A HISTORY OF THE PEOPLES OF PALESTINE. New York: Taplinger, 1971 [c1970]. 333 p. Paper. Bibliog. Maps.

One of many discussions of who has the right to live in Palestine. The author takes a historical perspective toward the current stalemate.

4145 Polk, William R.; Stamler, David M.; and Asfour, Edmund. BACKDROP TO TRAGEDY: THE STRUGGLE FOR PALESTINE. Boston: Beacon Press, 1957. 399 p. Bibliog. Illus. Index. Maps. Tables.

An American scholar, a British Zionist, and a Palestinian jointly review the historical background of Palestine, and individually analyze Arab and Jewish politics and the economic setting. An excellent documented introduction to the Mandate period.

4146 Ra'anan, Uri. THE FRONTIERS OF A NATION: A REEXAMINATION OF THE FORCES WHICH CREATED THE PALESTINE MANDATE AND DETERMINED ITS TERRITORIAL SHAPE. 1955. Reprint. Westport, Conn.: Hyperion, 1975. Bibliog. Index.

4147 Razzūk, Ass'ad. GREATER ISRAEL: A STUDY IN ZIONIST EXPANSIONIST THOUGHT. Palestine Book, 13. Beirut: Palestine Liberation Organization Research Center, 1970. 326 p. Paper. Bibliog. Maps.

Original text sources. Traces the roots of the 1967 war to early Zionist thought and its development during the Mandate. Does not examine Arab state policies.

Arab-Israeli Conflict

4148 Rodinson, Maxime. ISRAEL: A COLONIAL-SETTLER STATE? Translated by David Torsted. New York: Monad, 1973. 120 p. Paper. Bibliog. fnn. Index. Maps.

    A French Marxist scholar concludes that Israel's existence is a phenomenon of colonialism.

4149 Rose, Norman Anthony. THE GENTILE ZIONISTS: A STUDY IN ANGLO-ZIONIST DIPLOMACY, 1929-1939. London: Frank Cass, 1973. xiii, 242 p. Bibliog. Illus.

    A scholarly analysis of the non-Jewish movement to influence British policy in Palestine.

4150 Royal Institute of International Affairs. Information Department. GREAT BRITAIN AND PALESTINE, 1915-1945. Information Papers, 20. London and New York: 1946. xii, 177 p. Maps.

    Digest of relevant portions of the Institute's SURVEY OF INTERNATIONAL AFFAIRS, which was first published in 1937.

4151 Sacher, Harry. ISRAEL, THE ESTABLISHMENT OF A STATE. New York: British Book Centre; London: Weidenfeld and Nicolson, 1952. 332 p. Index. Maps.

    The United Nations' Partition Plan, the ensuing negotiations and war, and intermittent peace-keeping efforts by international negotiators. No documentation or references.

4152 Sakran, Frank C. PALESTINE DILEMMA: ARAB RIGHTS VERSUS ZIONIST ASPIRATIONS. Washington, D.C.: Public Affairs Press, 1948. 230 p. Bibliog. Maps.

    Local politics and external power strategies described by a Christian Arab who emigrated from Palestine before the Mandate.

4153 Samuel, Herbert Louis. MEMOIRS. London: Cresset, 1945. viii, 304 p. GROOVES OF CHANGE. New York: Bobbs-Merrill, 1946. 378 p. Front. Plates. Ports.

    Recollections of the first and controversial High Commissioner to Palestine 1920-25. Only a portion of the autobiography deals with Samuel's years in Palestine, but that portion provides valuable background to the aftermath of the Balfour Declaration.

4154 Samuel, Maurice. HARVEST IN THE DESERT. Philadelphia: Jewish Publication Society, 1944. 316 p.

    Diplomacy and economic progress in Palestine. Conflict attributed to the Arab Higher Committee and forced upon the Arab laborer.

Arab-Israeli Conflict

4155 _____. LEVEL SUNLIGHT. New York: Knopf, 1953. 302 p. Index.

> Sympathetic recounting of Chaim Weizmann's activities on behalf of Zionism and his role in the U.N. Special Committee on Palestine. Written by a friend and associate.

4156 _____. ON THE RIM OF THE WILDERNESS: THE CONFLICT IN PALESTINE. New York: Horace Liveright, 1931. 247 p.

> Views the major problem confronting Jewish Palestine as social conflict, particularly between Arab employers and laborers. Information on economic inequality. No sources cited.

4157 Sharef, Zeev. THREE DAYS. Translated by J[ulian].L. Meltzer. Garden City, N.Y.: Doubleday, 1962. 298 p.

> Three days leading up to the establishment of Israel--internal and external events, undocumented.

4158 Stein, Leonard J. THE BALFOUR DECLARATION. New York: Simon and Schuster, 1961. xiv, 681 p. Bibliog. fnn.

> The most extensive and scholarly treatment of the (1917) Balfour Declaration available. Focuses upon British policy-making processes. The author concludes that the motivations behind the declaration were manifold and that British policy was characterized by ambiguity.

4159 Storrs, Sir Ronald. THE MEMOIRS OF SIR RONALD STORRS. New York: G.P. Putnam, 1937. xvii, 563 p. Illus. Index. Maps. Ports. Plates.

> Storrs, who was military governor of Jerusalem after World War I, recollects British Policy, Arab nationalism, and Zionist politics during this period. A slightly longer version was published as ORIENTATIONS (London: Ivor Nicolson and Watson, 1937).

4160 A SURVEY OF PALESTINE. 2 vols. Jerusalem: Government Printer, 1946. 1,145 p. Illus. Index.

> Prepared for the information of the Anglo-American Committee of Inquiry. Volume 1 surveys the history, political structure, and, in detail, economic conditions. Volume 2 describes community and social affairs, political parties, and further economic issues. This is a government publication which is not critical of the Mandate. A supplement of notes was also published in 1947.

4161 Sykes, Christopher. CROSSROADS TO ISRAEL: 1917-1948. London: Collins, 1965; Bloomington: Indiana University Press, 1973. xii, 404 p. Bibliog. Illus. Index. Maps. Ports.

Conflicts in British policy in Palestine and Zionist strategy.
Less on Arab politics, which the author found to be passive.
Well-documented with a good bibliography of secondary sources.

4162 Taylor, Alan R. PRELUDE TO ISRAEL: AN ANALYSIS OF ZIONIST
DIPLOMACY, 1897-1947. New York: Philosophical Library, 1959.
136 p. Bibliog. Illus. Index. Ports.

Introduction to the diplomatic activities of Zionist leaders
especially in the United States and Britain. Primarily based
upon English language secondary sources, with extensive documentation.

4163 U.N. Special Committee on Palestine (UNSCOP). REPORT TO THE
GENERAL ASSEMBLY. 5 vols. General Assembly Official Records:
Second Session. Supplement 11. Lake Success, N.Y.: 1947. Index.

The hearings and recommendations of UNSCOP, related government documents and statements, and background information.
The last volume is an index.

4164 Van Passen, Pierre. THE FORGOTTEN ALLY. New York: Dial, 1943.
343 p. Map.

The Palestinian Jew is the ally who is forgotten by the British
and the U.N.

4165 Weizman, Chaim. TRIAL AND ERROR; THE AUTOBIOGRAPHY OF CHAIM
WEIZMAN. 1949. Reprint. New York: Schocken, 1972. xviii, 493 p.
Index. Map.

The evolution of Zionism in Palestine and the West from the
recollections of the chief spokesman for the Zionist cause before and during the Mandate years. Describes the author's
negotiations with British leaders, the formation of the Zionist
Commission, and the Palestine landscape.

4166 Williams-Thompson, Richard. THE PALESTINE PROBLEM. London and
New York: A. Melrose, 1946. x, 127 p. Illus. Ref.

Reviews the Mandate period from an essentially pro-Arab
perspective.

4167 Ziff, William Bernard. THE RAPE OF PALESTINE. New York and Toronto:
Longmans, Green, 1938. 616 p. Apps. Bibliog.

The author's arguments of anti-Zionist bias in British mandate
policy. Mandate instrument appended.

4168 ZIONISM AND PALESTINE BEFORE THE MANDATE: A PHASE OF WESTERN IMPERIALISM. Edited by Richard P. Stevens. Anthology Series, 5.

Arab-Israeli Conflict

Beirut: Institute for Palestine Studies, 1972. xiii, 153 p. Index.

A collection of essays originally published in the United States at the end of World War I which both support and criticize the Zionist movement and British policy.

DOCUMENTS

4201 Cordier, Andrew, and Foote, Wilder, eds. PUBLIC PAPERS OF THE SECRETARIES-GENERAL OF THE UNITED NATIONS. Vol. III: DAG HAMMARSKJOLD, 1956-57. New York and London: Columbia University Press, 1973. 729 p.

> The 123 papers in this volume are principally concerned with the Suez crisis and the Hungarian issue. Covers the events leading up to the invasion of Egypt by Israel, France, and Britain and the creation of UNEF. The editors both served in the United Nations Secretariat and have written a long introductory note. The third volume of four on Hammarskjold.

4202 Dodd, Charles, and Sales, Mary, comps. ISRAEL AND THE ARAB WORLD. London: Routledge and Kegan Paul; New York: Barnes and Noble, 1970. xvi, 247 p. Bibliog. Illus. Index. Maps.

> A collection of documents and essay excerpts topically organized, with concluding discussion questions. Covers the major Mandate period documents, the first three wars, and various negotiating efforts. Useful introductory material. Short bibliography.

4203 Higgins, Rosalyn. UNITED NATIONS PEACEKEEPING, 1946-1967: DOCUMENTS AND COMMENTARY. Vol. 1: THE MIDDLE EAST. London and New York: Oxford University Press for the Royal Institute of International Affairs, 1969. xiv, 669 p. Bibliog. Index. Maps.

> Separate sections on the U.N. Truce Supervision Organization (UNTSO, 1949-), the U.N. Emergency Force (UNEF, 1956-67), U.N. Observer Group in Lebanon (UNOGIL, 1958), and the U.N. Yemen Observation Mission (UNYOM, 1963-64). The case studies extend from enabling legislation to financing and implementation and offer checklists of documents relating to each. A valuable reference.

4204 Hyamson, Albert Montefiore, ed. THE BRITISH CONSULATE IN JERUSALEM IN RELATION TO THE JEWS OF PALESTINE, 1838-1914. 2 vols. London: Edward Goldston for the Jewish Historical Society of England, 1936. 594 p.

> Records from British Archives arranged chronologically relating to Jewish affairs in Palestine.

Arab-Israeli Conflict

4205 Indian Society of International Law. THE ARAB-ISRAELI CONFLICT, DOCUMENTS AND COMMENTS. New Delhi: Scandia House, 1967. 306 p. Apps. Bibliog.

 The comments are summaries of the documents, not analyses. Eighteen documents concerned primarily with the Suez and 1967 wars.

4206 Ingrams, Doreen, comp. PALESTINE PAPERS, 1917-1922: SEEDS OF CONFLICT. New York: George Braziller, 1973 [c1972]. xii, 198 p. Apps. Bibliog. ref. Index. Map.

 A first review of the archival material of the Public Records Office in London concerned primarily with British policy toward Palestine. Omits some of the Palestinian record. Many documents undated. Annotated.

4207 INTERNATIONAL DOCUMENTS ON PALESTINE, 1967. Compiled by Fuad A. Jabber. Palestine Before the United Nations Series, vol. 4. Beirut: Institute for Palestine Studies, 1970. 800 p. Index.

 Sections on international, United Nations, and Arab world documents, arranged chronologically. Joint declarations, communiques, U.N. resolutions, and statements of the secretary general and other U.N. officials. Translations from Arabic and Russian.

4208 Israel. Ministry of Foreign Affairs. ISRAEL'S PEACE OFFERS TO THE ARAB STATES, 1948-1963: THE RECORD. Jerusalem: Jerusalem Post Press, 1963. 97 p.

 Texts of approximately one hundred official Israeli statements made to various forums. General peace settlements and specific aspects of the conflict. Chronologically ordered.

4209 Lauterpacht, Elihu, comp. THE UNITED NATIONS EMERGENCY FORCE: BASIC DOCUMENTS. London: Stevens; New York: Praeger, 1960. 49 p.

 The creation and functioning of UNEF.

4210 Sayegh, Fayez [Abdullah], and Soukkary, Sohair A. PALESTINE: CONCORDANCE OF THE UNITED NATIONS RESOLUTIONS, 1967-1971. New York: New World Press, 1971. 93 p.

 Classified by topic; seventy-four listings. Resolutions cover refugees, cease-fires, Jerusalem, occupation, and definitions of future accommodation.

4211 United Nations. DOCUMENTS ON THE ARAB-ISRAEL CONFLICT. THE RESOLUTIONS OF THE UNITED NATIONS ORGANIZATION. Edited by

Arab-Israeli Conflict

Wilhelm Wengler and Joseph Tittle. Berlin: Berlin Verlag, 1971. 207 p.

4212 UNITED NATIONS RESOLUTIONS ON PALESTINE, 1947-1972. Compiled by Sami Musallam. Rev. ed. Beirut: Institute for Palestine Studies, 1973. xxiii, 225 p. Maps.

> Revised from previous versions (compiled by Sami Hadawi and Mundhir Anabtawi). Resolutions related to various aspects of the Palestine question since the partition.

4213 Watt, D.C., ed. DOCUMENTS ON THE SUEZ CRISIS, 26 JULY TO 6 NOVEMBER 1956. London: Royal Institute of International Affairs, 1957. 88 p. Illus.

JERUSALEM

4301 Bovis, H. Eugene. THE JERUSALEM QUESTION, 1917-1968. Hoover Institution Studies, 29, Policy 7. Stanford, Calif.: Hoover Institution Press, 1971. xiii, 175 p. Apps. Bibliog. Illus. Index. Maps.

> History of control over Jerusalem and proposals for its disposition. Author concludes with his own evaluation of alternatives, an extensive bibliography of official documents and other sources, and maps of the city's sectors. Originally presented as author's thesis, American University, 1968.

4302 Holz, Abraham, ed. THE HOLY CITY: JEWS ON JERUSALEM. New York: Norton, 1971. 187 p. Bibliog.

4303 Mohn, Paul. JERUSALEM AND THE UNITED NATIONS, pp. 421-71. International Conciliation, 464. New York: Carnegie Endowment for International Peace, May 1952. Map.

> Background on administration of the holy places and negotiations on various internationalization plans. By a member of the U.N. Palestine Commission and consultant to Count Bernadotte. U.N. documentation.

4304 Pfaff, Richard H. JERUSALEM: KEYSTONE OF AN ARAB-ISRAELI SETTLEMENT. Legislative and Special Analyses, 91st Congress, 1st session, no. 13. Washington, D.C.: American Enterprise Institute for Public Policy Research, 1969. 56 p. Bibliog. fnn. Maps.

> Discussion of the religious significance of Jerusalem and evaluation of alternative proposals for resolving its status. Author's analysis of U.S. interests in the area is the weakest part of the monograph.

4305 Tibawi, Abdul Latif. JERUSALEM, ITS PLACE IN ISLAM AND ARAB

Arab-Israeli Conflict

HISTORY. Beirut: Institute for Palestine Studies, 1969. 45 p.

> Published originally in THE ARAB WORLD 14, no. 10-11 (1967). A history summary.

4306 U.S. Congress. House. Committee on Foreign Affairs. JERUSALEM: THE FUTURE OF THE HOLY CITY FOR THREE MONOTHEISMS. Hearings before the Subcommittee on the Near East, 92d Cong., 1st. sess., July 1971. Washington, D.C.: Government Printing Office, 1971. 226 p.

> Testimony and appended statements from representatives of the three religions.

4307 Wilson, Evan M. JERUSALEM: KEY TO PEACE. The James Terry Duce Memorial Series, 2. Washington, D.C.: Middle East Institute, 1970. xi, 176 p. Bibliog. Illus. Maps.

> An account, by the former American consul general in Jerusalem, of the history of that divided city and its reunification in 1967. Reviews the problems encountered by the U.N. Truce Supervision Organization.

4308 Zander, Walter. ISRAEL AND THE HOLY PLACES OF CHRISTENDOM. London: Weidenfeld and Nicolson; New York: Praeger, 1971. viii, 148 p. Bibliog. ref. Index.

> Basically a history of Christian attitudes toward the Holy Land, including Jerusalem. The author explains why he prefers the establishment of condominium rule over Jerusalem to internationalization.

JORDAN RIVER

4401 Doherty, Kathryn B. JORDAN WATERS CONFLICT. International Conciliation, 553. New York: Carnegie Endowment for International Peace, 1965. 66 p. Map. Bibliog. fnn.

> The focus is upon the international legal aspects of the Jordan River problem, which, the author concludes, give few guidelines to resolving the conflict.

4402 Rizk, Edward. THE RIVER JORDAN. Information Papers, 23. New York: Arab Information Center, 1964. 61 p.

> The perspective is Arab and the argument is that the conflict over the river is political, not economic or legal, and bound up with the Palestinian question.

4403 Saliba, Samir N. THE JORDAN RIVER DISPUTE. The Hague: Martinus Nijhoff, 1968. ix, 167 p. Bibliog. Maps.

Arab-Israeli Conflict

A careful study of the "hydropolitics" (the author's term) of the river which links water needs and settlement strategies to their military repercussions. Includes relevant legal materials.

4404 Stevens, Georgiana G. JORDAN RIVER PARTITION. Hoover Institution Studies, 6. Stanford, Calif.: Hoover Institution on War, Revolution and Peace, 1965. x, 90 p. Bibliog. Illus. Map.

The 1955 Johnston proposals for water division and Arab state and Israeli plans. Points out the variety of Arab positions, and the official recognition of Israel's riparian rights. English language sources.

PEACEKEEPING AND NEGOTIATIONS

4501 al-Abid, Ibrahim. ISRAEL AND NEGOTIATIONS. Palestine Essays, 20. Beirut: Palestine Liberation Organization Research Center, 1970. 29 p. Paper.

The issue of direct negotiations and their implications for the Arab state and the Palestinian positions regarding Israel.

4502 Azcarate y Florez, Pablo de. MISSION IN PALESTINE, 1948-1952. Washington, D.C.: Middle East Institute, 1966. 211 p.

Memoirs of the Secretary of the U.N. Palestine Conciliation Commission. Traces the establishment of the commission, the fighting in Jerusalem and the subsequent ceasefire.

4503 Bar-Yaccov, Nissen. THE ISRAEL-SYRIAN ARMISTICE: PROBLEMS OF IMPLEMENTATION 1949-1966. Jerusalem: Magnes, 1967. 377 p. App. Bibliog. Index. Tables.

A critical analysis of the armistice structure, particularly the demilitarized zone, based on U.N. documents, records of interviews with Israeli government officials, and unpublished Israeli government documents. Also reviews experiences with demilitarized zones in other parts of the world. The treatment is usually balanced and does not duplicate other published materials.

4504 Ben-Gurion, David. MY TALKS WITH ARAB LEADERS. Translated by Aryeh Rubinstein and Misha Louvish. Edited by Misha Louvish. New York: Third Press, 1973 [c1972]. x, 342 p. Bibliog. Notes. Map. Ports.

Updated from the 1967 Hebrew edition. Covers the period from World War I to 1939 in detail and the post-independence years (during which Ben-Gurion was Prime Minister) more briefly. TALKS includes correspondence, some not reciprocal.

Arab-Israeli Conflict

4505 _____. NEGOTIATIONS WITH NASSER. Jerusalem: Israel Information Center, n.d. 64 p. Paper.

>Ben-Gurion's account of secret negotiations with the late Egyptian President Nasser through an American emissary in the early months of 1956, with correspondence exchanged between Ben-Gurion and Eisenhower. The printer misdates the talks on the inside cover.

4506 Bernadotte, Folke. TO JERUSALEM. Translated by Joan Bulman. London: Hodder and Stoughton, 1951. viii, 280 p. Port.

>The author reports his experiences as U.N. mediator in the 1948 war. A documentary account.

4507 Bowett, D. W. UNITED NATIONS FORCES: A LEGAL STUDY. New York: Praeger, 1964. xxiv, 579 p. Bibliog. fnn. Illus. Index. Maps.

>A legal approach to analyzing observer groups and peacekeeping forces (UNOGIL and UNEF included). Problems of consent and logistics.

4508 Boyd, James M. UNITED NATIONS PEACE-KEEPING: A MILITARY AND POLITICAL APPRAISAL. Special Studies in International Politics and Public Affairs Series. New York: Praeger, 1971. 261 p.

>A study of the military and administrative aspects of U.N. peacekeeping operations, mainly UNEF (1956-67), UNOC (Congo, 1960-64), and UNICYP (Cyprus, 1964-). The author, former U.S. Air Attache in Cairo (1956-59) and Chief of Staff to the U.N. Military Staff Committee (1965-69), reviews the legal bases for such operations and makes recommendations for restructuring peacekeeping forces to enhance their effectiveness.

4509 Brook, David. PREFACE TO PEACE: THE UNITED NATIONS AND THE ARAB-ISRAEL ARMISTICE SYSTEM. Washington, D.C.: Public Affairs Press, 1964. 151 p. Bibliog. Index.

>The armistice regime from 1948 to 1956--historical foundations, functions of observers, local commanders' relations, and Security Council supervision. Extensive documentation from U.N. records.

4510 Burns, Arthur Lee, and Heathcote, Nina. PEACEKEEPING BY U.N. FORCES FROM SUEZ TO THE CONGO. New York: Frederick A. Praeger for the Center for International Studies, Princeton, 1963. 256 p. Bibliog.

>A brief chapter on the Suez, Lebanon, and Jordan experiences and the late U.N. Secretary General Hammarskjold's evaluations of them. Primarily a critical study of the Congo from

Arab-Israeli Conflict

official documents and press releases.

4511 Burns, Edson L. M. BETWEEN ARAB AND ISRAELI. London: G.G. Harrap, 1962; New York: Astor-Honor, 1963. 336 p. Bibliog. Illus. Maps.

>An account of the U.N. Truce Supervision Organization (UNTSO) and of the U.N. Emergency Force (UNEF) in Egypt by General Burns, who headed both. The author's description of the experience of the first major U.N. peacekeeping effort is detailed and covers the period surrounding the Suez invasion.

4512 Elkordy, Abdul Hafez. CRISIS OF DIPLOMACY: THE THREE WARS AND AFTER. San Antonio, Tex.: Naylor, 1971. 296 p. App. Bibliog.

>A study of the failures of successive attempts to negotiate solutions to the Arab-Israeli conflict, from the pre-1947 "diplomacy of alienation" (the author's term) to the post-1967 "diplomacy of peacemaking." The author focuses upon the role of the U.N. as observer and peacekeeper, rather than on power politics and war making.

4513 Fisher, Roger. DEAR ISRAELIS, DEAR ARABS: A WORKING APPROACH TO PEACE. New York: Harper and Row, 1972. 166 p. Apps. Bibliog. ref. Index.

>The author turns his general interest in the process of creating solutions to international conflicts toward the Arab-Israeli conflict. The author is a lawyer, but the treatment is political, not legalistic.

4514 Forsythe, David P. UNITED NATIONS PEACEMAKING: THE CONCILIATION COMMISSION FOR PALESTINE. Baltimore and London: Johns Hopkins Press in cooperation with the Middle East Institute, 1972. xvii, 195 p. App. Bibliog. Index.

>An analysis of one of several organizations created by the U.N. to deal with the Arab-Israeli conflict, using a concept of peacemaking to evaluate the commission's performance. Based upon documents and interviews.

4515 Gordenker, Leon. THE U.N. SECRETARY GENERAL AND THE MAINTENANCE OF PEACE. Columbia University Studies in International Organization, 4. New York: Columbia University Press, 1967. xx, 380 p. Bibliog. ref.

>Useful references to the Middle East conflict.

4516 Hamzeh, Fuad Said. INTERNATIONAL CONCILIATION, WITH SPECIAL REFERENCE TO THE WORK OF THE UNITED NATIONS CONCILIATION COMMISSION FOR PALESTINE. The Hague: Drukberij Pasmans, 1963.

177 p. Bibliog. Index.

One-half of the study is concerned with international conciliation as a technique; the second half, with the failure of the Commission for Palestine (1948). Focuses upon the commission's formal terms of reference.

4517 Horn, Carlson Von. SOLDIERING FOR PEACE. New York: McKay, 1967. 402 p. London: Cassell, 1966. 372 p. Illus. Maps. Ports.

Recollections of the (Swedish) chief of the United Nations Truce Supervisory Organization in Palestine (1958-63).

4518 Hutchison, E. H. VIOLENT TRUCE, A MILITARY OBSERVER LOOKS AT THE ARAB-ISRAELI CONFLICT 1951-1955. New York: Devin-Adair, 1956. 199 p. App. Illus.

The American author served as observer and chairman to the Jerusalem Mixed Armistice Commission. These are his accounts of specific border incidents and of the conflict in general. Commission documents are appended.

4519 James, Alan. THE POLITICS OF PEACE-KEEPING. Studies in International Security, 12. New York: Praeger for the Institute for Strategic Studies, 1969. 452 p. Bibliog. Index.

Numerous cases of U.N. activities in the Middle East are indexed, including the Suez crisis, the Lebanese civil war and Yemen, placed in an international political context.

4520 Kadi, Leila S. THE ARAB-ISRAELI CONFLICT: THE PEACEFUL PROPOSALS, 1948-1972. Beirut: Palestine Research Center, 1973. 108 p.

4521 Kimche, Jon. PALESTINE OR ISRAEL: THE UNTOLD STORY OF WHY WE FAILED, 1917-1923; 1967-1973. London: Secker and Warburg, 1973. 360 p. Apps. Bibliog. notes.

Documented review of (author's view) two critical periods in the conflict. New records on the Palestinian nationalism. The great powers, oil, and internal politics.

4522 Lall, Arthur. THE U.N. AND THE MIDDLE EAST CRISIS, 1967. New York, London: Columbia University Press, 1968. 322 p. Apps. Bibliog. fnn. Index.

United Nations resolutions and draft resolutions concerning the 1967 conflict. Detailed description of Security Council and Assembly cease-fire proceedings.

4523 Merlin, Samuel. THE SEARCH FOR PEACE IN THE MIDDLE EAST: THE

Arab-Israeli Conflict

STORY OF PRESIDENT BOURGUIBA'S CAMPAIGN FOR A NEGOTIATED SETTLEMENT BETWEEN ISRAEL AND THE ARAB STATES. South Bruswick, N.J.: Yoseloff, 1968. 490 p.

> A detailed account of the mediation efforts of Bourguiba in 1965. The author, an Israeli citizen, also comments on Bourguiba's political philosophy. A useful addition to the "negotiation literature."

4524 THE MIDDLE EAST: PROSPECTS FOR PEACE. Edited by Isaac Shapiro. Dobbs Ferry, N.Y.: Oceana, 1969. 113 p. Apps. Bibliog.

> Background papers and proceedings of the Thirteenth Hammarskjold Forum (1968); working paper by Quincy Wright. Legal issues and the United Nations' role in the Arab-Israeli conflict. The comments of discussants (not identified) are included. Bibliography includes official documents classified by topic.

4525 Mohn, Paul. PROBLEMS OF TRUCE SUPERVISION, pp. 51-99. International Conciliation, 478. New York: Carnegie Endowment for International Peace, February 1952.

> An early critical evaluation of the operation of the U.N. supervisory mission. By the mediator's Tel Aviv representative.

4526 Reisman, Michael. THE ART OF THE POSSIBLE: DIPLOMATIC ALTERNATIVES IN THE MIDDLE EAST. Princeton, N.J.: Princeton University Press, 1970. 161 p. Paper. Apps. Index. Map.

> A series of proposals for accommodation in the several contested territories; imaginative, but not evaluated in light of past proposals. Four major U.N. documents are appended.

4527 Robinson, Jacob. PALESTINE AND THE UNITED NATIONS, PRELUDE TO A SOLUTION. 1947. Reprint. Westport, Conn.: Greenwood, 1971. 269 p. Bibliog. refs. Index.

> Debates in the 1947 Special Session of the United Nations to "consider" the Palestine question, advocates' cases, and outside agencies' roles. Based upon official documentary material with little analysis.

4528 Rosenne, Shabtai. ISRAEL'S ARMISTICE AGREEMENTS WITH THE ARAB STATES; A JURIDICAL INTERPRETATION. Tel Aviv: Blumstein's Bookstores, for the International Law Association, 1951. 93 p.

> By a former legal adviser to the Ministry of Foreign Affairs (Israel) and representative to the United Nations.

4529 Rosner, Gabriella. THE UNITED NATIONS EMERGENCY FORCE. Columbia University Studies in International Organization, 2. New York:

Columbia University Press, 1963. 294 p. Bibliog.

Legal, financial, and political background.

4530 Shoukry, Kamel Shoukry Abdelhamid. "The Economic Issues of Conflict Resolution in the Middle East." Ann Arbor, Mich.: University Microfilms. Doctoral dissertation, University of Southern California, 1972. 339 p. Bibliog. Maps.

Game strategy, war economics, and national power in the Arab-Israeli conflict covering the 1967 war and the Jarring mission.

4531 U.S. Congress. House. Committee on Foreign Affairs. APPROACHES TO PEACE IN THE MIDDLE EAST. Hearings before the Subcommittee on the Near East, 92d Cong., 2d sess., February 22-May 18, 1972. x, 166 p. Apps. Maps.

A series of proposals for peace settlements by nonofficial witnesses. Further proposals appended. The largest collection available.

4532 _____. UNITED NATIONS PEACEKEEPING IN THE MIDDLE EAST. Hearings before the Subcommittee on International Organizations and Movements and the Subcommittee on the Near East and South Asia, 93d Cong., 1st sess., December 5-6, 1973. Washington, D.C.: Government Printing Office, 1973. 105 p. App. Maps.

Official and academic testimony on the history of peacekeeping and the terms of reference for UNEF-II (1973).

4533 Wainhouse, David W. INTERNATIONAL PEACE OBSERVATION, A HISTORY AND FORECAST. Baltimore: Johns Hopkins Press, 1966. 663 p.

An encyclopedia of case studies including UNEF, UNOGIL, Yemen, and Cyprus. Suggestions for strengthening operations.

PALESTINIAN NATIONALISM

4601 Abcarius, Michel Fred. PALESTINE THROUGH THE FOG OF PROPAGANDA. London and New York: Hutchinson, 1946. 240 p. Bibliog. fnn.

A Palestinian Arab, a civil servant for twenty-three years in the Palestinian government, discusses the rise of Arab nationalism in Palestine.

4602 al-Abid, Ibrahim. A HANDBOOK TO THE PALESTINE QUESTION,

Arab-Israeli Conflict

QUESTIONS AND ANSWERS. Palestine Books, 17. Beirut: Palestine Liberation Organization Research Center, 1969. 198 p. Bibliog.

    Questions collected from Arab students in the West cover the Palestinian resistance movement, Arab state-Israeli relations, Arabs in occupied territories; answers are documented and "express the views of the Palestine national movement" (foreword). Varied bibliography.

4603 Abu Ghazaleh, Adnan Mohammad. ARAB CULTURAL NATIONALISM IN PALESTINE, 1919-1948. Ann Arbor, Mich.: University Microfilms, 1967. 178 p. Bibliog.

    The role of Zionism in the development of Arab nationalism as seen by the writers of Palestine. Extensive Arabic bibliography.

4604 Alush, Najii. ARAB RESISTANCE IN PALESTINE, 1914-1948. Beirut: Palestine Liberation Organization Research Center, 1967. 199 p.

4605 Aruri, Naseer, ed. THE PALESTINIAN RESISTANCE TO ISRAELI OCCUPATION. Arab-American University Graduates Monograph Series, 2. Wilmette, Ill.: Medina University Press, 1970. 171 p. Paper. App. Bibliog. notes.

    Papers presented at the second annual convention of the AAUG in 1969, covering occupied Palestine and relations among Palestinians and external actors. Sympathetic to the Palestinian dilemmas, but scholarly.

4606 Buehrig, Edward H. THE U.N. AND THE PALESTINIAN REFUGEES: A STUDY IN NONTERRITORIAL ADMINISTRATION. Studies in Development, 3. Bloomington: Indiana University, International Development Research Center, 1971. xvi, 215 p. Bibliog. ref. Map.

    An account of the foundation, structure, and activities of the UNRWA based upon U.N. documents, particularly UNRWA reports.

4607 Carre, Oliver. L'IDEOLOGIE PALESTINIENNE DE RESISTANCE; ANALYSE DE TEXTES 1964-1970. Travaux et Recherches de Science Politique, 20. Paris: Armand Colin for the Foundation Nationale des Sciences Politiques, 1972. 163 p. Paper. Apps. Bibliog. ref. Illus.

    Content analysis of Palestinian political and literary works: class revolution, the Arab states, Israel, religious themes. Selected texts appended.

4608 Chaliand, Gerard. THE PALESTINIAN RESISTANCE MOVEMENT. Translated by Michael Perl. Harmondworth, Eng. and Baltimore, Md.: Penguin, 1972. 190 p. Bibliog. ref.

Arab-Israeli Conflict

The ideology of the Palestinian movement. A useful source for materials on (1) the diversity of the movement, (2) resistance organization and recruitment, and (3) the relationship between world events and Palestinian tactics and strategy.

4609 Cooley, John K. GREEN MARCH, BLACK SEPTEMBER: THE STORY OF THE PALESTINIAN ARABS. London: Frank Cass, 1973. xi, 263 p. Bibliog. Illus. Index. Maps. Ports.

A journalist's account of the recent activities of Palestinian leaders. History, reports of firsthand conversations with leaders, and the author's judgments of what peace in Palestine would require.

4610 Dobson, Christopher. BLACK SEPTEMBER: ITS SHORT, VIOLENT HISTORY. New York: Macmillan, 1975. 179 p.

A British journalist discusses Palestinian organizations, tactics, and relations with Arab governments.

4611 Dodd, Peter, and Barakat, Halim. RIVER WITHOUT BRIDGES, A STUDY OF THE EXODUS OF THE 1967 PALESTINIAN ARAB REFUGEES. Monograph Series, 10. Beirut: Institute for Palestine Studies, 1968. xii, 64 p. Paper. Apps. Fold. map. Illus.

Two sociologists interview the 1967 Palestinian refugees and survey other reports to explain the exodus. Interview schedule appended and methodology discussed.

4612 Fath. LA REVOLUTION PALESTINIENNE ET LES JUIFS. Paris: Les Editions de Minuit, 1970. 71 p. Paper.

Published originally in Beirut in three parts. The characteristics of a democratic and nonconfessional state in Palestine by (unidentified) spokesmen for Fatah.

4613 Furlonge, Sir Geoffrey Warren. PALESTINE IS MY COUNTRY: THE STORY OF MUSA ALAMI. London: John Murray, 1969; New York: Praeger, 1970. 242 p. Bibliog. Illus. Maps. Plates. Ports.

The author's rendition of the reminiscences of Musa Alami, Palestinian Arab whose experiences include the final days of the Ottoman Empire, the British mandate, the partition, and the consolidation of the State of Israel. Infrequently documented historical background by a former British foreign service officer in the Middle East.

4614 Hadawi, Sami. BITTER HARVEST; PALESTINE BETWEEN 1914-1967. New York: New World Press, 1967. xx, 335 p. Maps. Ref.

A history, including the Mandate years (1920-48), and a statement of Israel's violations of the resident Arabs' rights. Hadawi

Arab-Israeli Conflict

served in the Mandate government, became a refugee in 1948 and is a well-known publicist of the Palestinian condition. Extensive documentation from public records and Israeli and Arab authors. Recommended by former UNRWA commissioner.

4615 Harkabi, Yehoshafat. FEDAYEEN ACTION AND ARAB STRATEGY. Adelphi Papers, 53. London: Institute for Strategic Studies, 1968. 43 p. Paper. Bibliog.

Analysis of Arab writings on guerrilla warfare by an Israeli scholar of military-strategic issues.

4616 _____. THE MIDDLE EAST: PALESTINIANS AND ISRAEL. New York: Halsted Press, 1975. 285 p.

A collection of articles by an Israeli focusing on Palestinians' internal politics, military strategies, images of the future, and obstacles to a settlement.

4617 Howley, Dennis C. THE UNITED NATIONS AND THE PALESTINIANS. Hicksville, N.Y.: Exposition Press, 1975. 135 p. App.

UNRWA and the growth of Palestine nationalism. Does not take analysis through the 1973 war.

4618 Jiryis, Sabri. THE ARABS IN ISRAEL, 1948-1966. Translated by Meric Dobson. Beirut: Institute for Palestine Studies, 1969. 180 p. Bibliog. fnn. Illus.

Hebrew source material, primarily official Israeli documents. Living conditions of Arabs in Israel, by a Palestinian lawyer who is an Israeli citizen. Omits guerrilla activities.

4619 Khaled, Leila. MY PEOPLE SHALL LIVE: THE AUTOBIOGRAPHY OF A REVOLUTIONARY. Edited by George Hajjar. Foreword by [Sir] John Glubb. London: Hodder and Stoughton, 1973. 223 p. Illus. Ports.

Leila Khaled's years as a Palestinian activist and revolutionary with her observations on Arab and western state policies and the Palestinian movement.

4620 Laffin, John. FEDAYEEN: THE ARAB-ISRAELI DILEMMA. New York: Tree Press, 1973. xii, 171 p. Bibliog. refs. Illus. Map.

The Palestinian resistance from 1965-73--its leaders, organizations, tactics, and ideology, which the author feels are typical of a dying movement. Popularly written. Based upon the newspaper accounts, interviews, and resistance publications.

4621 O'Ballance, Edgar. ARAB GUERILLA POWER, 1967-1972. Hamden: Conn.: Archon, 1974. 246 p. Index. Maps.

Arab-Israeli Conflict

Description of the several Palestinian guerrilla organizations, their military tactics, relations with Arab governments, and rivalry. Few notes, much historical detail.

4622 O'Neill, Bard E. REVOLUTIONARY WARFARE IN THE MIDDLE EAST: THE ISRAELIS VS. THE FEDAYEEN. Boulder, Colo.: Paladin Press, 1974. 140 p. Apps. Bibliog. fnn.

An analysis of the Palestinian guerrilla movement based largely upon Israeli data and written by an American military officer.

4623 Peretz, Don. ISRAEL AND THE PALESTINE ARABS. Washington, D.C.: Middle East Institute, 1958 [c1956]. 264 p. Bibliog. Index.

A long-time student of the Arab refugee problem discusses the history of various refugee policies, Israel's internal security and the Arab minority, and compensation and integration issues. Also cited in No. 2641.

4624 Peretz, Don; Wilson, Evan [M.]; and Ward, Richard J. A PALESTINE ENTITY? Washington, D.C.: Middle East Institute, 1970. 114 p. Bibliog. ref. Tables.

The history and goals of Palestinian nationalism. Possible solutions which would include a Palestinian community are explored.

4625 Porath, Yehoshua. THE EMERGENCE OF THE PALESTINIAN ARAB NATIONAL MOVEMENT, 1918-1929. London: Frank Cass, 1974. 412 p.

Focuses on the early period in the development of Palestinian nationalism.

4626 Pryce-Jones, David. THE FACE OF DEFEAT: PALESTINIAN REFUGEES AND GUERRILLAS. New York: Holt, Rinehart and Winston, 1973 [c1972]. 179 p. Maps.

By a journalist concerned with Palestinian attitudes following the 1967 war and the dilemmas faced by Palestinian leaders in the occupied territories and refugee communities. Little attention to resistance leaders or to the growth of resistance organizations during that period. Sketch of Arab status in Israel and list of Israeli organizations active in Arab-Jewish relations.

4627 Quandt, William B.; Jabber, Fuad [A.]; and Lesch, Ann Mosely. THE POLITICS OF PALESTINIAN NATIONALISM. Berkeley: University Press, 1973. ix, 234 p. Paper. Bibliog. Figures. Maps. Tables.

Three monographs in one: "The History of the Nationalist Movement under the Mandate" (Lesch), "Palestinian Organizations and Strategies" (Quandt), and "The Relationship between the Palestinians and the Arab Regimes" (Jabber).

Arab-Israeli Conflict

4628 el-Rayyes, Riad N., and Nahas, Dunia, eds. GUERILLAS FOR PALESTINE. A STUDY OF THE PALESTINIAN COMMANDO ORGANIZATIONS. Beirut: al-Nahar, 1974. 303 p.

>Palestinian commando organizations, their leaders, and relations with regional and external states. Includes discussion of a prospective Palestinian state. Compiled by the AN-NAHAR ARAB REPORT staff.

4629 Rosen, Harry M. THE ARABS AND JEWS IN ISRAEL: THE REALITY, THE DILEMMA, THE PROMISE. Jerusalem: Israel Office, Foreign Affairs Department and American Jewish Committee, 1970. 114 p. Paper.

4630 Schiff, Zeev, and Rothstein, Raphael. FEDAYEEN: THE STORY OF THE PALESTINIAN GUERILLAS. New York: McKay, 1972. 246 p. Bibliog. Illus. Refs.

>Popularly written account of the Fedayeen from 1956 from an Israeli perspective.

4631 Schwartz, Walter. THE ARABS IN ISRAEL. London: Faber and Faber, 1959. 172 p. Illus.

>Official Israeli policies toward the Arab population--land ownership, local government, education; Arab attitudes toward Israeli rule.

4632 Sharabi, Hisham. PALESTINE GUERRILLAS, THEIR CREDIBILITY AND EFFECTIVENESS. Monograph Series, 5. Beirut: Institute for Palestine Studies, 1970. 64 p. Paper. Apps. Plates.

>Structure, doctrine, and effectiveness of Palestinian organizations. Most prior assessments emphasize their ineffectiveness; Sharabi points to the meager evidence for that viewpoint. References to relevant Fatah documents.

4633 "Since Jordan: The Palestine Fedayeen." CONFLICT STUDIES. 38 (September 1973): 18.

>A report by the research department of the (London) Institute for the Study of Conflict. Organization and relations with Arab and Communist states.

4634 Stetler, Russell, comp. PALESTINE: THE ARAB ISRAELI CONFLICT. A Ramparts Press Reader. San Francisco: Ramparts Press, 1972. 297 p. Bibliog. ref. Illus. Maps.

>Collection of articles primarily concerned with the Palestinian resistance movements; previously published, seldom documented, and uncritical of the Palestinian perspective.

4635 Turki, Fawaz. THE DISINHERITED; JOURNAL OF A PALESTINIAN EXILE. New York: Monthly Review Press, 1972. 156 p. Bibliog. refs.

    Recollections of a Palestinian's youth as a refugee.

4636 Waines, David. THE UNHOLY WAR: ISRAEL AND PALESTINE, 1897-1971. Wilmette, Ill.: Medina University Press International, 1971. 208 p. Bibliog. ref. Index.

    The Palestinian community over time--its leaders, ideology, and negotiating strategies--and the response of Israel and the great powers to its demands. The author argues that the Palestinian movement can withstand future Israeli victories.

MILITARY ENGAGEMENTS

4701 Bell, J. Bowyer. THE LONG WAR; ISRAEL AND THE ARABS SINCE 1946. Englewood Cliffs, N.J.: Prentice-Hall, 1969. 467 p. Bibliog. Illus. Ports.

    Particularly noteworthy for its descriptions of the prosecution of the three wars in which the author commends Israeli military performance.

4702 Ben-Dak, Joseph D., and Azar, Edward E., eds. "Research Perspectives on the Arab-Israeli Conflict: A Symposium." JOURNAL OF CONFLICT RESOLUTION. 16 (June 1972): 131-296.

    Eleven articles on topics related to armed conflict escalation and adversaries' mutual images that are useful methodologically and substantively.

4703 Browne, Harry, comp. SUEZ AND SINAI. London: Longman, 1971. 117 p. Bibliog. Map. Ref.

    Also cited in No. 2604.

4704 Byford-Jones, W. FORBIDDEN FRONTIERS. London: Robert Hale, 1958. 188 p. Index.

    The popularly written report of a British journalist's tour of Israel's frontiers. Describes the terrain and movement across the borders.

4705 Whetten, Lawrence L. THE CANAL WAR: FOUR-POWER CONFLICT IN THE MIDDLE EAST. Cambridge, Mass.: M.I.T. Press, 1974. 520 p.

    Military, political, and diplomatic detail of relations among the United States, Soviet Union, Egypt, and Israel from 1967 through 1973, by a military strategist.

4706 Yale, Wesley W., et al. ALTERNATIVE TO ARMAGEDDON; THE PEACE

Arab-Israeli Conflict

POTENTIAL OF LIGHTNING WAR. New Brunswick, N.J.: Rutgers University Press, 1970. xii, 257 p. Illus. Maps.

A review of "limited" wars in Vietnam, Korea, Israel-Palestine, Biafra, and Czechoslovakia that have occurred in the context of the nuclear stalemate. The authors' perspective is the potential of lightning war to restore initiative to the Western powers. Useful background for superpower strategic issues in the Arab-Israeli conflict.

1948-49 War

4707 Collins, Larry, and Lapierre, Dominique. O JERUSALEM! New York: Simon and Schuster, 1972. 637 p. App. Bibliog. Illus. Index. Photos.

Two journalists' account of the 1948 struggle for Jerusalem, based upon interviews and unpublished diaries and papers. Generally, although not consistently, sympathetic to the Jewish position. A good bibliography.

4708 Eliot, George Fielding. HATE, HOPE, AND HIGH EXPLOSIVES. Indianapolis, Ind.: Bobbs, 1948. 284 p.

Firsthand account of the situation in the Middle East in 1948 by a journalist.

4709 Garcia-Granados, Jorge. THE BIRTH OF ISRAEL; THE DRAMA AS I SAW IT. New York: Alfred A. Knopf, 1948. 291 p. Index.

A primary source for events in the period immediately preceding Israel's independence authored by a member of the U.N. Special Committee on Palestine. Critical of the United Nations' failure to enforce the partition.

4710 Kimche, Jon, and Kimche, David. A CLASH OF DESTINIES; THE ARAB-JEWISH WAR AND THE FOUNDING OF THE STATE OF ISRAEL. New York: Praeger, 1960. BOTH SIDES OF THE HILL: BRITAIN AND THE PALESTINE WAR. London: Secker and Warburg, 1960. 287 p. Maps.

An account of the 1948-49 war, including the authors' assessments of military organization and strategic and tactical decisions on both sides. The authors experienced the war firsthand as journalist and Israeli soldier, respectively; their sources include interviews and documents.

4711 Kurzman, Dan. GENSIS 1948; THE FIRST ARAB-ISRAELI WAR. New York: World, 1970. xviii, 750 p. Bibliog. Illus. Maps. Plans. Ports.

Battles and personalities with little documentation, but a useful

Arab-Israeli Conflict

bibliography. Based upon interviews and private papers. Popularly written.

4712 Lorch, Netanel. THE EDGE OF THE SWORD; ISRAEL'S WAR OF INDEPENDENCE. New York: G.P. Putnam's Sons, 1961. 475 p. Illus.

   Israel's first official military historian authors this detailed treatment of the military aspects of the first war.

4713 O'Ballance, Edgar. THE ARAB-ISRAELI WAR, 1948. London: Faber and Faber, 1956. 220 p. Illus.

   Military strategy and tactics in the 1948 war.

1956 and the Suez Canal

4714 Abi-Mershed, Walid. ISRAELI WITHDRAWAL FROM SINAI. Series No. 1. Beirut: Institute for Palestine Studies, 1965. 144 p. Bibliog. Maps.

   Based upon primary U.N. documents and secondary sources. The author is a Lebanese government official who has provided a balanced review of the origins of the 1956 war and its aftermath which led to the withdrawal of Israeli forces from the Sinai Peninsula in 1957.

4715 Bar-Zohar, Michel. SUEZ: ULTRA-SECRET. Paris: Fayard, 1964. 317 p. Bibliog. refs. Map.

   Also cited in No. 2604.

4716 Barker, A. J. SUEZ: THE SEVEN DAY WAR. London: Faber and Faber, 1965 [c1964]. 223 p. Bibliog. Illus. Maps. Plans. Ports.

   Describes the invaders' tactics, the terrain and the UNEF operation. Chronicle of events and short bibliography (with incomplete citations).

4717 Beaufre, Andre. THE SUEZ EXPEDITION, 1956. Translated by Richard Barry. New York: Praeger, 1969. 161 p. Illus. Index. Maps.

   A memoir of the invasion by the French general who was second in command of the Allied operation and who concludes that "anything would have been better" than the 1956 war. He details pre-invasion preparations which began, he argues, before the Egyptian nationalization of the Suez Canal. The tactical detail is exceptional.

4718 Bowie, Robert R. SUEZ 1956, INTERNATIONAL CRISIS AND THE ROLE OF LAW. New York: Oxford University Press, 1974. xix, 148 p. Apps. Bibliog. ref. Index.

   Law and the interplay of regional and external interests in the

1956 crisis. The creation of UNEF and the U.N. secretary general's role. International documents appended.

4719 Browne, Harry, comp. SUEZ AND SINAI. London: Longman, 1971. 117 p. Bibliog. Map. Ref.

Historical summary and relevant documents combined in textbook form.

4720 Dayan, Moshe. DIARY OF THE SINAI CAMPAIGN. New York: Schocken Books, 1967. 236 p. Illus. Maps.

A former Israeli defense minister reviews the relationship between Israel's political goals and military strategies, the causes of the Egyptian defeat, and Israel's military leaders.

4721 Farnie, D. A. EAST AND WEST OF SUEZ: THE SUEZ CANAL IN HISTORY, 1854-1956. Oxford: Clarendon Press, 1969. ix, 860 p. Bibliog. Maps.

An extensive bibliography and a detailed well-documented study of the economic and political significance of the Suez Canal over a century. Excellent chronicle for events related to the canal, the Canal Co., and Egyptian politics.

4722 Finer, Herman. DULLES OVER SUEZ: THE THEORY AND PRACTICE OF HIS DIPLOMACY. Chicago: Quadrangle, 1964. xix, 538 p. Bibliog. fnn. Index. Ports. Maps.

Sets out to prove that the Suez crisis was a debacle for American foreign policy, using nonattributable interview material. Also cited in No. 3813.

4723 Longgood, William Frank. SUEZ STORY: KEY TO THE MIDDLE EAST. New York: Greenberg, 1957. 174 p. Illus. Index. Maps.

A history of the canal up to the 1956 crisis, with particular attention to its role in international politics.

4724 Love, Kennett. SUEZ: THE TWICE-FOUGHT WAR; A HISTORY. New York: McGraw-Hill, 1969. xxv, 767 p. Bibliog. Index. Maps. Ref.

An indispensable study of the 1956 war based upon interviews, published sources, and the Dulles and Eisenhower papers. The author, former NEW YORK TIMES Middle East correspondent, gives more of the American view than the other Suez analyses.

4725 Nutting, Anthony. NO END OF A LESSON: THE STORY OF SUEZ. London: Constable; New York: C.N. Potter, 1967. 205 p. Map.

The lesson which the author takes from the abortive Suez invasion is that British policymakers, specifically Anthony Eden, ignored the possibility of cooperating with the late President

Arab-Israeli Conflict

Nasser's decision to nationalize the Canal. There is little documentation or discussion of alternative views that (1) the invasion was justified or (2) it was not but cooperation with Nasser was impossible. Nutting had advised against the invasion; the book is his vindication.

4726 O'Ballance, Edgar. THE SINAI CAMPAIGN 1956. London: Faber and Faber, 1959. 223 p. App. Illus.

    The author's second analysis of military performance in the Arab-Israeli conflict. Based upon Israeli sources with little documentation.

4727 Obieta, Joseph A. THE INTERNATIONAL STATUS OF THE SUEZ CANAL. 2d ed. The Hague: Martinus Nijhoff, 1970. 164 p. Bibliog.

4728 Public Affairs Institute. REGIONAL DEVELOPMENT FOR REGIONAL PEACE: A NEW POLICY AND PROGRAM TO COUNTER THE SOVIET MENACE IN THE MIDDLE EAST. Washington, D.C.: 1957. 332 p. Paper.

    Account of events surrounding the Suez conflict of 1956 in terms of Soviet and Chinese relations with various Middle Eastern states and Western reactions. Sources are chiefly news dispatches and documents, used to develop the theme that Arab nationalism and communism are the major encumbrances.

4729 Robertson, John Henry. THE MOST IMPORTANT COUNTRY; THE TRUE STORY OF THE SUEZ CRISIS AND THE EVENTS LEADING UP TO IT. London: Cassell, 1957. 240 p. Illus. Index. Maps.

    The Suez invasion from a British perspective--a decision taken in response to British strategic interests without regard to the Arab-Israeli conflict. Background from British-Egyptian negotiations and British domestic politics.

4730 Robertson, Terence. CRISIS: THE INSIDE STORY OF THE SUEZ CONSPIRACY. New York: Atheneum, 1965. xvi, 349 p. Bibliog.

    The international diplomatic setting of the war rather than its military aspects, focusing upon the Canadian government's role at the U.N. and as intermediary between the United States and its European allies. Based upon extensive interviews of involved policy makers, especially Israeli and French officials, the account is thorough and insightful.

4731 Schonfield, Hugh J. THE SUEZ CANAL IN WORLD AFFAIRS. London: Constellation, 1952. 174 p.

    A critical study of the canal in international politics and British strategy.

Arab-Israeli Conflict

4732 SUEZ TEN YEARS AFTER: BROADCASTS FROM THE B.B.C. THIRD PROGRAMME. By Peter Calvocoressi, et al.; edited and introduced by Anthony Moncrieff. London: British Broadcasting Corporation, 1967. xvi, 160 p. Bibliog. Map.

> Broadcasts from BBC's third program moderated by Peter Calvocoressi. Extensively documented examination of the roots of the invasion, including French commentators. The participants highlight the importance of the invasion to France's Algerian policy.

4733 Thomas, Hugh. SUEZ. New York: Harper and Row, 1967. 261 p. Illus. Maps. Ports.

> Britain's role in the 1956 crisis. A well-documented study in which the author argues that the Suez invasion was based upon an inflated view among British policy-makers of that country's military strength. Little on Soviet or U.S. involvement.

4734 Wint, Guy, and Calvocoressi, Peter. MIDDLE EAST CRISIS. Harmondsworth, Engl.: Penguin Books, 1957. 141 p. Illus.

> Focuses upon the causes of the Suez crisis and the involvement of the great powers in the Arab-Israeli conflict.

1967 War

4735 Agwani, Mohammed Shafi, comp. THE WEST-ASIAN CRISIS. Meerut, India: Meenakshi Prakashan, 1968. 196 p. Apps.

> Essays by Indian analysts on the roles of several countries in the 1967 War—the United States, the Soviet Union, Turkey, Iran, and India.

4736 THE ARAB-ISRAELI CONFLICT: THE 1967 CAMPAIGN. Keesing's Research Report. New York: Scribner's, 1968. 55 p. Maps. Bibliog.

> A day-by-day account of the war.

4737 THE ARAB-ISRAELI CONFRONTATION OF JUNE, 1967: AN ARAB PERSPECTIVE. Edited by Ibrahim Abu-Lughod. Evanston, Ill.: Northwestern University Press, 1970. xiv, 201 p. Bibliog. Index. Maps.

> Collection of nine excellent and original articles by recognized scholars who are also Arab-Americans (with one exception). The essays cover topics such as the place of Jerusalem in Islamic and Arab history, the antecedents of the 1967 war, and the treatment of Israelis and Arabs in the mass media in the United States. The articles are well-documented and pertinent and the bibliography, extensive and balanced.

Arab-Israeli Conflict

4738 "The Arab-Israeli War." FOREIGN AFFAIRS. 46 (January 1968): 304-46.

> Consists of three articles: Charles Yost, "How It Began"; Bernard Lewis, "The Consequences of Defeat"; and Don Peretz, "Israel's Administration and Arab Refugees."

4739 Bar-Zohar, Michael. EMBASSIES IN CRISIS; DIPLOMATS AND DEMAGOGUES BEHIND THE SIX-DAY WAR. Translated by Monroe Stearns. Englewood Cliffs, N.J.: Prentice-Hall, 1971. 279 p.

> By an Israeli soldier in the 1967 war, the volume is a detailed presentation of Israel's perspective of the diplomatic context of the military engagement.

4740 Burdett, Winston. ENCOUNTER WITH THE MIDDLE EAST, AN INTIMATE REPORT ON WHAT LIES BEHIND THE ARAB-ISRAELI CONFLICT. New York: Atheneum, 1969. 384 p.

> Description, some firsthand, some not, of the events leading up to the 1967 war, focusing on the late Egyptian President Nasser's domestic and international dilemmas. A journalist who has spent much time in the Middle East, Burdett deals with diplomacy and military strategy, ideology and personalities.

4741 Byford-Jones, W. THE LIGHTNING WAR. Indianapolis, Ind.: Bobbs-Merrill, 1968. 229 p. Apps. Illus. Index. Maps.

> A firsthand account of the 1967 war from the Israeli lines with the author's observations of the international political context.

4742 Churchill, Randolph S., and Churchill, Winston S. THE SIX DAY WAR. London: Heinemann, 1970. 261 p. Apps. Map. Tables.

> Prelude to and execution of the 1967 war using Israeli accounts. More material on specific engagements is included than on overall strategy or planning. A few glaring errors, such as the reference to (former Prime Minister) Mossadegh of "Iraq" (Iran), are distracting. Recounts diplomatic activities within the United Nations and between the United States and the Soviet Union during June and July of 1967. This is a reprint of the 1967 edition (Boston: Houghton Mifflin) with a postscript added.

4743 Donovan, Robert J., et al. SIX DAYS IN JUNE: ISRAEL'S FIGHT FOR SURVIVAL. New York: New American Library, 1967. 160 p. Illus. Photos.

> A journalist's popularized view of the 1967 war.

4744 Douglas-Home, Charles. THE ARABS AND ISRAEL. Rev. ed. London and Sydney: Bodley Head, 1970. 127 p. Maps.

> Criticizes Israel's decision to go to war in 1967, arguing that the conflict must be resolved politically by "dezionizing" Israel.

Arab-Israeli Conflict

4745 Draper, Theodore. ISRAEL AND WORLD POLITICS: ROOTS OF THE THIRD ARAB-ISRAELI WAR. New York: Viking, 1968. x, 278 p. Ref.

> Half text, half documents. Based on published materials. The 1967 war is viewed against the backdrop of the two previous confrontations.

4746 Howard, Michael, and Hunter, Robert [E.]. ISRAEL AND THE ARAB WORLD: THE CRISIS OF 1967. Adelphi Press, 41. London: Institute for Strategic Studies, 1967. Beirut: Institute for Palestine Studies, 1968. 51 p. Paper. Bibliog. Maps. Tables.

> The background of the war and its prosecution. Sources include confidential interviews.

4747 ISRAEL AND THE ARABS: THE JUNE 1967 WAR. Edited by Hal Kosut. New York: Facts on File, 1967. 216 p. Paper. Index. Maps.

> Chronology of events leading up to the 1967 war, and the aftermath--United Nations activity, border fighting, and refugees. No references.

4748 Irving, Clifford. THE BATTLE OF JERUSALEM; THE SIX DAY WAR OF JUNE, 1967. New York: Macmillan, 1970. 88 p. Illus. Maps.

4749 Kemp, Geoffrey. ARMS AND SECURITY: THE EGYPT-ISRAEL CASE. Adelphi Papers, 52. London: Institute for Strategic Studies, 1968. 26 p. Bibliog. fnn. Illus.

> Arms and strategy in the 1967 war. Argues that the Israeli victory was a result of its successful strategies rather than Egypt's failures. States that prospects are slim for arms control without political agreements.

4750 Kimche, David, and Bawly, Dan. THE SANDSTORM; THE ARAB-ISRAELI WAR OF JUNE 1967: PRELUDE AND AFTERMATH. Rev. ed. New York: Stein and Day, 1968. 319 p. Illus. Maps.

> The third war by two Israeli journalists who fought in it. A historical view which is primarily a reflection of the author's national perspectives, but contains much information. Revised and expanded in a 1971 volume by the same publisher.

4751 Laqueur, Walter [Ze'ez]. THE ROAD TO JERUSALEM: THE ORIGINS OF THE ARAB-ISRAELI CONFLICT, 1967. New York: Macmillan, 1968. 368 p. Bibliog. Map.

> The author chronicles the immediate antecedents of the 1967 war, using published news sources. Focuses upon Israeli attitudes

Arab-Israeli Conflict

and policies. An introduction rather than a searching analysis, Laqueur's works are useful as prompt reviews of contemporary history.

4752 MacLeish, Roderick. THE SUN STOOD STILL. New York: Atheneum, 1967. xiv, 174 p.

A journalist's account of the last days before the 1967 war, in Cairo, and the war itself, in Tel Aviv. Based upon conversations with diplomats and journalists as well as secondary sources.

4753 Marshall, Samuel L. A. SINAI VICTORY. West Caldwell, N.J.: William Morrow, 1971. 280 p. Illus. Maps.

A descriptive celebration of Israel's victory, expanded from a 1967 volume published by American Heritage.

4754 O'Ballance, Edgar. THE THIRD ARAB-ISRAELI WAR. Hamden, Conn.: Archon Books, 1972. 288 p. Bibliog. Maps.

Events leading up to the 1967 war and an account of the war emphasizing Israeli sources. The author discusses the role of Israeli counterintelligence in disrupting Arab military communications. Little attention is given to evaluating weapons' performance and much to the description of engagements.

4755 Rouleau, Eric, et al. ISRAEL ET LES ARABES, LE 3^e COMBAT. Paris: Editions du Seuil, 1967. 188 p. Chron. Index. Map.

An account of the events leading to the 1967 war by experienced French journalists who were uniquely exempt from wartime censorship. The authors report on the psychological pressures and political realities in both Cairo and Tel Aviv which lay behind the outbreak of a war which (in the authors' view) was unintentional.

4756 Samo, Elias, comp. THE JUNE 1967 ARAB-ISRAELI WAR: MISCALCULATION OR CONSPIRACY? Foreword by Eqbal Ahmad. Wilmette, Ill.: Medina University Press International, 1971. xv, 180 p. Bibliog.

A collection of previously published essays representing various viewpoints which make no new progress in answering the question posed in the title.

4757 Teveth, Shabtai. THE TANKS OF TAMMUZ. New York: Viking, 1969. 290 p. Illus. Index. Maps. Ports.

An account of the 1967 war by an Israeli journalist from the perspective of the Israeli Armoured Corps which he accompanied.

Arab-Israeli Conflict

4758 Young, Peter. THE ISRAELI CAMPAIGN, 1967. London: Kimber, 1967. 192 p. Bibliog. Maps. Plates. Tables.

> A military study by a British brigadier.

1973 War

4759 Barker, A. J. THE YOM KIPPUR WAR. Ballantine Books Campaign Book, 29. New York: Random House, 1974. 159 p. Maps. Ports.

> The 1973 war on both fronts. Weapons evaluation and military tactics, including those systems first used in 1973.

4760 Davis, Moshe, ed. THE YOM KIPPUR WAR; ISRAEL AND THE JEWISH PEOPLE. Seminar on World Jewry and the Yom Kippur War. New York: Arno, 1974. xviii, 362 p. Bibliog. ref.

> Based on a conference held in Jerusalem in December 1973, the volume focuses upon the relationships between Israel and the Diaspora, particularly as they emerged in the 1973 war. The perspectives of the contributors are part of the context of the contemporary crisis.

4761 Laqueur, Walter [Ze'ez]. CONFRONTATION: THE MIDDLE EAST AND WORLD POLITICS. New York: Quadrangle, 1974. 295 p. Index.

> A chronological review of the 1973 war. The author focuses upon the extra-regional context in which the recurrent Arab-Israeli wars take place; oil and the conflict; and Israeli military doctrine.

4762 Palit, D. K. RETURN TO SINAI: THE ARAB OFFENSIVE, 1973. Columbia, Ohio: South Asia Books, 1974. 172 p.

> Focuses on the canal crossing and based almost exclusively on Arab sources. The author is a former Indian military attache in Cairo.

4763 el-Rayyes, Riad N., and Nahas, Dunia, eds. THE OCTOBER WAR, DOCUMENTS, PERSONALITIES, ANALYSES AND MAPS. Compiled by al-Nahar Arab Report Staff. Beirut: Dar al-Nahar, 1973. 295 p.

4764 Sherman, Arnold. WHEN GOD JUDGED AND MEN DIED. New York: Bantam, 1974. 144 p.

> The 1973 war described by an Israeli government information officer.

4765 Sobel, Lester A., ed. ISRAEL AND THE ARABS: THE OCTOBER 1973 WAR. New York: Facts on File, 1974. 185 p. Index.

A record of the antecedents of the war, the war, and its aftermath (to March 1974) from the record compiled by FACTS ON FILE and edited to avoid duplication. Entries are noted by a description of the event rather than date of the event.

4766 SUNDAY TIMES. The Insight Team. INSIGHT ON THE MIDDLE EAST WAR. London: Andre Deutsch, 1974. 256 p. Illus.

Sound and comprehensive journalism, a collection of rewritten articles which originally appeared in the SUNDAY TIMES.

4767 U.S. Congress. House. Committee on Foreign Affairs. THE IMPACT OF THE OCTOBER MIDDLE EAST WAR. Hearings before the Subcommittee on Inter-American Affairs, 93d Cong., 1st sess., October 3-November 29, 1973. Washington, D.C.: Government Printing Office, 1973. 159 p. Apps. Illus. Maps.

Testimony primarily from academic witnesses (some with official experience) beginning before and ending after the war. Concerns external involvement in the conflict as well as the protagonists' interests. Related articles appended.

Chapter 6
PETROLEUM

Petroleum plays an important economic and political role in international affairs. During the first half of the twentieth century the Western powers' technology and political power enabled them to exercise control over the major petroleum resources in the world. Contemporary challenges to that control are linked to other international political questions, such as the Arab-Israeli conflict. Because petroleum is a major source of capital for several states in the Middle East, the structure of the market is of vital importance to internal development planning and to regional investment programs.

Books on oil politics and oil economics supplement one another. In addition, studies are included on (1) the international legal issues raised by production agreements and (2) the technological limitations which prevent Middle Eastern states from participating fully in the entire exploration-production-marketing process.

THE ECONOMICS OF OIL

Petroleum prices are determined by economic market forces as well as by political decisions. This section includes specialized studies of production costs, reserves, and the technology of petroleum field development. The most current and detailed analysis of the petroleum business is Adelman's THE WORLD PETROLEUM MARKET [5001]. THE ECONOMICS OF MIDDLE EASTERN OIL (Issawi and Yeganeh [5005]) is less technical but thorough. The possible future oil import needs of the Soviet Union are a major factor in explaining its present interest in the region. Thus, the COMMUNIST TRADE IN OIL AND GAS (Ebel [5002]) is a good supplement to Adelman's volume.

The economics of oil from the producer country's viewpoint is covered in both Ashraf Lutfi's OPEC OIL [5008] and, more extensively, in Zuhayr Mikdashi's A FINANCIAL ANALYSIS OF MIDDLE EASTERN OIL CONCESSIONS [5009].

Longrigg's OIL IN THE MIDDLE EAST [5007] is a comprehensive description of the oil industry's performance in concession countries. A more rigorous analysis of industrial organization, useful for decision-making studies, has been written by Edith Penrose (THE GROWTH OF FIRMS [5010]).

OIL PRODUCER-CONSUMER RELATIONS

Shifts in demand and supply conditions occurred during the 1960s in tandem with legal changes in concession agreements and with OPEC's active participation in pricing negotiations. Accordingly many books on petroleum issues are neither technical nor industry-oriented. Most cover political, economic, and legal relationships among producers and consumers.

Benjamin Shwadran wrote a basic review of the political economy of petroleum in 1955. The third edition, revised in terms of recent developments, was published in 1973 (THE MIDDLE EAST, OIL, AND THE GREAT POWERS [5125]). Shwadran's volume is both extensive and it also provides a good bibliography for further research. MIDDLE EAST OIL (Stocking [5126]) is an earlier but similar work and has good regional references. For a more integrated analysis the third choice is Michael Tanzer's THE POLITICAL ECONOMY OF INTERNATIONAL OIL AND THE UNDERDEVELOPED COUNTRIES [5127] even though it does not concentrate on the Middle East. Lastly, Issawi's OIL, THE MIDDLE EAST, AND THE WORLD [5110] is a brief but clear summary by an economist who specializes in the Middle East.

In addition to general reviews and historical descriptions of the oil industry in the Middle East, there are case studies on producer-consumer disputes and energy development problems. The longest oil production dispute to date is still the Anglo-Iranian confrontation over nationalization which lasted from 1951 to 1954. Ford's THE ANGLO-IRANIAN OIL DISPUTE OF 1951-1952 [5106] brings out the legal issues; Elwell-Sutton (PERSIAN OIL [5102]) and Fatemi (OIL DIPLOMACY [5103]) concentrates on the history of the dispute. Studies of the foreign policy of Iran and of other producer states are particularly useful to understand the political implications of oil.

Oil flows were interrupted for brief periods following the 1956, 1967, and 1973 Arab-Israeli wars. The Organization for European Economic Cooperation met the disruption in 1956 with proposals to distribute the limited supplies among the member states. EUROPE'S NEED FOR OIL [5123] reviews the fate of those proposals.

The U.S. Department of the Interior published an extensive two-volume study of the 1967 war. And the 1973 boycott is appropriately placed in the context of the overall changes in producer-consumer relations by the American Universities Field Staff's OIL PRODUCERS AND CONSUMERS [5122] and by THE ENERGY CRISIS AND U.S. FOREIGN POLICY (Szyliowicz and O'Neill [5124]). The former is a conference report which is limited in coverage but which includes the views of both producers and consumers. The latter is a comprehensive scholarly study of short-term policy problems.

Historical descriptions include Leonard Mosley's POWER PLAY [5119], a popular account of the host countries, oil companies, and individual political leaders. Less informative are Finnie [5104], Hamilton [5107], and Vicker [5131].

RELATIONS AMONG OIL PRODUCING STATES

Several studies of the history and development of the Organization of the Petroleum Exporting Countries have been published. The most current of these is Mana al-Otaiba's OPEC AND THE PETROLEUM INDUSTRY [5205]. The author is the minister of petroleum and mineral resources for the United Arab Emirates. The author of the other major book also is an Arab oil economist (Mikdashi, COMMUNITY OF OIL EXPORTING COUNTRIES [5203]). Mikdashi documents his analysis extensively and provides good access to primary source documents. None of the OPEC analyses takes a particularly critical look at the performance of OPEC in terms of relationships among the member states and intraorganization politics. Kemal Sayegh wrote OIL AND ARAB REGIONAL DEVELOPMENT [5207] before the major price hikes in 1971. Sayegh makes an interesting statement of the potential for extending cooperation among the petroleum-producing states into new areas. The two earliest books which covered producer relations, Hirst [5201] and Lenczowski [5202], are not as positive about producer cooperation, but their conclusions are limited by the time period they cover. Hirst's book, however, is important for its coverage of the Arabic-language press and Iraq-IPC relations, and is a good supplement to the regional economists' studies.

PETROLEUM SERIALS

Petroleum serials which give significant coverage to the international oil industry are listed in chapter 8. Among these, the serials of most interest to readers focusing upon international politics are: THE PETROLEUM ECONOMIST, the annual TWENTIETH CENTURY PETROLEUM STATISTICS, and WORLD OIL. The ECONOMIST is most inclusive in terms of international oil news and reports on oil policy and production. The annual TWENTIETH CENTURY PETROLEUM STATISTICS is a data source. It does not summarize news. A combination of the two would meet the needs of many researchers.

THE ECONOMICS OF OIL

5001 Adelman, Morris A. THE WORLD PETROLEUM MARKET. Baltimore and London: Johns Hopkins University Press for Resources for the Future, 1972. xviii, 438 p. Apps. Bibliog. ref. Illus.

>Production costs, market structure, and market price trends-- past and future. Extensive technical information appended on development, operating, and transport costs; taxation policies; quantities produced and traded.

5002 Ebel, Robert E. COMMUNIST TRADE IN OIL AND GAS: AN EVALUATION OF THE FUTURE EXPORT CAPABILITY OF THE SOVIET BLOC.

Petroleum

Special Studies. New York: Praeger, 1970. 447 p. Apps. Bibliog. Illus. Maps.

> The oil and natural gas industry in the Soviet Union and East Europe--production trend data, trade and competition with Middle East countries, and Soviet press statements on Western oil involvement. Bibliographic essay and Russian language sources.

5003 Frank, Helmut J. CRUDE OIL PRICES IN THE MIDDLE EAST; A STUDY OF OLIGOPOLISTIC PRICE BEHAVIOR. Special Studies. New York: Praeger, 1966. 209 p. Bibliog. fnn.

> Revision of a doctoral dissertation; discusses the petroleum industry and trade.

5004 Hartshorn, J. E. POLITICS AND WORLD OIL ECONOMICS, AN ACCOUNT OF THE INTERNATIONAL OIL INDUSTRY IN ITS POLITICAL ENVIRONMENT. New York: Praeger, 1962. 364 p. Bibliog. Illus. Index. Map.

> Popularly written discussion of petroleum pricing with no documentation. Reviews the various nonmarket influences upon prices. A short bibliography.

5005 Issawi, Charles, and Yeganeh, Mohammed. THE ECONOMICS OF MIDDLE EASTERN OIL. New York: Praeger, 1963 [c1962]. 230 p. Apps. Bibliog. Illus.

> Petroleum industry structure; investment, income, and production trends; effects upon producing economies from 1948-60. Thorough bibliography.

5006 Leeman, Wayne A. THE PRICE OF MIDDLE EAST OIL: AN ESSAY IN POLITICAL ECONOMY. Ithaca, N.Y.: Cornell University Press, 1962. 274 p. App. Illus. Index. Sel. bibliog.

> Market structure, investments and profits, and producer-state participation. Written prior to OPEC's development. Little demand analysis.

5007 Longrigg, Stephen Hemsley. OIL IN THE MIDDLE EAST: ITS DISCOVERY AND DEVELOPMENT. 3d ed. London and New York: Oxford University Press for the Royal Institute for International Affairs, 1968. xii, 519 p. Apps. Illus. Index. Maps.

> Oil exploration, concession agreements, transport and labor issues, and company support facilities. Based upon the petroleum press and the author's recollections.

5008 Lutfi, Ashraf. OPEC OIL. Middle East Oil Monographs, 6. Beirut:

Petroleum

Middle East Research and Publishing Center, 1968. xiii, 120 p. Apps. Illus.

> The structure of the oil industry with respect to the possibility of nationalization, joint production programming (economic considerations); and profit-sharing arrangements. Company and country production data. No documentation.

5009 Mikdashi, Zuhayr. A FINANCIAL ANALYSIS OF MIDDLE EASTERN OIL CONCESSIONS: 1901-1965. Special Studies. New York: Praeger, 1966. xv, 340 p. Bibliog.

> Information on production costs, prices, and profit margins by company and producer state. Various methods of computing cost data.

5010 Penrose, Edith Tilton. THE GROWTH OF FIRMS: MIDDLE-EAST OIL AND OTHER ESSAYS. London: Frank Cass, 1971. ix, 336 p. Bibliog. ref. Illus.

> Largely reprints of previously published articles on oil companies operating in the Middle East as case studies of international firms--OPEC, vertical integration, governmental relations. Sees OPEC as an information clearinghouse with little impact on the structure of the market.

5011 Rifai, Taki. THE PRICING OF CRUDE OIL: ECONOMIC AND STRATEGIC GUIDELINES FOR AN INTERNATIONAL ENERGY POLICY. Special Studies. New York: Praeger, 1974. 378 p. Bibliog. Illus.

> Describes the oil pricing structure--a composite of economic, political, and strategic factors.

5012 Schurr, Sam. H., and Homan, Paul T. MIDDLE-EASTERN OIL AND THE WESTERN WORLD: PROSPECTS AND PROBLEMS. New York: American Elsevier, 1971. xii, 206 p. Bibliog. refs. Illus. Maps.

> The interdependence of petroleum producers and consumers, financial and contractual relationships, and the role of the United States in petroleum trade.

OIL PRODUCER-CONSUMER RELATIONS

5101 Denny, Ludwell. WE FIGHT FOR OIL. 1928. Reprint. Westport, Conn.: Hyperion, 1975. 297 p.

> Competition for control over oil resources between Great Britain and the United States, in several regions including Mesopotamia.

5102 Elwell-Sutton, Lawrence Paul. PERSIAN OIL: A STUDY IN POWER

Petroleum

POLITICS. London: Lawrence and Wishart, 1955. 343 p.

> A history and analysis of the first major oil concession conflict in the Middle East, between the Anglo-Iranian Oil Company and the Iranian government, culminating in the 1951 nationalization.

5103 Fatemi, Nasrollah Saifpour. OIL DIPLOMACY: POWDERKEG IN IRAN. New York: Whittier Books, 1954. 405 p.

> The historical background to the 1951 nationalization in Iran.

5104 Finnie, David H. DESERT ENTERPRISE; THE MIDDLE EAST OIL INDUSTRY IN ITS LOCAL ENVIRONMENT. Cambridge, Mass.: Harvard University Press, 1958. x, 224 p. Bibliog. refs. Illus. Map.

> The oil companies in the host environment.

5105 Fischer, Louis. OIL IMPERIALISM: THE INTERNATIONAL STRUGGLE FOR PETROLEUM. 1926. Reprint. Westport, Conn.: Hyperion, 1975. 256 p.

> A reprint of a journalist's view of oil concessions and international diplomacy. Includes Soviet documents.

5106 Ford, Alan W. THE ANGLO-IRANIAN OIL DISPUTE OF 1951-1952: A STUDY OF THE ROLE OF LAW IN THE RELATIONS OF STATES. Berkeley: University of California Press, 1954. xii, 348 p. Apps. Bibliog. Illus. Index.

> A review of the Iranian government's nationalization decree and the subsequent legal dispute in the World Court and the Security Council. Major documents connected with the case and a chronology are appended.

5107 Hamilton, Charles W. AMERICANS AND OIL IN THE MIDDLE EAST. Houston, Tex.: Gulf Publishing, 1962. 307 p. Bibliog.

> General survey of the oil industry, concessions, and impact on producer states.

5108 Hoskins, Halford Lancaster. MIDDLE EAST OIL IN UNITED STATES FOREIGN POLICY. Public Affairs Bulletin, 89. Washington, D.C.: 1950. 118 p. Illus. Maps.

> The author would like to separate U.S. foreign policy goals from energy demands and offers proposals to that end.

5109 Iskandar, Marwan. THE ARAB OIL QUESTION. Beirut: Middle East Economic Consultants, 1974. 138 p.

> The 1973 oil price rises with little historical background. The

Petroleum

author states that the producing states have an interest in international financial stability; the United States is viewed in monolithic perspective as the driving force behind price rises.

5110 Issawi, Charles. OIL, THE MIDDLE EAST, AND THE WORLD. Washington Papers, 4. New York: Library Press and The Center for Strategic and International Studies, Georgetown University, 1972. 86 p. Illus. Map. Sel. bibliog.

Surveys energy use trends, oil economics, and the influence of Middle Eastern regional politics on future oil supplies. Uses no OPEC publications.

5111 Kemp, Norman. ABADAN; A FIRST-HAND ACCOUNT OF THE PERSIAN OIL CRISIS. London: Allan Wingate, 1953. 270 p. Illus. Fold. map. Ports.

A journalist's firsthand report on the Iranian government's oil nationalization.

5112 Klebanoff, Shoshana. MIDDLE EAST OIL AND U.S. FOREIGN POLICY: WITH SPECIAL REFERENCE TO THE U.S. ENERGY CRISIS. Special Studies. New York: Praeger, 1974. 288 p. Illus.

Political control over multinational oil firms, competition for oil sources. Recommends a public agency to coordinate U.S. interests in the Middle East.

5113 Krueger, Robert B. THE UNITED STATES AND INTERNATIONAL OIL, A REPORT FOR THE FEDERAL ENERGY ADMINISTRATION ON U.S. FIRMS AND GOVERNMENT POLICY. New York: Praeger, 1975. 384 p.

U.S. energy needs and future policy options for relations with the oil producers.

5114 Landis, Lincoln. POLITICS AND OIL: MOSCOW IN THE MIDDLE EAST. New York and London: Dunellen, 1973. 201 p. Apps. Bibliog. Illus. Maps.

The Soviet Union's developing role as a middleman in international oil trade described with appended data and analyzed from official Soviet ideological pronouncements. Russian and English language sources; extensive bibliography.

5115 Lubell, Harold. MIDDLE EAST OIL CRISES AND WESTERN EUROPE'S ENERGY SUPPLIES. Baltimore: Johns Hopkins Press, 1963. xx, 233 p. Bibliog. Illus.

Discusses the stockpiling of coal and oil by Western industrial nations, and availability of American oil to European consumers.

Petroleum

5116 Lutfi, Ashraf. ARAB OIL, A PLAN FOR THE FUTURE. Translated from the Arabic. Middle East Oil Monographs, 3. Beirut: Middle East Research and Publishing Center, 1960. 96 p.

    Oil company-producer state relations with the author's proposals for future arrangements.

5117 Mikesell, Raymond F[rench]. ARABIAN OIL, AMERICA'S STAKE IN THE MIDDLE EAST. Chapel Hill: University of North Carolina Press, 1949. 201 p. Apps. Bibliog. fnn. Index.

    Survey of the structure of the oil industry in the Middle East with the author's recommendations for international controls on petroleum trade until "the present world shortage of petroleum comes to an end" (author's prediction).

5118 Mikesell, Raymond French, and Bartsch, William H., et al. FOREIGN INVESTMENT IN THE PETROLEUM AND MINERAL INDUSTRIES; CASE STUDIES OF INVESTOR-HOST COUNTRY RELATIONS. Baltimore: Johns Hopkins Press for Resources for the Future, 1971. 549 p. Bibliog. ref.

    Two relevant case studies--the Aramco concession and the oil industry in Iran's economy.

5119 Mosley, Leonard. POWER PLAY: OIL IN THE MIDDLE EAST. New York: Random House, 1973. xxi, 457 p. Bibliog. Illus.

    A popular history of the oil industry in the Middle East. Statistics and profiles of industrial and political leaders in the Middle East and the West.

5120 O'Connor, Harvey. WORLD CRISIS IN OIL. New York: Monthly Review, 1962. 433 p. Bibliog. ref. Illus. Index. Maps.

    Popularly written discussion of the politics and economics of the oil industry in Latin America and the Middle East; critical of the oil companies and producer state elites. Based upon interviews, and primary and secondary sources.

5121 Odell, Peter R. OIL AND WORLD POWER: BACKGROUND TO THE OIL CRISIS. New York: Taplinger, 1971 [c1970]. 188 p. Bibliog. Maps.

    A geographical description of the oil industry and its effect upon international relations--the United States and world oil, Soviet oil production, and oil policies in Western Europe.

5122 OIL PRODUCERS AND CONSUMERS: CONFLICT OR COOPERATION. Elizabeth Monroe and Robert Mabro, rapporteurs. Center for Mediterranean Studies Conference Series, 1. New York: American Universities Field Staff, 1974. 76 p. Paper. Apps. Bibliog. Illus. Map.

Synthesis of views expressed at a conference in Rome, June 1974, attended by oil specialists representing producing and consuming countries. Focuses upon possible international resource transfer arrangements, given increased petroleum prices.

5123 Organization for European Economic Cooperation. EUROPE'S NEED FOR OIL: IMPLICATIONS AND LESSONS OF THE SUEZ CRISIS. Paris: 1958. 106 p. Diagrs. Maps. Tables.

Petroleum consumption patterns in the OEEC countries prior to the 1956 Suez invasion, proposals to compensate for reduced supplies, and actual policies carried out in each country following the interruption of oil flows. Extensive, albeit dated, statistical information.

5124 Szyliowicz, Joseph S., and O'Neill, Bard E., eds. THE ENERGY CRISIS AND U.S. FOREIGN POLICY. Special Studies. New York: Praeger, 1975. 280 p.

The international politics of the energy crisis including chapters on the Arab-Israeli conflict, the Persian Gulf region, and OPEC.

5125 Shwadran, Benjamin. THE MIDDLE EAST, OIL, AND THE GREAT POWERS. 3d rev. ed. New York and Toronto: Halsted; Jerusalem: Israel Universities Press, 1973. 630 p. Bibliog. Illus. Index. Maps.

Encyclopaedic review of oil-producing countries in the Middle East--social and political background, concession arrangements, oil revenues and economies, regional relationships in OPEC and OAPEC, oil in world politics. Extensive English-language bibliography.

5126 Stocking, George Ward. MIDDLE EAST OIL: A STUDY IN POLITICAL AND ECONOMIC CONTROVERSY. Nashville, Tenn.: Vanderbilt University Press, 1970. xii, 485 p. Apps. Bibliog. ref. Index.

Issue-oriented survey of oil company-producer state relations. Focuses upon the post-World War II period and organized largely by producer states. The author brings in international political considerations and uses Middle Eastern sources.

5127 Tanzer, Michael. THE POLITICAL ECONOMY OF INTERNATIONAL OIL AND THE UNDERDEVELOPED COUNTRIES. Boston: Beacon, 1969. 435 p. Bibliog. fnn. Index.

Examines the relationships among international oil companies, their "home" governments, oil-exporting states, and underdeveloped oil-importing countries and discusses the economics of exploration, production, and transport. A case study of India's oil industry and shorter analyses of Iraq, China, and Mexico.

Petroleum

5128 U.S. Cabinet Task Force on Oil Import Control. THE OIL IMPORT QUESTION; A REPORT ON THE RELATIONSHIP OF OIL IMPORTS TO THE NATIONAL SECURITY. Washington, D.C.: Government Printing Office, 1970. 399 p. Bibliog. refs. Illus. Maps.

   Task force initiated in 1969; recommendations for changes in petroleum import controls.

5129 U.S. Congress. House. Committee on Foreign Affairs. OIL NEGOTIATIONS, OPEC AND THE STABILITY OF SUPPLY. Hearings before the Subcommittee on Foreign Economic Policy with the Subcommittee on the Near East and South Asia. 93d Cong., 1st sess., April-September 1973. Washington, D.C.: Government Printing Office, 1973. 300 p. Illus.

5130 U.S. Department of the Interior. Office of Oil and Gas. THE MIDDLE EAST PETROLEUM EMERGENCY OF 1967. 2 vols. Washington, D.C.: Government Printing Office, 1969. Apps. Bibliog. ref. Illus.

   The interruption of oil supplies following the 1967 war, compensatory policies, and statistics.

5131 Vicker, Ray. THE KINGDOM OF OIL; THE MIDDLE EAST: ITS PEOPLE AND ITS POWER. New York: Charles Scribner's Sons, 1974. 264 p. Index.

   A popularly written account of the petroleum producing countries, and the Soviet Union's petroleum policies. By an American journalist.

RELATIONS AMONG OIL PRODUCING STATES

5201 Hirst, David. OIL AND PUBLIC OPINION IN THE MIDDLE EAST. New York: Praeger, 1966. 127 p. Bibliog. fnn.

   The first section describes Arab leaders opinions on the oil companies and concession agreements; the second, the Iraqi-IPC negotiations under Qassem and the support for OPEC among member states. Uses Arabic press reports.

5202 Lenczowski, George. OIL AND THE STATE IN THE MIDDLE EAST. Ithaca, N.Y.: Cornell University Press, 1960. 379 p. Apps. Bibliog. Illus. Index.

   Survey of concession agreements, revenues in the petroleum exporting economies, and the early stages of producer cooperation. Relatively little documentation; apparently based upon primary and secondary sources in English, Persian, and Arabic.

5203 Mikdashi, Zuhayr. COMMUNITY OF OIL EXPORTING COUNTRIES: A STUDY IN GOVERNMENTAL COOPERATION. Ithaca, N.Y.: Cornell

Petroleum

University Press, 1972. 239 p. App. Bibliog. Index.

History, structure, and performance of OPEC and OAPEC (Arab) to 1971 including preferential price treatment for the less-developed countries. Extensive documentation from primary and secondary sources. Written by an Arab oil economist.

5204 Organization of the Petroleum Exporting Countries. OPEC AND THE PRINCIPLE OF NEGOTIATION. Geneva: OPEC Public Relations Department, 1965. 20 p. Paper.

Presented to the fifth Arab Petroleum Congress, Cairo, March 16-23, 1965. Reviews royalty negotiations between OPEC and the oil companies from 1960 until the end of 1964. Earlier petroleum congress reports in Arabic.

5205 al-Otaiba, Mana S. OPEC AND THE PETROLEUM INDUSTRY. New York: Halsted, 1975. 224 p. Bibliog.

The formation of OPEC, its structure and policies. Also covers the oil industry in each producer state and participation agreements. By the Minister of Petroleum and Mineral Resources, the United Arab Emirates.

5206 Rouhani, Fuad. A HISTORY OF O.P.E.C. Special Studies. New York: Praeger, 1971. xvi, 281 p. Bibliog. Illus.

Trends in oil company-producer state agreements, oil economics in OPEC member states, the structure of OPEC, and pricing trends through the 1971 Tehran agreements. Bibliography includes OPEC publications.

5207 Sayegh, Kemal S. OIL AND ARAB REGIONAL DEVELOPMENT. Special Studies. New York: Praeger, 1968. xix, 357 p. Bibliog. Maps.

Arab regional relations, especially economic and oil negotiations. Proposals for a potential Arab common market.

REFERENCE BOOKS

5301 HANDBOOK: OIL AND THE MIDDLE EAST. Rev. ed. Dhahran, Saudi Arabia: Arabian-American Oil Company, 1968. 269 p. Bibliog. Illus. Index. Maps.

A history of ARAMCO operations with concession descriptions and surveys.

5302 INTERNATIONAL PETROLEUM ENCYCLOPEDIA. Tulsa, Okla.: Petroleum Publishing, 1974. 478 p. Adv. Illus. Maps. Photos.

Country and regional industry surveys, with data on production,

Petroleum

shipping, transport, and consumption.

5303 Organization of Petroleum Exporting Countries. SELECTED DOCUMENTS OF THE INTERNATIONAL PETROLEUM INDUSTRY. Vienna: 1966- . Irregular.

    A 1968 collection was published under the editorship of Nameer Jawdet.

5304 Organization of Petroleum Exporting Countries. Public Relations Department. SOURCES OF PETROLEUM STATISTICAL INFORMATION. Vienna: August, 1966. 91 p. Index.

    Loose-leaf reference to serial sources for statistics on the various aspects of the international petroleum industry.

Chapter 7

REFERENCE MATERIALS

The English-language reference materials which cover the Middle East are more abundant and varied than they were before 1960. Several major gaps still exist. But in general, background information has grown to meet expanding interest in the region.

Reference materials have been classified into five categories--bibliographies, biographical indexes, chronologies, area studies programs, yearbooks and atlases, and weapons references. The categories overlap to some extent. Most of the yearbooks include bibliographies, a selected list of biographies, and very selective chronologies. The volumes listed in each section are devoted primarily to the topic of classification, not necessarily exclusively. The most comprehensive reference works are described in this essay.

BIBLIOGRAPHIES

The bibliography list covers contemporary Middle East affairs and diplomatic history. This excludes bibliographies and indexes which cover the social sciences and/or international politics generally and, in the process, reference works on the Middle East.

The sometimes tenuous relationship between the study of international politics and Middle Eastern area studies often makes it worthwhile to search bibliographies that are not specifically on the area. Many of these general bibliographies are widely known. Others may not be. For example, the relatively new (United States) National Technical Information Service maintains an ANNUAL INDEX which lists external research reports. The index is a fairly productive source for military and strategic reports. The U.S. Department of State also publishes a serial, EXTERNAL RESEARCH [6046], which includes a section on the Middle East. Similarly, the Rand Corporation provides SELECTED RAND ABSTRACTS to libraries without charge. The abstracts also list numerous monographs on topics in Middle Eastern politics.

Access to current materials on Middle Eastern international politics for undergraduate or less specialized graduate use can be gained through serial bibliographies in

Reference Materials

both regional publications and international affairs indexes and periodicals. The reader is referred to the International Politics section of chapter 8 for those periodicals which regularly include material on the Middle East. Of the area specific bibliographies, those published in the quarterly MIDDLE EAST JOURNAL [7011] are among the most complete for periodical literature. These listings are classified by topic (politics and history, the Arab-Israeli conflict) and also include non-English language articles. The Middle East Institute periodically duplicates bibliographies of books [6025, 6029] which are classified by region; most of these have been compiled by Harry N. Howard and also have appeared periodically in the MIDDLE EAST JOURNAL. Other serials which publish bibliographies and/or book reviews are listed in chapter 8. Beyond the serials, many of the books cited in the prior chapters of this guide provide extensive lists of references. Few are annotated, however.

The major continuous indexing of periodical literature dealing with the Middle East is INDEX ISLAMICUS [6017]. The index is compiled at the School of Oriental and African Studies in London and is published in yearly cumulations in paperback. It covers a wide variety of topics, but its index is detailed.

THE CONTEMPORARY MIDDLE EAST 1948-1973, compiled by George N. Atiyeh [6004], is annotated, unlike INDEX ISLAMICUS. The title refers to publication dates, not the dates of the events which the citations cover. Atiyeh's bibliography includes articles, monographs, and books; it is indexed by topic and author.

THE CONTEMPORARY MIDDLE EAST includes many headings and entries for international politics although its coverage is the social sciences in general. The only other comparable bibliography in comprehensiveness is PALESTINE AND THE ARAB-ISRAELI CONFLICT, edited by Khalidi and Khadduri [6019]. The editors of this bibliography have concentrated on the Arab-Israeli conflict and English-language studies. The volume is well-organized and thorough.

The remaining regional bibliographies cover significantly less material on foreign relations. MIDDLE EAST AND ISLAM [6026] emphasizes bibliographic essays with a selected number of entries on each topic. The bibliography compiled by Harry Howard (MIDDLE EAST AND NORTH AFRICA [6027]) is more extensive. This volume is specifically designed to serve as a guide to building an undergraduate library collection. The compiler also prepares bibliographies for the MIDDLE EAST JOURNAL and the Middle East Institute. Both bibliographies could be used for that purpose although the MIDDLE EAST AND ISLAM develops Islamic studies and Arabic language resources more intensively.

The American Universities Field Staff survey bibliography [6003] is limited in length. Field Staff publications cover a broad range of social and economic, as well as political, issues. The Human Relations Area Files follows the same pattern (Wilber [6050]). The U.S. Department of the Army's publication MIDDLE EAST: TRICONTINENTAL HUB [6045] is more current and more politically-focused.

Reference Materials

CHRONOLOGIES

The time lag between the occurrence of international events and the analysis of those events in periodical literature is often significant. A comprehensive collection will therefore include one or several sources which provide continuous data about international events involving the Middle East. Utilizing these resources, researchers can themselves update material accessed through the bibliographies and indexes. For information on the foreign relations of several countries in the region, regular news coverage may be the only source (see the essay opening chapter 3).

The two major questions determining which chronologies or news sources to use are: (1) where can one find the most comprehensive coverage of regional events? and (2) how is the information found to be used?

New types of event data analysis which were brought into use during the 1960s offer alternatives to more traditional library holdings. The alternatives are more often of methodological or manipulative concern than substantive.

The periodical CAHIERS DE L'ORIENT CONTEMPORAIN [7002] provides the most comprehensive coverage of Middle Eastern news. Second to that is the NEW YORK TIMES, whose INDEX can be used as a source for event data as well as accessing specific TIMES articles. These two sources are significantly more comprehensive than any other described.[1]

Many of the news sources have only marginal coverage, and many are duplicative. In other words, using several rather than one does not increase the number of events accessed. This is particularly true of DEADLINE DATA [6206], FACTS ON FILE [6207], KEESING'S ARCHIVES [6209], and the MIDDLE EAST JOURNAL chronology [7011].

Most of the news sources regularly devote disproportionate attention to particular issues or countries. One way of decreasing the probability of marked gaps in news covered is to balance the sources by place of publication. For example, the RECORD OF THE ARAB WORLD [6216] is published in Beirut and covers regional news sources, which are cited in the reports. An older, but nonregional, source which similarly focuses (not exclusively, however) on the Arab states is the (London) ARAB REPORT AND RECORD [6202]. SWASIA-NORTH AFRICA [6218] consists of bimonthly press digests from Israeli and surrounding Arab state newspapers. The translations are more opinion than news, and valuable for that. SWASIA does not often duplicate the records of events described

---

[1]An analysis of the coverage of particular serials and data sets was reported in the Middle East Studies Association BULLETIN, 5, 2 (May 1, 1971), pp. 54-71, by Robert Burrowes, et al. Most of the information in this section is drawn from that article.

Reference Materials

above. The MIDDLE EAST MONITOR is brief, like SWASIA, but presents more news in an in-depth fashion.

The BBC's SUMMARY OF WORLD BROADCASTS and the Foreign Broadcast Information Service DAILY REPORT both contain Middle East or Arab state sections and fall into the category of primary news sources and translations. The DAILY REPORT is available by subscription, but its cost suggests regional or interlibrary use. Given national controls over news, these sources are of mixed utility, primarily valuable for news interpretation.

In a different category are the data sets or compilations of international events which are designed to be used with mechanical aids. These sets include the WORLD EVENT INTERACTION SURVEY (WEIS), the CONFLICT AND PEACE DATA BANK (COPDAB), and the POLITICS AND DIPLOMACY IN THE ARAB WORLD PROJECT. The latter two are more inclusive than WEIS which is based on the NEW YORK TIMES. COPDAB uses regional sources and includes information on nation-state characteristics and images as well as events. POLITICS AND DIPLOMACY IN THE ARAB WORLD reproduces the documentary information in volumes and includes biographical sketches of persons in the news. Both archives are comprehensive; the COPDAB material is more immediately useful for computer analysis.

WEAPONS

A number of the books and monographs listed under Arab-Israel Military Engagements provide information on military tactics and weapons. The references listed here specifically focus upon the distribution of military weapons and weapons capabilities.

A series of three monographs (Tahtinen [6508-10]) examines the military weapons aspect of the Arab-Israeli conflict and the arms race in the Persian Gulf which began during the early 1970s. Tahtinen builds his 1974 study around the nature of the 1973 war and the relationship between weapons technology and military tactics.

As Tahtinen points out, the weapons available to the protagonists in the Arab-Israeli conflict are rapidly becoming more sophisticated. The major world suppliers of arms and weapons increased trade with the Middle East during the 1970s. Long-range missiles and electronic weapons systems were introduced into the Middle East. Trade in nuclear materials was discussed as a possibility.

Such transformations in the regional military environment illustrate the problem of keeping source materials current. The very comprehensive reference published by the Stockholm International Peace Research Institute (ARMS TRADE WITH THE THIRD WORLD [6504]) continues to be valuable for its thorough treatment of military trade and capabilities during the 1950s and 1960s as well as for the value of its bibliography. However, less detailed references become dated much more rapidly (Frank [6502], Joshua and Gilbert [6505], Martin [6506]).

Reference Materials

Some of the references are analytical as well as descriptive. Robert Harkavy's THE ARMS TRADE AND INTERNATIONAL SYSTEMS [6503] examines the interrelationship of trade, technology, and power. Similarly, Thayer's THE WAR BUSINESS [6511] examines the structure of the arms trade and its influence upon conflicts. Thayer uses numerous case studies to illustrate points and those which involve the Middle East are indexed.

BIBLIOGRAPHIES AND INDEXES

6001 Abdulrazak, Fawzi, comp. ARAB HISTORICAL WRITING, 1973. Cambridge, Mass.: Harvard University Library, 1974. 147 p. Mimeo. Index.

 Annotated bibliography of non-English language (primarily Arabic) sources for history and politics arranged alphabetically by authors' names. Consists of Widener Library acquisitions under Public Law 480.

6002 Alexander, Yonah. ISRAEL: SELECTED ANNOTATED AND ILLUSTRATED BIBLIOGRAPHY. Gilbertsville, N.Y.: Victor Buday, 1968. 116 p. Illus. Maps.

 Foreign relations section and listings on Zionism and the establishment of Israel. Books and monographs including publications by Arab authors.

6003 American Universities Field Staff. A SELECT BIBILIOGRAPHY: ASIA, AFRICA, EASTERN EUROPE, LATIN AMERICA. New York: 1960. 534 p. Supplement, 1961.

 One copy of this bibliography is supplied free of charge to every accredited four-year college in the United States. A Southwest-Asia section includes the Middle East (40 p.) and a North Africa section (14 p.). Broad topical coverage.

6004 Atiyeh, George N., comp. THE CONTEMPORARY MIDDLE EAST 1948-1973: A SELECTIVE AND ANNOTATED BIBLIOGRAPHY. Boston: G.K. Hall, 1975. xviii, 775 p. Index.

 The Middle East and North Africa; social, educational, political, and economic topics covering books, monographs, and journal articles. Most works covered are in European languages; some Middle Eastern language sources. Cross-referenced and indexed. Useful category headings, including several on International politics. The most comprehensive bibliography available, compiled by the Near East librarian of the Library of Congress.

6005 Bolton, Alexander Rollo Colin. SOVIET MIDDLE EAST STUDIES; AN ANALYSIS AND BIBLIOGRAPHY. Chatham House Memoranda. 8 parts.

Reference Materials

London: Oxford University Press for the Royal Institute of International Affairs, 1959. 203 p. Cum. indexes.

> The parts are structured by country with a general index volume, which also describes Middle East journals and institutes in the Soviet Union. Works covered are in Russian, but lengthy annotations, transliterated titles, and bibliographic essays make it useful to English language readers.

6006 Centre for Middle Eastern and Islamic Studies. CURRENT BRITISH RESEARCH IN MIDDLE EASTERN STUDIES. 2d rev. ed. Durham, Eng.: 1971. 92 p.

6007 Conover, Helen F. NORTH AND NORTHEAST AFRICA; A SELECTED, ANNOTATED LIST OF WRITINGS 1951-1957. Washington, D.C.: Library of Congress, 1957. 182 p.

> Listings (348) are in French and English.

6008 Dotan, Uri, comp. A BIBLIOGRAPHY OF ARTICLES ON THE MIDDLE EAST, 1959-1967. Edited by Avigdor Levy. Shiloah Center, Teaching and Research Aids, 2. Tel Aviv: Tel Aviv University, Shiloah Center for Middle Eastern and African Studies, 1970. 227 p.

> Most of the entries relate to Arab states in the immediate vicinity of Israel. Includes Hebrew and Arabic language sources and many misprints.

6009 Ettinghausen, Richard, ed. A SELECTED AND ANNOTATED BIBLIOGRAPHY OF BOOKS AND PERIODICALS IN WESTERN LANGUAGES DEALING WITH THE NEAR AND MIDDLE EAST WITH SPECIAL EMPHASIS ON MEDIEVAL AND MODERN TIMES, WITH SUPPLEMENT. 2d ed. Washington, D.C.: Middle East Institute, 1953. 137 p. Index.

> More than 2,000 classified and annotated listings including maps and serials. No international politics headings. Individual country sections and general studies.

6010 Fatemi, Ali Mohammad S., et al. POLITICAL ECONOMY OF THE MIDDLE EAST: A COMPUTERIZED GUIDE TO THE LITERATURE. 3 vols. Akron, Ohio: University of Akron, Department of Economics, 1970. 346, 326, 49 p.

> Over 2,000 listings of contemporary publications (1948-70). A user's guide accompanies the computerized information retrieval system.

6011 Geddes, Charles L. AN ANALYTICAL GUIDE TO THE BIBLIOGRAPHIES ON THE ARAB FERTILE CRESCENT (WITH A SECTION ON THE ARAB-ISRAELI CONFLICT). Bibliographic Series, 8. Denver, Colo.: American Institute of Islamic Studies, 1975. 131 p. Paper. Indices.

Reference Materials

Approximately 200 entries, with 40 on the Arab-Israeli conflict. Supersedes Geddes' earlier Arab-Israeli bibliographies. Includes non-English language titles.

6012 _____. AN ANALYTICAL GUIDE TO THE BIBLIOGRAPHIES ON THE ARABIAN PENINSULA. Bibliographic Series, 4. Denver, Colo.: American Institute of Islamic Studies, 1974. 50 p. Index.

Seventy entries in European languages. Brief annotations.

6013 _____. AN ANALYTICAL GUIDE TO THE BIBLIOGRAPHIES ON MODERN EGYPT AND THE SUDAN. Bibliographic Series, 2. Denver, Colo.: American Institute of Islamic Studies, 1972. 72 p.

Over one hundred bibliographies classified by author. Geographical topics excluded.

6014 "General Directory of the Press and Periodicals in the Arab World 1973." 2 vols. Damascus: Syrian Documentation Papers, 1973. Mimeo.

A directory of serials published in the Arab states in several languages. Arranged by country.

6015 Handley-Taylor, Geoffrey, comp. BIBLIOGRAPHY OF IRAN. 5th ed. Chicago: St. James Press, 1969. xviii, 150 p.

Topically organized list of books in a variety of fields including politics.

6016 Hill, Roy W. A BIBLIOGRAPHY OF LIBYA. Research Papers Series, 1. Durham, Eng.: University of Durham, Department of Geography, 1959. 100 p.

Lists works on bibliography; maps and periodicals; general studies, geography, and demography; and historical and political works--including military actions and the United Nations and Libya.

6017 INDEX ISLAMICUS; A CATALOGUE OF ARTICLES ON ISLAMIC SUBJECTS IN PERIODICALS AND OTHER COLLECTIVE PUBLICATIONS. Compiled by James Douglas Pearson. London: Mansell Information/Publication. Quinquennial. Index.

Covers articles published from 1906--over 900 sources. Yearly cumulations from 1971 to be published in paperback. (Formerly published in Cambridge by W. Heffer.)

6018 Kabeel, Soraya M., comp. SELECTED BIBLIOGRAPHY ON KUWAIT AND THE ARABIAN GULF. Bibliographic Series, 1. Kuwait: Kuwait University, Libraries Department, 1969. 104 p. Index.

Reference Materials

Lists 1,300 periodical articles, books, and public documents, arranged by country and topic with some useful international relations references.

6019 [el-] Khalidi, Walid, and Khadduri, Jill, eds. PALESTINE AND THE ARAB-ISRAELI CONFLICT; AN ANNOTATED BIBLIOGRAPHY. Beirut: Institute for Palestine Studies; Kuwait: University of Kuwait, 1974. 735 p. Index.

Classified by chronology and topic, the volume includes books, monographs, and articles. Most of the listings are in English. Includes reference books.

6020 King, R., and Stevens, J[ohn]. H[oward]. A BIBLIOGRAPHY OF OMAN, 1900-1970. Occasional Papers Series, 2. Durham, Eng.: University of Durham, Centre for Middle Eastern and Islamic Studies, 1973. 14 p.

General coverage, reproduced from typescript. Not annotated.

6021 Krikler, Bernard, and Laqueur, Walter [Ze'ez], eds. A READER'S GUIDE TO CONTEMPORARY HISTORY. Chicago, Ill.: Quadrangle, 1972. 259 p. Index.

Bibliographic essay including a section (16 p.) on the Middle East which covers international relations and military affairs.

6022 Lawless, Richard I. A BIBLIOGRAPHY OF WORKS ON ALGERIA PUBLISHED IN ENGLISH SINCE 1954. Occasional Papers Series, 1. Durham, Eng.: University of Durham, Centre for Middle Eastern and Islamic Studies, 1972. 39 p.

References include books, monographs, and periodical articles in the social sciences, divided by disciplinary focus. Approximately five hundred nonannotated references.

6023 Ljunggren, Florence, and Hamdy, Mohammed, comp. ANNOTATED GUIDE TO JOURNALS DEALING WITH THE MIDDLE EAST AND NORTH AFRICA. Cairo: American University in Cairo Press, 1964. 107 p. Indices.

A nonannotated list divided into Arabic and European language journals. Full citation information. Over 350 entries.

6024 Macro, Eric. BIBLIOGRAPHY OF THE ARABIAN PENINSULA. Coral Gables, Fla.: University of Miami Press, 1958. xiv, 80 p. Index.

Lists, by author, 2,380 titles on varying subjects. List of journals consulted.

6025 THE MIDDLE EAST; A SELECTED BIBLIOGRAPHY OF RECENT WORKS. 1973-74 SUPPLEMENT. Compiled by Harry N. Howard. Washington, D.C.: Middle East Institute, 1974. 24 p.

Reference Materials

Preceded by three volumes: volume 1 (1969) covers 1960-69, volume 2 covers 1970-71, and volume 3, 1972. Mimeographed. Annotated. Books organized by topic with a table of contents.

6026 MIDDLE EAST AND ISLAM: A BIBLIOGRAPHICAL INTRODUCTION. Edited by Derek Hopwood and Diana Grimwood-Jones. Bibliotheca Asiatica, 9. Switzerland: Inter Documentation, 1972. 368 p.

Bibliographical essays covering reference materials, Islamic studies, subject bibliographies, regional bibliographies, and Arabic language and literature. Works in several languages are cited. Coverage and format varies widely among the essays. Few political science entries.

6027 MIDDLE EAST AND NORTH AFRICA: A BIBLIOGRAPHY FOR UNDERGRADUATE LIBRARIES. Compiled by Harry N. Howard, et al. Occasional Publication, 14. Williamsport, Pa.: Bro-Dart and Foreign Areas Materials Center, University of the State of New York, 1971. xviii, 80 p. Index.

General and country classifications of listings in the humanities and the social sciences which the compilers have graded by importance for undergraduate collections. Author index; slightly over 1,000 entries.

6028 Nawabi, Y. M. A BIBLIOGRAPHY OF IRAN: A CATALOGUE OF BOOKS AND ARTICLES ON IRANIAN SUBJECTS, MAINLY IN EUROPEAN LANGUAGES. 2 vols. Tehran: Khajeh Press, 1969.

Mainly culture and history. More volumes forthcoming.

6029 NORTH AFRICA IN REGIONAL AND INTERNATIONAL AFFAIRS: A SELECTED BIBLIOGRAPHY. Compiled by John Duke Anthony. Washington, D.C.: Middle East Institute, 1974. 19 p.

Lists entries by author and includes articles as well as books.

6030 Patai, Raphael. JORDAN, LEBANON AND SYRIA; AN ANNOTATED BIBLIOGRAPHY. 1957. Reprint. Westport, Conn.: Greenwood Press, 1973. 289 p.

Primarily sociology and anthropology with some listings on Palestine before 1948.

6031 Pearson, James Douglas. ORIENTAL AND ASIAN BIBLIOGRAPHY; AN INTRODUCTION WITH SOME REFERENCE TO AFRICA. Hamden, Conn.: Anchor, 1966. xvi, 261 p.

A guide to Oriental studies including institutes and library collections.

Reference Materials

6032 QUARTERLY CHECK-LIST OF ORIENTAL STUDIES; AN INTERNATIONAL INDEX OF CURRENT BOOKS, MONOGRAPHS, BROCHURES AND SEPARATES. Darien, Conn.: American Bibliographic Service, 1959- . Quarterly. Bibliog. Index.

> Author-classified list emphasizing English-language books. Good coverage of the contemporary Middle East.

6033 Ragatz, Lowell. BIBLIOGRAPHY OF ARTICLES, DESCRIPTIVE, HISTORICAL AND SCIENTIFIC, ON COLONIES AND OTHER DEPENDENT TERRITORIES, APPEARING IN AMERICAN GEOGRAPHICAL AND KINDRED JOURNALS. 2 vols. Washington, D.C.: Educational Research Bureau, 1951. x, 214 p. and 149 p.

> Volume 1--through 1934; volume 2--1935-50. Available on microfiche from Inter-Documentation (Zug, Switzerland). No annotations or index.

6034 Reich, Bernard. ISRAEL IN PAPERBACK. Bibliographic Series, II. New York: Middle East Studies Association of North America, 1971. 26 p.

> Emphasizes politics and the Arab-Israeli conflict. Annotated and subject-classified.

6035 Saba, Mohsen. ENGLISH BIBLIOGRAPHY OF IRAN. PUBLICATION I. Tehran: Centre for Studies and Research on the Iranian Civilization, 196?. 313 p.

> Covers a variety of topics.

6036 Saint Joseph, University of. Centre d'Etudes Pour Le Monde Arabe Moderne. ARAB CULTURE AND SOCIETY IN CHANGE: A PARTIALLY ANNOTATED BIBLIOGRAPHY OF BOOKS AND ARTICLES IN ENGLISH, FRENCH, GERMAN AND ITALIAN. Beirut: Dar el-Mashreq, 1973. xi, 318 p. Indexes.

> Almost 5,000 listings of published and unpublished works covering conflict between Western and traditional values in Arab society.

6037 Schluter, Hans. INDEX LIBYCUS: BIBLIOGRAPHY OF LIBYA, 1957-1969, WITH SUPPLEMENTARY MATERIAL, 1915-1956. Boston: G.K. Hall, 1972. 305 p.

> Over 4,000 entries on various topics.

6038 SELECTED BIBLIOGRAPHY OF ARTICLES DEALING WITH THE MIDDLE EAST, 1955-1958. Vol. III. Jerusalem: Hebrew University, Economic Research Institute, 1955. x, 65 p. Paper. Index.

> Listed by country with subsections on foreign policy. The first volume (1950) covered the period 1939-50; the second volume, 1951-54. No annotations.

Reference Materials

6039 Selim, George Dimitri, comp. AMERICAN DOCTORAL DISSERTATIONS ON THE ARAB WORLD, 1883-1968. Washington, D.C.: Library of Congress, Near East section, Orientalia Division, 1970. 103 p. Paper. Index.

    One thousand entries arranged by author drawn from DISSERTATION ABSTRACTS.

6040 Shulman, Frank J. AMERICAN AND BRITISH DOCTORAL DISSERTATIONS ON ISRAEL AND PALESTINE IN MODERN TIMES. Ann Arbor, Mich.: Xerox University Microfilms, 1973. 25 p. Index.

    Annotated guide to dissertations which supplements AMERICAN DOCTORAL DISSERTATIONS ON THE ARAB WORLD [6039]. Also includes dissertations which deal with broader subjects but which devote substantial attention on the Middle East. Useful categorization and indexes.

6041 Stanford University. Hoover Institution on War, Revolution, and Peace. AFRICAN AND MIDDLE EAST COLLECTIONS: A SURVEY OF HOLDINGS AT THE HOOVER INSTITUTION ON WAR, REVOLUTION AND PEACE. Compiled by Peter Duigan, et al. Hoover Institution Survey of Holdings, 4. Stanford, Calif.: 1971. 37 p. Bibliog.

    One of a series of guides to the Hoover collection, which describes the scope of the holdings and special holdings.

6042 Stevens, John Howard, and King, R. A BIBLIOGRAPHY OF SAUDI ARABIA. Occasional Papers Series, 3. Durham, Eng.: University of Durham, Centre for Middle Eastern and Islamic Studies, 1973. 81 p.

    General coverage, reproduced from typescript. Not annotated.

6043 Tamkoc, Metin. A BIBLIOGRAPHY OF THE FOREIGN RELATIONS OF THE REPUBLIC OF TURKEY 1919-1967 AND BRIEF BIOGRAPHIES OF TURKISH STATESMEN. Faculty of Administrative Sciences Publication, II. Ankara: Middle East Technical University Press, 1968. xviii, 248 p.

    Almost 2,000 entries of monographs, documents, and biographical detail.

6044 United Arab Republic. Ministry of Culture and National Guidance. National Library. Reference Department. A BIBLIOGRAPHY OF WORKS ABOUT ARAB NATIONALISM. Cairo: National Library Press, 1959. 224 p. Index.

    One-third of the volume is an English language bibliography; the remainder is in Arabic. Lists works on colonialism and the Soviet Union as well as on Arab nationalism. Includes a few relatively unknown works by Arab authors in English, but citations are incomplete.

Reference Materials

6045 U.S. Department of the Army. Headquarters. MIDDLE EAST: TRICONTINENTAL HUB, A BIBLIOGRAPHIC SURVEY. Vol. 2. Washington, D.C.: 1968. 266 p. Fold. maps. Illus.

    Annotated list of periodical articles and books on various aspects of the region--primarily political--and on specific countries. Follows volume 1, published in 1965.

6046 U.S. Department of State. Bureau of Intelligence and Research. EXTERNAL RESEARCH: MIDDLE EAST, COMPLETED STUDIES. List 4.23. Washington, D.C.: 1960- . Annual. [S1.101]

    A list of current social science research by private scholars and academic centers. Books, monographs, articles, and dissertations classified by country. List numbers change.

6047 U.S. Foreign Service Institute. Center for Country and Area Studies. NEAR EAST AND NORTH AFRICA: A SELECTED FUNCTIONAL AND COUNTRY BIBLIOGRAPHY. Washington, D.C.: 1968. 43 p.

    A survey bibliography covering the region and the social sciences and the humanities.

6048 U.S. Library of Congress. Orientalia Division. THE ARABIAN PENINSULA: A SELECTED, ANNOTATED LIST OF PERIODICALS, BOOKS AND ARTICLES IN ENGLISH. Washington, D.C.: 1951. 111 p. Paper. Index.

    Reference works and serials, and country and region entries. Useful for diplomatic history.

6049 U.S. Library of Congress. Reference Department. THE ARABIAN PENINSULA. A SELECTED ANNOTATED LIST OF PERIODICALS, BOOKS, AND ARTICLES IN ENGLISH. 1951. Reprint. Hamden, Conn.: Greenwood Press, 1969. 111 p.

    Monographs and periodicals on various topics.

6050 Wilber, Donald Newton. ANNOTATED BIBLIOGRAPHY OF AFGHANISTAN. New Haven, Conn.: Human Relations Area Files, 1956. 220 p. Bibliog. Index.

    Works in numerous languages, including Persian, Pushtu, and Arabic. Fourteen pages of political sources, most in English.

6051 Zuwiyya, Jalal, comp. THE NEAR EAST (SOUTH-WEST ASIA AND NORTH AFRICA): A BIBLIOGRAPHIC STUDY. Metuchen, N.J.: Scarecrow, 1973. 392 p.

    Includes 3,616 titles, based upon holdings of State University of New York, Binghamton. Indexed by author and title, arranged by region and country.

Reference Materials

BIOGRAPHICAL INDEXES

6101 Adamec, Ludwig W. WHO'S WHO IN AFGHANISTAN. Graz, Austria: Akademische Druck-u. Verlags-anstalt, 1974. 500 p. Tables.

> Four parts: part 1 presents historical information about influential families, part 2 focuses upon contemporary leaders, part 3 lists the composition of post-1901 governments, and part 4 provides genealogical tables of important Afghan families.

6102 Bidwell, Robin, ed. BIDWELL'S GUIDES TO GOVERNMENT MINISTERS. Vol. 2: THE ARAB WORLD, 1900-1972. London: Frank Cass, 1973. 128 p.

> Lists names of occupants of ranking ministerial posts and dates of incumbency.

6103 IRAN WHO'S WHO. Tehran: Echo of Iran, 1972. 480 p.

> Alphabetically lists leading Iranians in various fields, providing short biographies.

6104 WHO'S WHO IN THE ARAB WORLD. 3d ed. Beirut: Publitec Editions, 1971. 1567 p.

> First published in 1965/66. General reference for Arab states--internal and international--as well as biographical information on approximately 3,000 Arab leaders.

6105 WHO'S WHO IN ISRAEL, AND IN THE WORK FOR ISRAEL ABROAD, 1973-74. 16th ed. Tel Aviv: Bronfman and Cohen, 1975. 680 p.

> Two-thirds of the volume is devoted to the biographical directory. The majority of the entries are Israeli. The remainder of the volume is an annotated guide to public and private organizations in Israel, including names of current officeholders. Descriptions of major public and quasi-public institutions add to its usefulness. Published regularly.

6106 WHO'S WHO IN LEBANON, 1973-74. 5th ed. Beirut: Imm. Gideon, n.d. 820 p.

> Includes a political guide with the names of past and present cabinet members and representatives to the National Assembly, political parties, diplomatic missions, as well as the Constitution of Lebanon and the current social security code and a few current demographic statistics. Standard biographical sketches.

Reference Materials

CHRONOLOGIES

6201 AN-NAHAR ARAB REPORT; A WEEKLY ANALYSIS OF POLITICAL AND ECONOMIC DEVELOPMENTS. Beirut: Al-Nahar Press Services Dept., 1970- .

> Press translations. Sometimes a brief discussion accompanies the press report.

6202 ARAB REPORT AND RECORD. Edited by Peter Kilner. London: 1966- . Bimonthly. Loose-leaf. Index.

> Summaries of domestic and foreign economic and political events by country, with a section on Arab-Israeli conflict. Sources cited include Arabic press and radio. Cabinet changes documented.

6203 BRIEF: MIDDLE EAST HIGHLIGHTS. Tel Aviv: Middle East Information Media. Fortnightly.

> Summaries of news of Middle Eastern international affairs, particularly the Arab-Israeli conflict. Some sources mentioned.

6204 CONFLICT AND PEACE DATA BANK (COPDAB). Compiled by Edward E. Azar. Chapel Hill: University of North Carolina, Department of Political Science.

> Over 100,000 international events (1948-72) compiled from various public sources, including the NEW YORK TIMES, FACTS ON FILE, THE SWISS REVIEW OF WORLD AFFAIRS, and AL-AHRAM. Stored on computer tapes and available for use.

6205 CURRENT HISTORY ANNUAL. Philadelphia: Current History, 1970-72. Maps.

> Three volumes appeared before the ANNUAL ceased publication. Each volume consisted of approximately 130 pages and was organized by country and "international crises, conflicts and organizations." Daily summaries of Middle Eastern events included the U.S. peace initiatives in the Arab-Israeli conflict (the Rogers plan).

6206 DEADLINE DATA ON WORLD AFFAIRS. Edited by Paul L. Pearson. Greenwich, Conn.: DMS, 1956- . Weekly. Index. Stat.

> Domestic and foreign relations of all countries and international organization activities. Chronologies, basic country data, governmental information. Based on press and periodical sources. Subject indexed. Available in microform.

Reference Materials

6207 FACTS ON FILE. Edited by Henry H. Schulte, Jr. New York: Facts on File, 1940- . Weekly. Cum. index.

> Cross-listing, contents. No sources. Annual index. Loose-leaf.

6208 FACTS ON FILE MASTER INDEX. 5 vols. New York: Facts on File, 1946-70.

> Guides to back volumes of FACTS ON FILE, which also serve as aids to using back newspapers and periodicals. Useful cross-references and many entries related to the Middle East. Sub-headings for event classifications are not always consistent and cross-references are not always complete.

6209 KEESING'S CONTEMPORARY ARCHIVES: WEEKLY INDEXED DIARY OF WORLD EVENTS. Edited by H. C. Tobin and R. J. Fraser. Bristol, Eng.: Kessing's Publications, 1931- . Weekly. Charts. Index.

> Country and personal name index, with section on the Arab-Israeli conflict. Loose-leaf. Entries are cross-referenced. Primarily British sources. Includes statistics.

6210 MAGHREB/MACHREK; MONDE ARAB-ETUDES ET DOCUMENTS. Paris: Fondation Nationale des Politiques et Direction de la Documentation, Documentation Francaise, 1958- . Bimonthly. Bibliog. Bk. rev. Cum. index.

> Summaries of events, people in the news, documents, and decrees. Classified by country.

6211 Mansoor, Menahen, comp. POLITICAL AND DIPLOMATIC HISTORY OF THE ARAB WORLD. 1900-1967: A CHRONOLOGICAL STUDY. 7 vols. Washington, D.C.: NCR Microcard Editions, 1972.

> Chronology and cross-listing of events, documents, and persons gathered from sources in the Middle East, Europe, the United States, and the Soviet Union. Two index volumes.

6212 MIDDLE-EAST INTELLIGENCE SURVEY. Tel Aviv: Middle East Information Media, 1973- . Semimonthly.

> News and news analysis on Arab state foreign and domestic policies and external powers. No sources.

6213 MIDDLE EAST MONITOR. 1971. Washington, D.C.: Middle East Institute, 1971- . Semimonthly. Index.

> Political and economic news summaries from Middle Eastern European, and English language press and foreign broadcast translations. Middle East leaders' major policy statements.

Reference Materials

6214 NEWS DICTIONARY, AN ENCYCLOPEDIC SUMMARY OF CONTEMPORARY HISTORY. New York: Facts on File, 1964- . Annual. Index.

Organized as a dictionary, with sufficient cross-references to be useful. Coverage of Middle East events is minimal with the exception of petroleum issues and the Arab-Israeli conflict.

6215 ORIENTE MODERNO. Edited by Paolo Minganti. Rome: Instituto per L'Oriente, 1921- . Monthly. Bk. rev. Cum. index. Index.

Events classified by country. Includes documents.

6216 RECORD OF POLITICAL OPINIONS AND EVENTS IN THE ARAB WORLD. Edited by Gibran Chamieh. Beirut: Research and Publishing House, 1969- . Monthly. Index.

Arabic and foreign news sources for events--internal, intra-Arab, international. Published in Arabic and English, with the (1972) title: RECORD OF THE ARAB WORLD (DOCUMENTS, EVENTS, POLITICAL OPINIONS). Arranged by country and region. Documents and analyses in Vol. 2 (1972). Sources cited. Name and subject index.

6217 SURVEY OF INTERNATIONAL AFFAIRS. London: Oxford University Press for the Royal Institute of International Affairs, 1920- . Irregular.

The latest volume of the Institute's annual coverage of international events appeared in 1965 under the editorship of D. C. Watt. Volumes have appeared irregularly; some are under specific titles, as THE MIDDLE EAST IN THE WAR, edited by George Kirk (see No. 1018).

6218 SWASIA-NORTH AFRICA. New York: National Council of Churches, 1973- . Bimonthly.

Translations from the Arabic and Hebrew language press, and news analysis. Focuses on the Arab-Israeli conflict.

6219 U.S. Foreign Broadcast Information Service. DAILY REPORT. Vol. 5: THE MIDDLE EAST AND NORTH AFRICA. Springfield, Va.: National Technical Information Service. Daily.

News and commentary monitored by FBIS from foreign broadcasts, newspapers, and periodicals. Available by subscription from NTIS.

6220 U.S. Library of Congress. A SELECT CHRONOLOGY AND BACKGROUND DOCUMENTS RELATING TO THE MIDDLE EAST. 1st rev. ed. Washington, D.C.: Government Printing Office, 1969. 287 p. Bibliog. fnn.

Prepared for the Senate Committee on Foreign Relations. Chronology and basic documents focusing upon the Arab-Israeli conflict 1947-69.

Reference Materials

6221 WORLD EVENT/INTERACTION SURVEY. 1966- . Directed by Charles McClelland. Los Angeles: University of South California, 1966- .

> Nation-state event/interactions from periodical sources coded and recorded on tape. Covers 1966-69. To be updated. Codebooks and two programs available to accompany the tape.

AREA STUDIES IN THE UNITED STATES

Guides

6301 MIDDLE EAST AREA STUDY PROGRAMS AT AMERICAN UNIVERSITIES AND COLLEGES, 1970, AN OUTLINE GUIDE. 5th ed. Washington, D.C.: Middle East Institute, 1970. 70 p.

6302 Middle East Studies Association of North America. BULLETIN, DIRECTORY OF GRADUATE AND UNDERGRADUATE PROGRAMS AND COURSES IN MIDDLE EAST STUDIES IN THE UNITED STATES, CANADA AND ABROAD. Biannual.

Study Programs

6303 Brandeis University. Near Eastern and Judaic Studies Program. Waltham, Mass. 02154. Chr.: Nahum M. Sarna.

> Ancient Near East and Modern Jewish history. Library collection of materials on contemporary international politics in the region.

6304 Columbia University. Middle East Institute, 420 West 118th Street, New York 10027. Dir.: Jacob Coleman Hurewitz.

> Contemporary history and languages. Graduate and undergraduate. Part of Columbia University's School of International Affairs. Publishes the Modern Middle East Studies Series.

6305 Harvard University. Center for Middle Eastern Studies. 1737 Cambridge Street, Cambridge, Mass. 02138. Dir.: Nur Yalman.

> Humanities, languages, and social science. Publishes the Middle Eastern Monograph Series.

6306 Johns Hopkins University. Center for Middle East Studies. 1740 Massachusetts Avenue, Washington, D.C. 20036. Dir.: Majid Khadduri. 1960.

> Unit of JHU School of Advanced International Studies. Speciality in contemporary politics and economics. Graduate.

Reference Materials

6307 New York University. Hagop Kevorkian Center for Near Eastern Studies. 50 Washington Square S., New York 10003. Dir.: R. Bayly Winder.

Political science, languages, humanities, social sciences. Graduate, undergraduate.

6308 Pennsylvania State University. Middle East Studies Committee. 601 Liberal Arts Tower, University Park, Pa. 16802. Chr.: Arthur Goldschmidt, Jr.

Anthropology, history. Graduate, undergraduate.

6309 Portland State University. Middle East Studies Center. Portland, Oreg. 97207. Dir.: Frederick J. Cox. Established 1959.

Social sciences, humanities, language. Middle East library collection.

6310 Princeton University. Program in Near Eastern Studies. 110 Jones Hall, Princeton, N.J. 08540. Dir.: Morroe Berger. Established 1947.

Humanities, social sciences, and languages. Undergraduate and graduate. PROCEEDINGS OF ANNUAL NEAR EAST CONFERENCE (annual); PRINCETON NEAR EAST PAPERS (irregular); and PRINCETON STUDIES IN THE MODERN NEAR EAST (irregular).

6311 Southwest Texas State University. Coord.: Elmer DeShazo. San Marcos, Tex. 78666.

Political science, geography, Turkish. Graduate, undergraduate.

6312 State University of New York, Binghamton. Program in South West Asia/North Africa Studies. Binghamton, N.Y. 13901. Dir.: Don Peretz.

Political science, social sciences, Near Eastern languages and literature, art, ethnomusicology.

6313 University of California at Los Angeles. Near Eastern Center. 405 Hilgard Avenue, Los Angeles, Calif. 90024. Dir.: Speros Vryonis, Jr. Established 1957.

Social sciences, humanities, language, monographs, and books. Near Eastern section in library.

6314 University of Chicago. Center for Middle Eastern Studies, 1130 East 59th Street, Chicago, Ill. 60637. Dir.: Leonard Binder. Established 1961.

Social sciences, humanities, language. Middle East area library. Graduate, undergraduate.

Reference Materials

6315 University of Michigan. Center for Near Eastern and North African Studies. 144 Lane Hall, Ann Arbor, Mich. 48104. Dir.: Kenneth Allin Luther.

> Humanities, languages, social sciences, contemporary and ancient history. Graduate and undergraduate. Reference library and university collection. Occasional papers.

6316 University of Pennsylvania. Near East Center. 847 Williams Hall, Philadelphia, Pa. Dir.: Thomas Naff.

> Social sciences, language and Oriental studies, including Central Asia. Cross-disciplinary. Graduate and undergraduate.

6317 University of Texas. Center for Middle Eastern Studies. Austin, Tex. 78712. Dir.: Paul Ward English. Established 1960.

> Formerly Middle East Center. Humanities, social sciences, and language. Undergraduate and graduate.

6318 University of Utah. Middle East Center. Salt Lake City, Utah 84112. Dir.: Khosrow Mostofi.

> Language and area studies training. Middle East Library collection (Marian Sheets). Collaborates with the university's Division of International Education. Undergraduate and graduate.

YEARBOOKS AND ATLASES

6401 ANNUAIRE DE L'AFRIQUE DU NORD. Aix-en-Provence, France: Centre d'Etudes Nord-Africaines, 1962. Annual.

> General reference--articles, book reviews, lengthy bibliographies, and chronologies.

6402 Barbour, Nevill, ed. A SURVEY OF NORTHWEST AFRICA, THE MAGHRIB. 2d ed. London and New York: Oxford University Press, 1962. xi, 411 p. Bibliog. Maps.

> A general reference work on Morocco, Algeria, Tunisia, and Libya, including bibliography.

6403 The Economist (London). THE MIDDLE EAST AND NORTH AFRICA. London: Oxford University Press, 1960. 135 p. Col. maps. Illus. Index.

> [Oxford Regional Economic Atlas.] Prepared by Economist Intelligence Unit and the Cartographic Department of the Clarendon Press. Regional and country political maps; economic, communications, transportation, and petroleum maps; information

Reference Materials

on oil concessions; and an appended gazeteer.

6404 Gilbert, Martin. ATLAS OF THE ARAB-ISRAELI CONFLICT. New York: Macmillan, 1975. 101 p. Maps.

    Numerous maps tracing the conflict through the twentieth century up to 1974. Notes inserted on maps emphasize an Israeli perspective, but the collection of negotiating and military maps is the largest available.

6405 IRAN ALMANAC, AND BOOK OF FACTS. 12th ed. Edited by Jahangir Behrouz. Tehran: Echo of Iran, Kucheh Khalkhali, 1973. 800 p. Illus. Index. Maps.

    Basic political, historical, economic, and demographic information.

6406 Iraq. Ministry of Planning. Central Statistical Organization. Publication and Public Relations Department. ANNUAL ABSTRACT OF STATISTICS 1972. Baghdad: n.d. 479 p. Illus. Index.

    English and Arabic. Business, economic (including trade), and social data.

6407 Israel. Central Bureau of Statistics. STATISTICAL ABSTRACT OF ISRAEL 1974. Jerusalem: n.d. 732 and 172 p. Illus. Index.

    Hebrew and English. Geography, demography, business, economic, and political data.

6408 Jordan. Department of Statistics. STATISTICAL YEARBOOK 1972. No. 23. Amman: 1972. 239 p. Illus. Index.

    English and Arabic. Economic, demographic, and social statistics.

6409 Kuwait. Fund for Arab Economic Development. THE ARAB WORLD: KEY INDICATORS. Kuwait: April 1975.

    English. Social, trade, investment, and other economic data. Sources given, primarily United Nations.

6410 THE MIDDLE EAST AND NORTH AFRICA; SURVEY AND DIRECTORY OF LANDS OF MIDDLE EAST AND NORTH AFRICA. London: Europa Publications, 1948- . Annual. Maps.

    A comprehensive reference. Includes survey articles on religion, oil, and the Arab-Israeli conflict; Middle Eastern states in international organizations; country surveys with statistics, diplomatic information, and bibliographies; a biographical directory; and a directory of research institutions concerned with the Middle East.

Reference Materials

6411 THE MIDDLE EAST: A POLITICAL AND ECONOMIC SURVEY. 4th ed. Edited by Peter Mansfield. London and New York: Oxford Univeristy Press, 1973. xi, 591 p. Bibliog. Maps.

> Includes historical background chapters and essays reviewing the Palestine conflict; Soviet and U.S. involvement in the Middle East, and the oil industry. Previous editions prepared by the Royal Institute of International Affairs and edited by Sir Reader Bullard.

6412 MIDDLE EAST ANNUAL REVIEW. Essex, Eng.: Middle East Review Co., 1974- . Maps.

> Prepared by the Economist Intelligence Unit and the publisher. Area political and economic trends and country surveys with domestic and international trade data.

6413 MIDDLE EAST RECORD, 1968. Edited by Daniel Dishon. Jerusalem: Israel Universities Press, the Shiloah Center for Middle Eastern and African Studies, 1968. 889 p. Illus. Index. Maps. Notes.

> The fourth volume to appear (1, 1960; 2, 1961; 3, 1967). Articles summarizing major international and domestic events (not including North Africa). Briefly annotated list of sources consulted. Includes discussion of military-strategic issues.

6414 Pounds, Norman John Grenville. AN ATLAS OF MIDDLE EASTERN AFFAIRS. Praeger Series of World-Affairs Atlases. Text by Norman J. G. Pounds. Maps by Robert C. Kingsbury. New York: Praeger, 1963. 117 p. Illus. Index. Maps.

> General background atlas with demographic, geographic, petroleum, and historical maps; country chapters including some diplomatic history.

6415 Shimoni, Yaacov, and Levine, Evyatar, eds. POLITICAL DICTIONARY OF THE MIDDLE EAST IN THE TWENTIETH CENTURY. London: Weidenfeld and Nicolson, 1972. 434 p. Illus. Maps. Ports.

> The detail encompassed in this volume makes it all the more unfortunate that there is no table of contents nor an index. Countries, organizations, and prominent leaders are described. The biographical information is the most complete available for the Middle East.

6416 Turkey. State Institute of Statistics. STATISTICAL YEARBOOK OF TURKEY 1973. 710. Ankara: 1974. 524 p. Illus. Index.

> Turkish and English. Geographic, demographic, social, political, economic, and resource data. Data sources listed.

Reference Materials

WEAPONS

6501 Ashkar, Riad, and Khalidi, Ahmed. WEAPONS AND EQUIPMENT OF THE ISRAELI ARMED FORCES. Monograph Series, 27. Beirut: Institute for Palestine Studies, 1971. xi, 86 p. Illus.

    Guide to Israel's weapons, their country of origin, capabilities, and use in combat. No source references.

6502 Frank, Lewis A. THE ARMS TRADE IN INTERNATIONAL RELATIONS. Special Studies. New York: Praeger, 1969. xviii, 266 p. Apps. Bibliog. Illus.

    Private and public arms flows during the 1950s and 1960s. Describes secondary suppliers including Israel, the United Arab Republic, Iran, and Turkey. Good bibliography.

6503 Harkavy, Robert E. THE ARMS TRADE AND INTERNATIONAL SYSTEMS. Cambridge, Mass.: Ballinger, 1975. 325 p.

    Historical view of arms trade, and the weapons technology changes and its impact upon the distribution of military power.

6504 International Institute for Peace and Conflict Research. THE ARMS TRADE WITH THE THIRD WORLD. By Stockholm International Peace Research Institute. New York: Humanities Press; Stockholm, Sweden: Almquist and Wiksell, 1971. xxxi, 910 p. Bibliog. Charts. Tables. Map.

    The most comprehensive work in print on the movement of major weapons--planes, tanks, ships, and missiles--to the developing countries between 1950 and 1969. Country registers list arms received by country, supplier, and year of delivery. Indigenous defense production in Israel. A chapter on the Middle East covering the demand for weapons, proposals for controls, and country-by-country defense reviews. The bibliography is comprehensive and well organized.

6505 Joshua, Wynfred, and Gilbert, Stephen P. ARMS FOR THE THIRD WORLD: SOVIET MILITARY AID DIPLOMACY. Baltimore: Johns Hopkins Press, 1969. x, 169 p. Bibliog. Illus. Index.

    A survey of Soviet policy directions in and military aid to major regions, including the Middle East. Arms aid data covers the 1955-67 period and is readily available from other sources. The bibliography is sketchy.

6506 Martin, Laurence. ARMS AND STRATEGY: THE WORLD POWER STRUCTURE TODAY. New York: David McKay, 1973. 320 p. Illus. Index.

    Survey of military capabilities--weapons and troops--with short section on the Middle East (Arab-Israeli arena). Introductory, with no documentation.

Reference Materials

6507 Sutton, John Lawrence, and Kemp, Geoffrey. ARMS TO DEVELOPING COUNTRIES, 1945-1965. Adelphi Papers, 28. London: Institute for Strategic Studies, 1966. 45 p. Bibliog. fnn. Illus.

6508 Tahtinen, Dale R. THE ARAB-ISRAELI MILITARY BALANCE SINCE OCTOBER, 1973. Foreign Affairs Studies, 11. Washington, D.C.: American Enterprise Institute for Public Policy Research, 1974. 43 p. Paper. Bibliog. ref.

> Updates the 1973 monograph [6509]. Does not include several major new arms sales agreements negotiated during the latter half of 1974.

6509 _____. THE ARAB-ISRAELI MILITARY BALANCE TODAY. Foreign Affairs Studies, 9. Washington, D.C.: American Enterprise Institute for Public Policy Research, 1973. 37 p. Paper. Bibliog. ref.

> Military data from numerous published sources compiled and analyzed. The author argues that the spiraling arms race increased the likelihood of war.

6510 _____. ARMS IN THE PERSIAN GULF. Foreign Affairs Studies, 10. Washington, D.C.: American Enterprise Institute for Public Policy Research, 1974. Paper. Bibliog. Illus. Map. Refs.

> A review of military developments in the Gulf and accumulated military data from a variety of public sources. The commentary focuses upon U.S. arms sales and interests in the region.

6511 Thayer, George. THE WAR BUSINESS, THE INTERNATIONAL TRADE IN ARMAMENTS. New York: Simon and Schuster, 1969. 417 p. Bibliog. ref.

> The mechanics of international arms sales and the influence of sales upon armed conflicts. Numerous cases involving countries within the Middle East are indexed. Analysis of recipients' defense needs and appropriateness of supplies.

6512 Wood, David H. THE MIDDLE EAST AND THE ARAB WORLD: THE MILITARY CONTEXT. Adelphi Paper, 20. London: Institute for Strategic Studies, 1965. 26 p. Illus.

Chapter 8
SERIALS

Four kinds of periodicals regularly carry information on international political issues involving the Middle Eastern region. Periodicals devoted to petroleum issues are discussed in the earlier essay preceding chapter 6. The journals of international politics listed here are those which frequently publish articles focusing upon the Middle East.

Serials collections can be based upon methodological and/or geographic balance. The international journals listed occupy almost the entire range of the spectrum from news analysis to those emphasizing methodological concerns. ROUND TABLE [7117], the SWISS REVIEW OF WORLD AFFAIRS [7119], and WORLD TODAY [7122] provide in-depth reporting and carry relatively short articles. FOREIGN AFFAIRS [7104], ORBIS [7115], FOREIGN POLICY [7105], and SURVIVAL [7118] are policy-oriented journals. The last two are more academic but not to the same degree as COOPERATION AND CONFLICT [7103] or INTERNATIONAL STUDIES QUARTERLY [7111]. Both these journals are concerned with advancing the technique of international political analysis. ROUND TABLE, WORLD TODAY, and SURVIVAL are all published in England. Their coverage is geographically broader than that of most American journals.

The list of Middle Eastern studies journals is varied also. In addition to serials which cover Middle Eastern topics exclusively, several Jewish studies periodicals are included. Each of these publishes articles frequently (at least two each year) on some aspect of the Arab-Israeli conflict. Other journals occasionally carry relevant articles although their focus is not international politics (such as JEWISH SOCIAL STUDIES [7006]).

The news magazines in the list are individually designated by a "J" following the annotation. Other regular sources of news about the Middle East are referenced under "Chronologies" in chapter 7. THE MIDDLE EAST [7009] has the broadest geographic and topical coverage, but the quality of the articles varies widely. NEW OUTLOOK [7018] and THE JOURNAL OF PALESTINE STUDIES [7007] publish longer documented analyses of current events usually written by scholars.

The MIDDLE EAST JOURNAL [7011] is the oldest journal in the field. The

Serials

JOURNAL is a multipurpose publication for students of international politics. It publishes a bibliography and a more limited chronology of current events. Articles in the JOURNAL cover political, economic, and, less often, international affairs. It is published by the Middle East Institute (Washington, D.C.) which also distributes its annual conference proceedings and brief, pamphlet, discussions of current events.

The INTERNATIONAL JOURNAL OF MIDDLE EAST STUDIES [7003] and MIDDLE EASTERN STUDIES [7014] emphasize historical topics and scholarly approaches. The INTERNATIONAL JOURNAL is the publication of the Middle East Studies Association of North America (see also the M.E.S.A. BULLETIN [7015]). It rarely contains articles on international affairs, but publishes book reviews on world politics as does MIDDLE EASTERN STUDIES.

Continuity is often difficult to maintain in a field in which many periodicals are short-lived. This list is intended to be current, but one or two of the periodicals cited may have ceased publication by the time this book appears. The journals which publish scholarly articles have been the best candidates for survival.

Rapid changes in military capabilities necessitate recourse to serial literature. Some of the serials listed below are primarily data sources; others, discussions of military tactics. The most helpful data sources are the JANE'S series [7210-12], THE MILITARY BALANCE [7208], the WORLD ARMAMENTS AND DISARMAMENTS [7207], SIPRI YEARBOOK [7207] and WORLD WIDE MILITARY EXPENDITURES [7217]. THE MILITARY BALANCE supplies basic information about military capabilities for each Middle Eastern state. The SIPRI YEARBOOK includes essays on military issues.

The tactical literature is accessed through the AIR UNIVERSITY LIBRARY INDEX [7201]. Military serial literature is dominated by U.S. service organs, such as the U.S. NAVAL INSTITUTE PROCEEDINGS [7218], ARMY [7202], MILITARY REVIEW [7213], and so forth. The quality of articles in these serials varies widely. Often, though, they present information on tactical issues in the Middle East region which are not discussed elsewhere. All the serials listed frequently publish articles dealing with the Middle East.

MIDDLE EAST AREA

7001 AFRO-ASIAN ECONOMIC REVIEW. Edited by Emad el Rashidi. Cairo: Afro-Asian Organization for Economic Cooperation, 1959- . Bimonthly.

>Articles concerning domestic and international economic issues, country profiles, special country reports, and trade agreement news. Little documentation.

7002 Centre d'Etudes de L'Orient. Institut d'Etudes Islamique. University of Paris. CAHIERS DE L'ORIENT CONTEMPORAIN. Edited by N. Tomiche.

Paris: Documentation Francaise. 5/yr. Bk. rev.

Chronology and documents.

7003 INTERNATIONAL JOURNAL OF MIDDLE EAST STUDIES. Edited by Stanford J. Shaw. New York: Middle East Studies Association of North America, 1970- . Quarterly. Adv. Bk. rev.

Primarily contemporary topics and history.

7004 IRANIAN STUDIES. Edited by Ali Banuazizi. Chestnut Hill, Mass.: Society for Iranian Studies, 1968- . Quarterly. Adv. Bk. rev. Charts. Illus. Index.

Literature, history, contemporary political, social, and economic topics.

7005 JEWISH OBSERVER AND MIDDLE EAST REVIEW. Edited by Maurice Samuelson. London: Zionist Review, 1952- . Weekly. Adv. Bk. rev. Charts. Illus.

News summaries and articles on topics including international political issues in the Middle East.

7006 JEWISH SOCIAL STUDIES. Edited by Carol Diament. New York: Conference on Jewish Social Studies, 1939- . Quarterly. Bk. rev. Cum. index (5 years).

Some coverage of the Palestine conflict.

7007 JOURNAL OF PALESTINE STUDIES. Edited by Hisham Sharabi. Beirut: Institute of Palestine Studies and Kuwait University, 1971- . Quarterly. U.S. Distributor: Institute for Palestine Studies, Oxford, Pa. Adv. Bk. rev.

The Arab-Israeli conflict, including documentary material and regional press reviews.

7008 M.E.N. ECONOMIC WEEKLY. Cairo: Middle East News Agency. Weekly. Charts. Stat.

Centers upon Egypt--internal economic programs, foreign economic relations, and the legal position of foreign investors. (Formerly M.E.N. WEEKLY REVIEW OF WORLD AND ARAB AFFAIRS.) Microfilm available.

7009 THE MIDDLE EAST; AN INTERNATIONAL BUSINESS, ECONOMIC AND POLITICAL MONTHLY. Edited by Richard Purdy. London: International Communications, 1974- . Monthly. Adv. Illus.

Political news analysis and briefs. Business reports. Broad coverage.

Serials

7010 MIDDLE EAST INTERNATIONAL. Edited by Michael Adams. London: Middle East International Publishers, 1971- . Monthly. Adv. Bk. rev.

    Short articles and book reviews on contemporary politics and economics. Documents. Draws upon the Arab and Israeli press.

7011 THE MIDDLE EAST JOURNAL. Edited by William Sands. Washington, D.C.: Middle East Institute, 1947- . Quarterly. Adv. Bibliog. Bk. rev. Charts. Chron. Index.

    Contemporary politics and economics, occasional articles on international affairs. The bibliography of periodical literature is extensively organized by topic and includes Middle East language periodicals. Brief chronology of current events. Twenty-year cumulative index available.

7012 MIDDLE-EAST RESEARCH AND INFORMATION PROJECT REPORTS. Washington, D.C.: Middle East Research and Information Project, 1971- . Monthly. Bk. rev. Bibliog.

    One or two major articles on contemporary issues, a book review, and a brief summary of a few events--varying documentation.

7013 MIDDLE EAST REVIEW. Edited by Anne Sinai. New York: American Academic Association for Peace in the Middle East, 1974- . Quarterly.

    Brief, summary essays focusing upon the Arab-Israeli conflict and internal problems confronted by the Arab states. Some are documented. (Supercedes MIDDLE EAST INFORMATION SERIES.)

7014 MIDDLE EASTERN STUDIES. Edited by Elie Kedourie. London: Frank Cass, 1964- . 3/year. Adv. Bk. revs.

    Modern history and area studies with occasional articles relevant to international affairs.

7015 Middle East Studies Association. BULLETIN. Edited by I. W[illia]m. Zartman. New York: Middle East Studies Association of North America, 1967- . Quarterly. Abstr. Adv. Bibliog.

    News of the profession, bibliography, syllabi, short articles on research facilities.

7016 NEAR EAST REPORT (WASHINGTON LETTER ON AMERICAN POLICY IN THE NEAR EAST). Edited by I. L. Kenen. Washington, D.C.: 1957- . Weekly. Illus. Index.

    Summary and analysis of news from a perspective sympathetic to Israel. Sources generally documented.

Serials

7017 THE NEW MIDDLE EAST. Edited by Dan Gillon. London: Middle East Magazine, 1968- . Monthly. Abstr. Bk. rev. Charts. Illus. Stat.

    Features political news articles, energy and business reports, news briefs. Broad coverage.

7018 NEW OUTLOOK; MIDDLE EAST MONTHLY. Edited by Simhan Flapan. Tel Aviv: Herrat Tazpiot, 1975- . Monthly. Adv. Bibliog. Bk. rev. Cum. index. Stat.

    Articles focus on the Arab-Israeli conflict--superpower involvement, Palestinian and Israeli public opinion, accommodation plans. Limited reviews.

7019 PRESENT TENSE, THE MAGAZINE OF WORLD JEWISH AFFAIRS. Edited by Murray Polner. New York: American Jewish Committee, 1973. Quarterly. Adv. Bk. rev. Illus.

    Designed to inform the American Jewish community's "understanding of the condition of World Jewry" (masthead). Feature journalism including Middle-East affairs.

7020 TIMES OF ISRAEL AND WORLD JEWISH REVIEW. Edited by Stanley Goldfoot. Tel Aviv and Beverly Hills, 1970- . Weekly. Adv. Bk. rev. Charts. Film rev. Illus.

    Includes topics relevant to Israel's foreign policy and the occupied territories, including U.S. foreign policy.

7021 THE WIENER LIBRARY BULLETIN. Edited by Robert S. Wistrich and Ernest Hearst. London: Institute of Contemporary History, 1974- . Quarterly. Adv. Book list.

    Topics of general interest to the Jewish community with one essay/issue on international politics and Israel.

INTERNATIONAL POLITICS

7101 AMERICAN JOURNAL OF INTERNATIONAL LAW. Edited by R. R. Baxter. Washington, D.C.: American Society of International Law, 1907- . 5/year. Adv. Bibliog. Bk. rev. Cum. index.

    Regional legal issues.

7102 THE ANNALS OF THE AMERICAN ACADEMY OF POLITICAL AND SOCIAL SCIENCE. Edited by Richard D. Lambert. Philadelphia: 1891- . Bimonthly. Adv. Bk. rev. Index.

    Domestic and international. Issues on specific topics.

Serials

7103 COOPERATION AND CONFLICT. NORDIC STUDIES IN INTERNATIONAL POLITICS. Oslo: Norwegian Institute of International Affairs, 1965- . Quarterly. Adv. Bk. rev. Charts. Index.

7104 FOREIGN AFFAIRS, AN AMERICAN QUARTERLY REVIEW. Edited by William P. Bundy. New York: Council on Foreign Relations, 1922- . Quarterly. Adv. Bk. rev. Index.

7105 FOREIGN POLICY. Edited by Samuel P. Huntington and Warren D. Manshel. New York: National Affairs, 1970- . Quarterly.

7106 INTERNATIONAL AFFAIRS. London: Royal Institute for International Affairs, 1922- . Quarterly.

7107 INTERNATIONAL AFFAIRS, A JOURNAL OF POLITICAL ANALYSIS. Edited by Nikolai V. Alepov. Moscow: All-Union Society Znaniye, 1955- . Monthly.

Editions in English, French, Russian.

7108 INTERNATIONAL AND COMPARATIVE LAW QUARTERLY. Edited by K. K. Simmonds. London: British Institute of International and Comparative Law, 1952- . Quarterly. Adv. Bibliog. Bk. rev. Index.

7109 INTERNATIONAL ORGANIZATION. Edited by David Kan. Madison: University of Wisconsin, 1947- . Quarterly. Adv. Bk. rev. Bibliog. Charts. Index.

7110 INTERNATIONAL PROBLEMS. Edited by Marion Mushkat. Tel Aviv: Israeli Institute of International Affairs, 1963- . 2-4/year. Bk. rev. Index. (Tabloid format.)

7111 INTERNATIONAL STUDIES QUARTERLY. Edited by K. J. Holsti. Beverly Hills, Calif.: Sage Publications for the International Studies Association, 1957- . Quarterly. Adv. Charts.

Cross-national, interdisciplinary.

7112 JERUSALEM JOURNAL OF INTERNATIONAL RELATIONS. Edited by Dan V. Segre. New York: Holmes and Meier for the Leonard Davis Institute for International Relations, Hebrew University of Jerusalem, 1975- . Quarterly. Bk. rev. Index.

Conflict research.

7113 JOURNAL OF INTERNATIONAL AFFAIRS. Edited by Brian Connelly. New York: Columbia University School of International Affairs, 1947- . Semiannual. Adv. Bk. rev.

7114 JOURNAL OF PEACE RESEARCH. Edited at International Peace Research Institute. Oslo: Universitetsforlaget, 1964- . 4/year. Adv. Charts. Illus. Index. Stat.

7115 ORBIS, A QUARTERLY JOURNAL OF WORLD AFFAIRS. Edited by William R. Kintner. Philadelphia: Foreign Policy Research Institute, 1957- . Quarterly. Adv. Bk. rev. Index.

7116 REVIEW OF POLITICS. Edited by M.A. Fitzsimons. Notre Dame, Ind.: University of Notre Dame, 1939- . Quarterly.

7117 ROUND TABLE, THE COMMONWEALTH JOURNAL OF INTERNATIONAL AFFAIRS. Edited by Robert Jackson. London: Round Table, 1910- . Quarterly. Index.

7118 SURVIVAL. Edited by Christoph Bertram. London: International Institute for Strategic Studies, 1959- . Bimonthly. Adv. Bk. rev. Index.

> Documents and articles on conflicts.

7119 SWISS REVIEW OF WORLD AFFAIRS. Edited by M. Luchsinger. Zurich: Neue Zuercher Zeitung, 1951- . Weekly. Adv. Charts. Illus.

7120 WORLD AFFAIRS. Edited by Cornelius Vahle, Jr. Washington, D.C.: American Peace Society, 1837- . Quarterly. Bk. rev.

7121 WORLD POLITICS, A QUARTERLY JOURNAL OF INTERNATIONAL RELATIONS. Edited by Klaus Knorr. Princeton, N.J.: Princeton University Press, 1948- . Quarterly. Adv. Book rev. Index.

7122 WORLD TODAY. Edited by Margaret Cornell. London: Oxford University Press for the Royal Institute of International Affairs, 1945- . Monthly. Adv. Index.

MILITARY

7201 AIR UNIVERSITY LIBRARY INDEX TO MILITARY PERIODICALS. Edited by Frances B. Rucks. Maxwell Air Force Base, Ala.: Air University Library, 1949- . Quarterly. Cum. index. Index.

> A subject index to significant articles, news items. Several sections of articles dealing with the Middle East, drawing upon an extensive list of military and strategic periodicals. Useful subheads.

Serials

7202 ARMY. Edited by L. James Binder. Washington, D.C.: Association of the United States Army, 1950- . Monthly. Adv. Bibliog. Bk. rev. Illus. Index. Maps.

7203 AVIATION WEEK AND SPACE TECHNOLOGY. Edited by Robert B. Holtz. New York: McGraw-Hill, 1916- . Weekly. Adv. Charts. Illus.

7204 THE DEFENSE MONITOR. Washington, D.C.: Center for Defense Information. Quarterly.

> Review of arms production, deployment, and trade with frequent attention to the Middle East.

7205 INSTITUTE FOR DEFENSE STUDIES AND ANALYSIS JOURNAL. Edited by K. Subrahmanyam. New Delhi: Institute for Defense Studies and Analysis, 1970- . Quarterly.

> Strategic and tactical focuses with frequent essays on the Middle East.

7206 INTERNATIONAL DEFENSE REVIEW. Geneva, Switzerland: Interavia, 1968- . Bimonthly. Abstr. Adv. Bk. rev. Charts. Illus. Stat. index.

> Text in English, French, German, and Spanish.

7207 International Institute for Peace and Conflict Research. WORLD ARMAMENTS AND DISARMAMENTS, SIPRI YEARBOOK. By Stockholm International Peace Research Institute. Cambridge and London: M.I.T. Press; Stockholm: Almquist and Wiksell, 1968/69- . Apps. Illus. Index. Maps.

> (Earlier title: SIPRI YEARBOOK OF WORLD ARMAMENTS AND DISARMAMENTS.) Essays and data concerning developments in military technology, specific armed conflicts, strategic issues, military expenditures, the arms trade, and disarmament negotiations. Indexed for identifying country and region reports. Extensive discussion of sources.

7208 International Institute for Strategic Studies. THE MILITARY BALANCE. London: 1959- . Annual. Illus.

> (Supersedes a publication with the same title issued by the institute under its earlier name: INSTITUTE FOR STRATEGIC STUDIES.) The section on the Middle East and the Mediterranean includes a description of major current defense agreements and country-by-country military force information. Tabular comparative data appended. Table of contents.

7209 _____. STRATEGIC SURVEY. London: 1967- . Annual. Chron. Illus.

Serials

Regional surveys of current strategic issues with special attention to specific conflicts. 1973 issue devoted largely to the Middle East War. Carries reports of arms agreements.

7210 JANE'S ALL THE WORLD'S AIRCRAFT. Edited by John W. R. Taylor. London: B.P.C. Publishing; New York: McGraw-Hill, 1909- . Annual. Adv. Illus. Index.

Aircraft and missile capabilities classified by country of manufacture. (Earlier editions of JANE'S yearbooks distributed in the United States by McGraw-Hill.)

7211 JANE'S FIGHTING SHIPS. Edited by John Moore. London: B.P.C. Publishing; New York: McGraw-Hill, 1898- . Annual. Adv. Illus. Index.

Title varies: ALL THE WORLD'S FIGHTING SHIPS. The 1974-75 volume contains information on naval forces of countries, classified alphabetically, including numbers of ship types and ship capabilities.

7212 JANE'S WEAPONS SYSTEMS. Edited by R. T. Bretty and D. H. R. Archer. London: Macdonald and Jane's; New York: McGraw-Hill, 1969/70- . Annual.

7213 MILITARY REVIEW. Edited by Col. V. W. Martin, Jr. Fort Leavenworth, Kans.: U.S. Army Command and General Staff College, 1922- . Monthly. Abstr. Bk. rev. Charts. Illus. Index. Maps.

Editions in English, Portuguese, and Spanish.

7214 NAVAL WAR COLLEGE REVIEW. Edited by Commander R. M. Lask, USN. Newport, R.I.: Naval War College, 1948- . Bimonthly. Bk. rev. Cum. index. Index.

7215 Sellers, R. C., et al. ARMED FORCES OF THE WORLD: A REFERENCE HANDBOOK. Edited by Robert C. Sellers. 3d ed. Special Studies in International Politics and Public Affairs Series. New York: Praeger, 1973. Apps. 296 p.

Earlier title: THE REFERENCE HANDBOOK OF THE ARMED FORCES OF THE WORLD, pub. by R. C. Sellers. Begun as an annual publication; now appears irregularly. Military forces by country with defense treaty and military production capacity appended. No index or table of contents.

7216 STRATEGIC REVIEW. Edited by Thomas Lane. Washington, D.C.: U.S. Strategic Institute, 1973- . Quarterly.

Serials

7217 U.S. Arms Control and Disarmament Agency. Bureau of Economic Affairs. WORLD WIDE MILITARY EXPENDITURES. Washington, D.C.: Government Printing Office, 1970- . Annual.

> Supersedes world military expenditures and related data issued by the Economic Bureau of the Arms Control and Disarmament Agency. Government expenditures on military and other public functions related to population and production. Classified by country.

7218 U.S. NAVAL INSTITUTE PROCEEDINGS. Edited by Robert P. Brewer. Annapolis, Md.: U.S. Naval Institute, 1873- . Monthly. Adv. Bk. rev. Charts. Illus. Index.

PETROLEUM

7301 ARAB PETROLEUM CONGRESS, PAPERS AND DISCUSSIONS. Beirut: Bureau des Documentations Libanaises et Arabes, 1959- . Annual.

> Proceedings of annual congresses, consisting of papers read on various petroleum issues.

7302 ARAB PETROLEUM DIRECTORY. Kuwait: Trade and Marketing Bureau, 1972- . Annual.

> Economic and technical information, including statistics, on the petroleum and petrochemical industry.

7303 BP STATISTICAL REVIEW OF THE WORLD OIL INDUSTRY. London: British Petroleum Company, 1974- . Annual.

> Data presented in various ways on reserves, production, consumption, trade, refining, tankers, energy. Brief.

7304 IRAN OIL JOURNAL. Tehran: National Iranian Oil Co., 1970- . Monthly. Illus.

> World oil news and technical information.

7305 OFFSHORE: THE JOURNAL OF OCEAN BUSINESS. Edited by Robert G. Burke. Tulsa, Okla.: Petroleum Publishing Co., 1954- . Monthly. Adv. Photos. Stats.

> Technical.

7306 THE OIL AND PETROLEUM INTERNATIONAL YEARBOOK. Edited by Wm. G. Nightingale. London: FT Business Publications, 1910- . Annual. Adv.

> Lists more than 1,400 petroleum companies' assets and holdings.

Serials

7307 Organization of Petroleum Exporting Countries. RESOLUTIONS OF THE (year) CONFERENCE. Vienna: 1960- . Annual.

    Available for conferences from 1960 on. Resolutions are presented without analysis or background.

7308 Organization of Petroleum Exporting Countries. Statistics Unit. ANNUAL STATISTICAL BULLETIN. Vienna: Bors & Muller, 1973- . Annual. Illus.

    Data on international oil industry provided by country with regional comparisons--production, transport, and revenues. Sources cited.

7309 THE PETROLEUM ECONOMIST. Edited by E. Stanley Tucker. London: Petroleum Press Foundation, 1934- . Monthly. Book lists. Index. Statistics.

    Articles, country news summaries, consumption and production forecasts. Continues PETROLEUM PRESS SERVICE. OPEC coverage. Published in six languages.

7310 TWENTIETH CENTURY PETROLEUM STATISTICS. Dallas, Tex.: DeGolyer, 1945- . Annual.

    Compilation of petroleum and natural gas statistics by country and region. Data includes production, reserves, tank fleets, and refining capacity. Posted oil price and general commodity price trend data summarized. Annual 1974 issue included 102 loose-leaf pages.

7311 WORLD OIL. Edited by Robert W. Scott. Houston, Tex.: Gulf Publishing Co., 1959- . Monthly. Adv.

    The August issue is the annual international outlook issue of WORLD OIL. It surveys developments in the petroleum industry by region and country and focuses on exploration and production contracts. February issue is a forecast and review annual.

7312 WORLD PETROLEUM REPORT, AN ANNUAL REVIEW OF INTERNATIONAL OIL OPERATIONS. Edited by William C. Uhl. New York: Mona Palmer Publishing. Annual. Adv. Illus.

    Reviews contractual, production, and refining development by country and region.

AUTHOR INDEX

Included in this index are all authors, editors, compilers, and translators whose works are cited in this bibliography. References are to entry numbers unless the number is preceded by a "p" (to indicate the reference is to a page number). This index is alphabetized letter by letter.

A

Abboushi, W.F. 2001, 4001
Abcarius, Michel Fred 4601
Abdulrazak, Fawzi 6001
al-Abid, Ibrahim 4501, 4602
Abidi, Aqil H.H. p. 39, 2701
Abi-Mershed, Walid 4714
Abir, Mordechai 1301, 4043
Abu Ghazaleh, Adnan Mohammad 4603
Abu Jaber, Kamel S. 3201
Abu-Laban, Baha 4066
Abu-Lughod, Ibrahim p. 10, p. 97, 1101, 4066, 4069, 4737
Acheson, Dean G. p. 7, 3801
Adamec, Ludwig W. p. 41, 2101-2, 6101
Adamiyat, Fereydun 1302
Adams, Michael 1201, 7010
Adamson, David 2501
Adelman, Morris A. p. 153, 5001
Adenauer, Konrad 2651
Adie, W.A.C. 1303
Afifi, Mohamed El-Hadi 1202
Agwani, Mohammed Shafi 1501, p. 72, 3742, 4735
Ahmad, S. Maqbul 3601
al-Akhrass, Safouh 3202

Alepov, Nikolai V. 7107
Alexander, Sidney S. p. 3, p. 9, p. 37, 1010
Alexander, Yonah 4002-3, 6002
Allen, Sir Richard H.S. 4101
Allon, Yigal p. 40, 2601
Alroy, Gil Carl 4004, 4006
Alush, Najii 4604
Alwan, Mohamed 2201
American Academic Association for Peace in the Middle East 4005-7
American Assembly 3803
American Enterprise Institute for Public Policy Research 3804
American Friends Service Committee 4008
American Universities Field Staff p. 154, p. 166, 6003
Amin, Ab'dul Amir 3510
Amin, Samir 1401
Amuzegar, Jahangir 2401
Anabtawi, Mundhir 4212
Anderson, Matthew S. 1102, 1502
Anderson, Victor 3739
Andrews, Fannie Fern 4102
Anglo-American Committee of Inquiry on Jewish Problems in Palestine and Europe 4103
Anthony, John Duke 6029

Author Index

Antonius, George p. 10, 1103
Arab Office (London) 4104
Arab Republic of Egypt. Ministry of Information 1503
Arakie, Margaret 3838
Arberry, Arthur John p. 98, 4105
Archer, D.H.R. 7212
Aruri, Naseer 4605
Asfour, Edmund 4145
Ashkar, Riad 6501
Ata'ov, Turkkaya 3401
Atiyah, Edward 1104
Atiyeh George N. p. 166, 6004
Avineri, Shlomo 4010
Avnery, Uri 2602
Azar, Edward E. 4011, 4702, 6204
Azcarate y Florez, Pablo de 4502
Azzam, Abdel Rahman 1001

B

Baczkowski, Wlodzimierz 3701
Baddour, Abd el-Fattah Ibrahim el-Sayed p. 38, 2301
Badeau, John S. p. 70, 3805, 3814, 4048
al-Baharna, Husain M. 1305
Balabkins, Nicholas 2603
Balfour, John Patrick Douglas, Baron Kincross p. 41, 3402
Banerji, J.K. p. 9, 1002
Bank, Myra 2650
Banuazizi, Ali 7004
Barakat, Halim p. 101, 4611
Barbour, Nevill 4106, 6402
Barker, A.J. 4716, 4759
Barry, Richard 4717
Bartsch, William H. 5118
Bar-Yaccov, Nissen p. 100, 4503
Bar-Zohar, Michel 2604, 4715, 4739
Bauer, Yehuda 4107
Baulin, Jacques 3602
Bawly, Dan 4750
Baxter, R.R. 7101
al-Bazzaz, Abdul Rahman 1104
Beaufre, Andre p. 101, 4717
Becker, Abraham S. p. 71, 1306, 3702, 4012
Be'eri, Eliezer p. 37, 2002

Begin, Menahem 2605
Behrouz, Jahangir 6405
Beling, Willard A. 3818
Bell, J. Bowyer 4701
Ben-Abba, Dov 2002
Ben-Dak, Joseph D. 4702
Ben-Gurion, David p. 40, 2606-7, p. 100, 4504-5
Bentwich, Helen p. 99, 4108
Bentwich, Norman 1105, p. 99, 4013, 4108
Berger, Earl 4014
Berger, Elmer 3839, 4015, 4109
Berger, Morroe 2003
Bernadotte, Folke 4506
Berque, Jacques 1402
Bertram, Christoph 7118
Bidwell, Robin 6102
Bill, James A. 3806
Binder, L. James 7202
Binder, Leonard p. 39, 2801
Blair, Leon Borden 3854
Blaxland, Gregory 1003, 3502
Blum, Yehuda Z. 2608, 4043
Bober, Arie 2609
Bolton, Alexander Rollo Colin 6005
Bose, Tarun Chandra p. 97, 4016
Bovis, H. Eugene 4301
Bowett, D.W. 4507
Bowie, Robert R. 4718
Boyd, James M. p. 100, 4508
Brace, Richard M. 1403
Branyan, Robert L. 3865
Brecher, Michael p. 5, p. 6, p. 39, p. 41, 2610-12
Bretty, R.T. 7212
Brewer, Robert P. 7218
Brook, David 4509
Brown, Edward Hoagland p. 42, 3101
Brown, Neville 4017
Browne, Harry 4703, 4719
Buehrig, Edward H. 4606
Bullard, Sir Reader William 3503, 6411
Bullock, John 4018
Bulman, Joan 4506
Bundy, William P. 7104
Burdett, Winston 4740
Burke, Robert G. 7305

Author Index

Burns, Arthur Lee 4510
Burns, Edson L.M. p. 100, 4511
Burrell, Robert Michael p. 12, 1307-8, 1316, 1404, 2402
Burrowes, Robert 3203, p. 167
Busch, Briton Cooper 3511
Buss, Robin p. 72, 3703
Bustani, Emile p. 9, 1004-5
Byford-Jones, W. 4704, 4741

C

Calvocoressi, Peter 4732, 4734
Campbell, John Coert 3807-8, 3727
Carmichael, Joel 1106
Carre, Oliver p. 101, 4607
Cattan, Henry 4019-21
Cemal, Ahmed Pasha 3403
Centre d'Etudes de L'Orient. Institut d'Etudes Islamique. University of Paris 7002
Centre for Middle Eastern and Islamic Studies 6006
Chaliand, Gerard p. 101, 4608
Chamieh, Gibran 6216
Chevalier, Hoakon 1109
Childers, Erskine B. 1006
Chomsky, Norm 4022
Chouraqui, Andre p. 98, 4023
Christman, Henry M. 2623, 2638
Chubin, Shahram p. 5, p. 13, p. 41, 2403
Churchill, Randolph S. 4742
Churchill, Winston S. 4742
Cohen, Israel 4110
Cohen, R. 4043
Cohen, S. 4043
Collins, Larry p. 97, 4707
Collins, Robert O. 2302
Confino, Michael p. 71, 3730
Congressional Quarterly 3809
Connelly, Brian 7113
Conover, Helen F. 6007
Cooley, John K. 4609
Copeland, Miles p. 6, p. 38, 2303
Cordier, Andrew p. 99, 4201
Cornell, Margaret 7122
Cottam, Richard W. p. 70, 2404, 3834

Cottrell, Alvin J. p. 12, 1308, 1316, 1404-5, 2402
Cremeans, Charles D. p. 12, 1203
Crosbie, Sylvia K. p. 40, 2613, p. 70, 3603
Crossman, Richard p. 99, 4111
Crum, Bartley C. p. 99, 4112
Cumming, Henry H. p. 11, 1107
Curtis, Michael 4007
Curzon, George Nathaniel 1309

D

Dadant, Philip 3818
Dagan, Avigdor p. 40, 2614
Darby, Phillip p. 69, 3504
Davis, John H. 4025
Davis, Moshe 4760
Dawn, C. Ernest p. 10, 1108
Dayan, Moshe 4720
Deak, Francis p. 41, 3412
DeGaury, Gerald 3102
Dekmejian, R. Hrair p. 38, 2304
Denny, Ludwell 5101
De Novo, John A. 3860
Deutschkron, Inge p. 40, 2615
Diament, Carol 7006
Diamond, Robert A. 3809
Dib, G. Moussa 1204
Dickson, Harold R.P. p. 42, 3103
Dilke, Mary 1025
Dishon, Daniel 6413
Dobson, Christopher 4610
Dodd, Charles 4202
Dodd, Peter p. 101, 4611
Doherty, Kathryn B. 4401
Donovan, John 1031, 3810
Donovan, Robert J. 4743
Dotan, Uri 6008
Douglas, William O. 3409
Douglas-Home, Charles 4744
Dowty, A. 4043
Draper, Theodore 4745
Duigan, Peter 6041

E

Eban, Abba Solomon p. 40, 2616-18
Ebel, Robert E. p. 153, 5002

Author Index

Economist (London), The 6403
Ehrenfield, Alfred 4051
Elath, Eliahu p. 40, 2619-20
Eliav, Arie Lova p. 40, 2621
Eliot, George Fielding 4708
Elkordy, Abdul Hafez p. 100, 4512
Ellis, Harry B. 2622, 3811, 4026
Elon, Amos 4027
Elwell-Sutton, Lawrence Paul p. 154, 5102
Epstein, Leon D. p. 69, 3505
Erkin, Feridun Cemal p. 41, 3404
Esco Foundation for Palestine p. 98, 4113
Eshkol, Levi p. 40, 2623
Ettinghausen, Richard 6009
Evans, Lawrence 1033, 3856
Evron, Yair p. 97, 4028
Evyatar, Levine 6415
Eytan, Walter 2624

F

Faddah, Mohammad Ibrahim p. 39, 2702
Fanon, Frantz 1109
Farah, Caesar E. 1001
Faris, Nabih Amin 1205
Farnie, D.A. 4721
Farrel, Robert H. 3812
Fatemi, Ali Mohammad S. 6010
Fatemi, Nasrollah Saifpour 2405, p. 154, 5103
Fath p. 101, 4612
Feinberg, Nathan 4029
Feis, Herbert 3840
Field, James A., Jr. 3861
Finer, Herman 3813, 4722
Fink, Reuben 3841
Finnie, David H. p. 155, 5104
Fischer, Louis 5105
Fisher, Carol Ann 1007
Fisher, Roger p. 6, p. 100, 4513
Fisher, Sydney N. 3814
Fitzsimons, Matthew A. p. 69, 3512, 7116
Flapan, Simhan 7018
Foote, Wilder p. 99, 4201
Ford, Alan W. p. 154, 5106
Foroughy, Abbas 1311

Forrest, Alfred C. 4030
Forsythe, David P. p. 100, 4514
Frank, Helmut J. 5003
Frank, Lewis A. p. 168, 6502
Frankel, Joseph p. 6
Fraser, R.J. 6209
Freedman, Robert O. p. 71, 3704
Friedman, Isaiah p. 98, 4114
Friedrich, Carl J. 3842
Frye, Richard Nelson 1008, 3827
Furlonge, Sir Geoffrey Warren p. 101, 4613

G

Gabbay, Rony E. 4115
Gabrielli, Francesco 1110
Gallagher, Charles F. 1111
Garcia-Granados, Jorge p. 101, 4709
Gasteyger, C. 1406
Geddes, Charles L. 6011-13
Gendzier, Irene L. p. 97, 4031
Georgetown University. Institute of Ethnic Studies 1009
Gershman, Carl 4038
Gervasi, Frank H. 4116
Gilbert, Martin 6404
Gilbert, Stephen P. p. 168, 6505
Gillon, Dan 7017
Giritli, Ismet 3705
Glick, Edward B. 3604
Glubb, Sir John Bagot 1112, p. 39, 2703, 4032, 4619
Goitein, Solomon D. p. 98, 4117
Golan, Galia 3706
Goldfoot, Stanley 7020
Gordenker, Leon 4515
Gordon, David C. 2202
Gordon, Kermit 3808
Gordon, Leland James 3857
Goure, Leon p. 71, 3713
Grabill, Joseph L. 3862
Grassmuck, George p. 41, 2102
Great Britain. Palestine Royal Commission 4118
Grimwood-Jones, Diana 6026
Gugli, William 4023

Author Index

H

Hadawi, Sami p. 99, p. 101, 4033, 4129, 4212, 4614
Haddad, George M. p. 37, 2004
Hahn, Lorna 1113
Haim, Sylvia G. p. 11, 1114
Hajjar, George 4619
Halderman, John W. 4058
Hall, Luella 3855
Halpern, Ben p. 40, 2625
Hamdy, Mohammed 6023
Hamilton, Charles W. p. 155, 5107
Hammond, Paul Y. p. 3, p. 9, 1010, p. 37
Hamzeh, Fuad Said 4516
Handel, Michael I. p. 40, 2626
Handley-Taylor, Geoffrey 6015
Hansen, Bent 4012
Harari, Maurice 2005
Harkabi, Yehoshafat 4034, 4615-16
Harkavy, Robert E. p. 169, 6503
Harris, George Sellers p. 72, 3405, 3743
Hart, Parker T. 3802
Hartshorn, J.E. 5004
Harvey, Mose L. p. 71, 3713
Hassan, Sana 4027
Hatem, Abdel-Hatem 1011
Hattis, Susan Lee 4119
Hauer, Christian E., Jr. 4035
Hawley, Donald p. 13, 1313
Hay, Rupert 1314
Hearst, Ernest 7021
Heathcote, Nina 4510
Heikal, Mohammed Hassanein p. 38, 2306
Heradstveit, Daniel 4036
Hermassi, Elbak 1407
Herzl, Theodor 4120
Heyd, Uriel 3406
Higgins, Rosalyn p. 99, 4203
Hill, Roy W. 6016
Hirst, David p. 155, 5201
Hobeychi, General Abdullah 4037
Hocking, William Ernest p. 11, 1115
Hodes, Aubrey 2627
Holden, David p. 42, 3104
Holmes, John Haynes 4121

Holsti, K.J. 7111
Holt, P.M. p. 12, 1206
Holtz, Robert B. 7203
Holz, Abraham 4302
Homan, Paul T. 5012
Hopwood, Derek 1304, 3105, 3735, 6026
Horelick, Arnold I. p. 71, 3702
Horn, Carlson Von 4517
Horowitz, David 4122
Hoskins, Halford Lancaster 1012, 5108
Hostler, Charles W. 3407
Hourani, Albert H. p. 38, 3204, 4048
Howard, Harry N. p. 41, 3408, 3858, 4048, 4123, p. 166, 6025, 6027
Howard, Michael 4746
Howard, Peter 3732
Howe, Irving 4038
Howley, Dennis C. 4617
Hudson, Michael C. 2802
Humbaraci, Arslan 2203
Hunter, Robert E. 3707, 4746
Huntington, Samuel P. 7105
Hurewitz, Jacob Coleman 1028, 1207, 1315, 1505, p. 37, 2006, 2801, p. 71, 3708, 3815, p. 98, p. 99, 4124, 4129
Husayn, Mohammed Tawfik 1205
Hussein, King p. 7, 2704
Hutchison, E.H. 4518
Hyamson, Albert Montefiore 4125-26, 4204

I

Indian Society of International Law 4039, 4205
Ingrams, Doreen p. 99, 4206
Ingrams, William Harold 3106
Insight Team, Sunday Times 4766
Institute for Strategic Studies 4040
International Institute for Peace and Conflict Research 6504, 7207
International Institute for Strategic Studies 7208-9
International Peace Research Institute 7114

Author Index

Iraq. Ministry of Planning. Central Statistical Organization 6406
Ireland, Philip W. p. 38, 2502
Irving, Clifford 4748
Irwin, Frances H. 2102
Isard, Walter 4057
Iskandar, Marwan 5109
Ismael, Tareq Y. p. 3, pp. 9-10, 1013, p. 38, 2307
Israel. Central Bureau of Statistics 6407
Israel. Ministry of Foreign Affairs 3709, p. 99, 4208
Issawi, Charles p. 153, p. 154, 5005, 5110

J

Jabber, Fuad A. 2629, p. 99, 4207, 4627
Jackson, Robert 7117
Jacob, Abel 2630
Jacobs, Paul 4041
James, Alan 4519
al-Jamiyah al-Misriyah lil-Qanun al-Duwali 2308
Jansen, Godfrey H. p. 9, 1014, 2631
Jansen, Michael E. 3843
Japeth, Maurice David 4042
Jeffries, Joseph M. 4128
Jiryis, Sabri 4618
John, Robert p. 99, 4129
Joseph, Bernard 4130
Jordan. Department of Statistics 6408
Joshua, Wynfred 3710, p. 168, 6505
Jukes, Geoffrey 3711

K

Kabeel, Soraya M. 6018
Kadi, Leila S. p. 12, 1208, 4520
Kagan, Benjamin 2632
Kahler, Erich 2633
Kalb, Bernard 3816
Kalb, Marvin 3816
Kan, David 7109
Kanet, Roger E. 3727

Kantor, David Mark 4045
Kapur, Harish p. 72, 3736
Katz, Samuel 2605
Katznelson, Siegmund 4131
Kaushik, Devendra p. 12, 1317
Kazemian, Gholam H. 2406
Kazemzadeh, Firuz p. 41, 2407, 3737
Kedourie, Elie p. 11, 1116, 7014
Keesing's Research Report 1506
Kelly, George Armstrong 1117, 3605
Kelly, John Barrett p. 42, 3107
Kemp, Geoffrey 4749, 6507
Kemp, Norman 5111
Kenen, I.L. 4044, 7016
Kerekes, Tibor 1009
Kerr, Malcolm H. p. 3, p. 11, 1209-10, 3818, 4012, 4046-47
Kertesz, Stephen D. 3812
Khadduri, Jill p. 166, 6019
Khadduri, Majdia 4048
Khadduri, Majid 1015, p. 38, 2503-4, 2901
Khaled, Leila 4619
Khalidi, Ahmed p. 166, 6501
el-Khalidi, Walid 4132, 6019
Khalil, Muhammad 1211
Khalili, Joseph E. p. 70, 3606
Khouri, Fred J. p. 97, 4049
Kilic, Altemur 3409
Kilner, Peter 6202
Kimball, Lorenzo K. p. 38, 2505
Kimche, David p. 9, 1016, p. 101, 4710, 4750
Kimche, Jon p. 9, 1017, p. 101, 4050, 4133, 4521, 4710
King, Gillian 3506
King, R. 6020, 6042
Kingsbury, Robert C. 6414
Kintner, William R. 7115
Kirk, George Eden p. 4, 1018-19, 1212, 6217
Kirkbride, Alec p. 99, 4134
Kisch, Frederick H. 2634, 4135
Kittrie, Nicholas N. 102
Klebanoff, Shoshana 5112
Klieman, Aaron S. p. 69, 3513, 3712
Knorr, Klaus 7121

Author Index

el-Kodsy, Ahmad 4051
Koestler, Arthur 4136
Kohler, Foy D. p. 71, 3713
Kohn, Hans p. 11, 1118
Kosut, Hal 4747
Koury, Enver M. 1213, 1318
Krammer, Arnold 2635
Krikler, Bernard 6021
Krinsky, Fred 1007
Krueger, Robert B. 5113
Kulski, W.W. 3714
Kumar, Ravinder p. 4, p. 13, 1319
Kurzman, Dan 4711
Kuwait. Fund for Arab Economic Development 6409

L

Lacouture, Jean 4048
Laffin, John 4620
Lall, Arthur 4522
Lambert, Richard D. 7102
Landen, Robert G. 3108
Landis, Lincoln 3715, 5114
Lane, Thomas 7216
Lapierre, Dominique 4707
Laqueur, Walter Ze'ez p. 71, p. 72, 3716, 3744, p. 97, p. 101, p. 102, 4052, 4751, 4761, 6021
Larsen, Lawrence H. 3865
Lask, Commander R.M. USN 7214
Lauer, Pierre p. 39, 2706
Laufer, Leopold 2636
Lauterpacht, Elihu 4209
Lawless, Richard I. 6022
Lederer, Ivo J. p. 72, 3728, 3737
Leeman, Wayne A. 5006
Lenczowski, George p. 9, 1020, p. 70, p. 72, 3717, 3738, 3804, 3818, p. 155, 5202
Lesch, Ann Mosely 4627
Levin, Norman Gordon 4137
Lewis, Bernard p. 10, 1021, p. 41, 3410, 4738
Lilenthal, Alfred M. 4053
Ling, Dwight L. 1119, 3301
Liska, George 1408
Little, Tom p. 38, 2309-10, 3109
Litvinoff, Barnet 2637, 4138

Ljunggren, Florence 6023
Lobel, Eli 4051
Longgood, William Frank 4723
Longrigg, Stephen Hemsley p. 153, 5007
Lorch, Netanel 4712
Louvish, Misha 4504
Love, Kennett p. 102, 4724
Lowdermilk, Walter Clay 4139
Lubell, Harold 5115
Luchsinger, M. 7119
Lutfi, Ashraf p. 153, 5008, 5116

M

Mabro, Robert 5122
McClelland, Charles 6221
McDonald, James Grover 3844
MacDonald, Robert W. p. 3, p. 12, 1214
MccGwire, Michael p. 72, 3725
McLane, Charles B. 3718
MacLeish, Roderick p. 101, 4752
Macro, Eric 3110, 6024
Magnus, Ralph H. p. 71, 3867
Mansfield, Peter 1120, 2311, 6411
Manshel, Warren D. 7105
Mansoor, Menahem 6211
Manuel, Frank E. 3845
Ma'oz, M. 4043
al-Marayati, Abid A. p. 37, p. 38, 2007, 2506
Marlowe, John p. 10, p. 11, p. 12, 1121-22, 1320, 4140-41
Marshall, Samuel L.A. 4753
Martin, Col. V.W., Jr. 7213
Martin, Laurence p. 168, 6506
Mason, Herbert 4054
Mattison, Francis C. 3819
Mehdi, Mohammed Taki 3817, 4055
Meinertzhagen, Richard p. 99, 4142
Meir, Golda p. 40, 2638
Meltzer, Julian L. 4122, 4157
Meo, Leila M.T. p. 39, 2803
Merlin, Samuel p. 100, 4056, 4523
Meyers, Nechemia 2606
Michaels, Walter B. 2706
Middle East Institute 3819
Middle East Studies Association of North America 6302, 7015

Author Index

Mikdashi, Zuhayr p. 153, p. 155, 5009, 5203
Mikesell, Raymond French 5117-18
Millar, Thomas B. 1321, 3719
Miller, John Donald B. 1022
Millspaugh, Arthur Chester 3835
Minganti, Paolo 6215
Mohn, Paul 4303, 4525
Moncrieff, Anthony 4732
Monroe, Elizabeth 1322, 3507, 5122
Moore, Clement H. 1409
Moore, John 7211
Moore, John Norton 4059
Morris, James 1123
Mosley, Leonard p. 155, 5119
Murphy, Robert D. p. 6, 3820
Musallam, Sami 4212
Mushkat, Marion 7110
Musrey, Alfred G. 1215

N

el-Naggar, Said 2312
Nahas, Dunia 4628, 4763
Nawabi, Y.M. 6028
Nevakivi, Jukka p. 11, 1124
Nightingale, Wm. G. 7306
Nirumand, Bahman p. 41, 2408
Nollau, Gunther p. 72, 3739
Nolte, Richard H. 3803
Nuseibeh, Hazem Zaki pp. 10-11, 1125
Nutting, Anthony 4725
Nystar, Uzy 2606

O

O'Ballance, Edgar 2204, 3111, p. 101, 4621, 4713, 4726, 4754
Obieta, Joseph A. 4727
O'Connor, Harvey 5120
Odell, Peter R. 5121
Oden, David H. 2639
O'Neill, Bard E. 4622, p. 154, 5124
Organization for European Economic Cooperation 5123
Organization of Petroleum Exporting Countries 5204, 5303, 7307
Organization of Petroleum Exporting Countries. Public Relations Department 5304
Organization of Petroleum Exporting Countries. Statistics Unit 7308
al-Otaiba, Mana S. p. 155, 5205

P

Page, Stephen 3720
Palit, D.K. p. 101, 4762
Parkes, James W. 4143-44
Patai, Raphael 4120, 6030
Pearce, Brian 4051
Pearson, James Douglas 6017, 6031
Pearson, Paul L. 6206
Pelt, Adrian 2902
Pennar, Jaan 3721
Penrose, Edith Tilton p. 154, 5010
Peres, Shimon p. 40, 2640
Peretz, Don 1010, 2641, p. 101, 4623-24, 4738
Perl, Michael 1401, 4060, 4608
Perlmutter, Amos 2642
Permanent Organization for Afro-Asian People's Solidarity. Permanent Secretariat 1507
Petran, Tabitha p. 38, 3205
Pfaff, Richard H. 4304
Polk, William R. 3821, 4145
Polner, Murray 7019
Porath, Yehoshua 4625
Pounds, Norman John Grenville 6414
Pranger, Robert J. 3822
Proctor, Jesse Harris 1216
Pryce-Jones, David 4626
Public Affairs Institute 4728
Purdy, Richard 7009

Q

Quandt, William B. 1010, 3823, p. 100, 4627
Qubain, Fahim I. 1023

R

Ra'anan, Uri p. 71, 3722, 4146
Rabinovich, Itamar p. 39, 3206
Ragatz, Lowell 6033

Author Index

Rajiv, P.K. 4042
Ramazani, Rouhollah K. p. 13, 1024, 1324, 2409
Rand Corp. 165
el Rashidi, Emad 7001
el-Rayyes, Riad N. 4628, 4763
Razzūk, Ass'ad 4147
Reich, Bernard p. 12, 1323, 3846, 6034
Reisman, Michael p. 100, 4526
Reitzel, William 3824
Reppa, Robert B., Sr. 2410
Richards, Bernard G. 4110
Rifai, Taki 5011
Rikabi-Succari, Elizabeth Hart 1217
Rivlin, Benjamin 2008, 2903
Rizk, Edward 4402
Robanna, Adderrahman 1410
Roberts, Samuel J. 2643
Robertson, John Henry 4729
Robertson, Terence 4730
Robertson, Wilmot 3847
Robinson, Jacob 4527
Rodinson, Maxime 4060, 4148
Ro'i, Y. p. 72, 3723
Romeril, P.E.A. 3411
Rondot, Pierre 1025
Rose, Norman Anthony 4149
Rosen, Harry M. 4629
Rosenau, James N. p. 4
Rosenne, Shabatai 4528
Rosner, Gabriella 4529
Rostov, R. 3825
Rothstein, Raphael 2646, 4630
Rouhani, Fuad 5206
Rouleau, Eric p. 101, 4755
Royal Institute of International Affairs 3508
Royal Institute of International Affairs, Information Department 1026, 1126, 4150
Rubinstein, Aryeh 4504
Rucks, Frances B. 7201

S

Saab, Hassan p. 12, 1218
Sacher, Harry 4151
Sachar, Howard M. p. 10, 1027
Sadik, Mohammad T. 1325

Safran, Nadav p. 70, 3848, p. 97, 4061
Saint Joseph, University of 6036
Sakran, Frank C. p. 99, 4152
Saleh, Zaki 1127
Sales, Mary 4202
Saliba, Samir N. 4403
Salibi, Kamal S. 2801, 2804
Samo, Elias 4756
Samuel, Herbert Louis 4153
Samuel, Maurice 4154-56
Samuelson, Maurice 7005
Sands, William 1028-29, 7011
Sanger, Richard H. 3112
Sayegh, Fayez Abdullah p. 12, 1028, 1219-20, 2644-45, 4210
Sayegh, Kemal S. p. 155, 5207
Sayigh, Yusif A. 4033
al-Sayyid, Afaf Lutfi p. 11, 1128
Schechtman, Joseph B. p. 70, 3849
Schiff, Zeev 2646, 4630
Schleifer, Abdullah 4062
Schlesinger, Arthur M., Jr. 3868
Schluter, Hans 6037
Schmidt, Dana Adams 2507, 3113, 4063
Schonfield, Hugh J. 4731
Schulte, Henry H., Jr. 6207
Schurr, Sam H. 5012
Schwartz, Walter 4631
Scott, Robert W. 7311
Seale, Patrick p. 12, 1221
Segal, Ronald 4064
Segre, Dan V. 7112
Selim, George Dimitri 6039
Sellers, Robert C. 7215
Selzer, Michael 2647
Seminar of Arab Jurists on Palestine 4065
Shamir, Shimon p. 71, 3730
Shapiro, Isaac 4523
Sharabi, Hisham p. 10, 1129-30, p. 37, 2009, p. 100, 4067, 4632, 7007
Sharef, Zeev 4157
Shaw, Stanford J. 7003
Sheehan, Michael Karl p. 70, 3836
Sherman, Arnold 4764
Shimoni, Yaacov 6415
Shotwell, James T. p. 41, 3412

Author Index

Shoukry, Kamel Shoukry Abdelhamid 4530
Shulman, Frank J. 6040
Shwadran, Benjamin p. 154, 5125
Silverberg, Robert 3850
Simmonds, K.K. 7108
Sinai, Anne 4127, 7013
Sinai, I. Robert 4127
Singh, K. Rajendra p. 12, 1326
Smith, Gary V. 2654
Smolansky, Oles M. 3724
Snavely, William P. 1325
Snetsinger, John p. 70, 3851
Snow, Peter p. 39, 2705
Snyder, Richard C. p. 6
Sobel, Lester A. 4765
Sorensen, Reginald 1131
Soukkary, Sohair A. 4210
Southgate, Patsy 2632
Spanier, John p. 2
Spector, Bert 3203
Spector, Ivar p. 72, 3740
Speiser, Ephrem Avigdor 3863
Spencer, William 2010
Spielman, William Carl 3826
Staar, Richard F. 3745
Stamler, David M. 4145
Stanford University 6041
Stearns, Monroe 4739
Stebbins, Richard P. 3832
Stein, Leonard J. p. 98, 4158
Steiner, Morris Jacob 1132
Stephens, Robert H. 1222
Stetler, Russell 4634
Stevens, Georgiana 3803, 4404
Stevens, John Howard 6020, 6042
Stevens, Richard P. 3852, 4168
Stewart, Jean 1402
Stock, Ernest p. 40, 2648
Stockholm International Peace Research Institute 6504, 7207
Stocking, George Ward p. 154, 5126
Stookey, Robert W. 3806
Storrs, Sir Ronald p. 99, 4159
Subrahmanyam, K. 7205
Sulzberger, Cyns Leo 3607
Sumner, Benedict H. 3741
Sutton, John Lawrence 6507
Sykes, Christopher p. 98, 4161

Szyliowicz, Joseph S. 2008, p. 154, 5124

T

Tahtinen, Dale R. p. 168, 6508-10
Talmon, Jacob L. p. 40, 2649
Tamkoc, Metin 6043
Tanzer, Michael p. 154, 5127
Taylor, Alan R. 4068, 4162
Taylor, John W.R. 7210
Tetlie, Richard N. 4068
Teveth, Shabtai 2650, 4757
Thayer, George p. 169, 6511
Theberge, J. 1405
Thomas, Hugh 4733
Thomas, Lewis Victor 3827
Tibawi, Abdul Latif 4305
Tignor, Robert L. 2302
Tittle, Joseph 4211
Tobin, H.C. 6209
Tomiche, N. 7002
Torrey, Gordon H. p. 39, 3207
Torsted, David 4148
Touval, Saadia 1411
Trask, Roger R. 3859
Trevaskis, Sir Gerald Kennedy Nicolas 3114
Truman, Harry S. p. 7, 3828
Tucker, E. Stanley 7309
Tuma, Elias H. 4070
Turkey. State Institute of Statistics 6416
Turki, Fawaz 4635
Tutsch, Hans E. p. 11, 1133, 2011

U

Uhl, William C. 7312
U.N. See United Nations
United Arab Republic. Ministry of Culture and National Guidance. National Library. Reference Department 6044
United Nations 4211
U.N. Special Committee on Palestine 4163
U.S. Arms Control and Disarmament Agency. Bureau of Economic Affairs 7217

Author Index

U.S. Cabinet Task Force on Oil Import Control 5128
U.S. Congress. House. Committee on Foreign Affairs p. 13, 1030, 1327-29, 1412, 3729, 3829-30, p. 100, 4071, 4306, 4531-32, 4767, 5129, 5432
U.S. Congress. Senate. Committee on Foreign Relations 3831, 3869
U.S. Department of State 3870-71
U.S. Department of State. Bureau of Intelligence and Research p. 165, 6046
U.S. Department of State. Bureau of Public Affairs. Office of Media Services 3872
U.S. Department of State. Historical Office 3873-75
U.S. Department of the Army. Headquarters 6045
U.S. Department of the Interior 5130
U.S. Foreign Broadcast Information Service 6219
U.S. Foreign Service Institute. Center for Country and Area Studies 6047
U.S. Library of Congress 6220
U.S. Library of Congress. Orientalia Division 6048
U.S. Library of Congress. Reference Department 6049
U.S. National Technical Information Service p. 165
University of Chicago Press p. 7
Upton, Joseph M. 2411
U.S. See United States
Utley, Freda 3833

V

Vahle, Cornelius, Jr. 7120
Vali, Ferenc A. p. 41, 3414-15
Vance, Vick p. 39, 2705
Van Passen, Pierre 4164
Van Wagenen, Richard W. 2412
Vatikiotis, Panayiotis, J. p. 39, 2313, 2707, 4072
Vicker, Ray p. 155, 5131
Vogel, Rolf 2651

Vucinich, Wayne S. p. 72, 3728

W

Wagner, Abraham R. p. 39, 2652
Wagner, Charles 3818
Waines, David 4636
Wainhouse, David W. 4533
Walichnowski, Tadeusz 2653
Warburg, James P. 4073
Ward, Richard J. 4624
Waterfield, Gordon 3115
Watt, D.C. 1504, 4213, 6217
Weisband, Edward 3416
Weizman, Chaim 4165
Welles, Sumner 3853
Wengler, Wilhelm 4211
Wenner, Manfred W. 3116
Wheelock, Keith p. 38, 2314
Whetten, Lawrence L. 3733, p. 101, 4705
Wiehe, Hans Jurgen p. 72, 3739
Wilber, Donald Newton p. 166, 6050
Wilkenfeld, Jonathan 3203
Williams, Ann p. 9, 1032
Williams-Thompson, Richard 4166
Wilmington, Martin W. 1033
Wilson, Evan M. 4307, 4624
Wilson, June P. 2706
Wint, Guy 4734
Winters, Alton, M. 4107
Wistrich, Robert S. 7021
Wolpert, Julian 4057
Wood, David H. 6512
Woodhouse, Christopher M. 3509
Wright, Quincy 4524
Wynn, Wilton p. 38, 2315

Y

Yale, Wesley W. 4706
Yalon, Judith 2621
Yamak, Labib Zuwiyya 3208
Yeganeh, Mohammed p. 153, 5005
Yeselson, Abraham 3837
Yodfat, Aryeh 3734
Yost, Charles 4738
Young, Peter 4758

Author Index

Z

Zabih, Sepehr p. 5, p. 13, p. 41, 2403, p. 72, 3746
Zander, Walter 4308
Zartman, I. William 3001, 7015

Zayid, Mahmud Y. 2316
Zeine, Zeine N. 1134, p. 38, 3209
Ziff, William Bernard 4167
Zohn, Harry 4120
Zoppo, Ciro 3818
Zuwiyya, Jalal 6051

TITLE INDEX

In addition to titles of books cited in the text, this index includes published reports, monographs, bulletins, directories, and journals and newsletters which are the main subject of an entry. Alphabetization is letter-by-letter and references are to entry numbers, unless preceded by a "p." (to indicate that reference is to a page number). In some cases, titles have been shortened.

A

Abadan; A First-Hand Account of the Persian Oil Crisis 5111
Aden, the Protectorates and the Yemen 1131
Afghanistan p. 41
Afghansitan: Some New Approaches 2102
Afghanistan's Foreign Affairs to the Mid-Twentieth Century p. 41, 2101
African and Middle East Collections 6041
Afro-Asian Economic Review 7001
Afro-Asian Movement, The p. 9, 1016
Air University Index to Military Periodicals p. 102
Air University Library Index p. 190, 7201
Algeria: A Revolution that Failed 2203
Algeria before the United Nations 2201
Algerian Insurrection, The 2204
Alternative to Armageddon 4706
America and Palestine 3841

America and the Mediterranean World 1776-1882 3861
America and the Middle East p. 70
American and British Doctoral Dissertations on Israel and Palestine in Modern Times 6040
American Approach to the Arab World, The p. 70, 3805
American Doctoral Dissertations on the Arab World, 1883-1968 6039
American Foreign Policy: Basic Documents 3873
Ameican Foreign Policy; Current Documents 3874
American Foreign Relations 3832, 3864
American Interests and Policies in the Middle East, 1900-1939 3860
American Journal of International Law 7101
American Policy for Peace in the Middle East 1969-1971 3822
American Policy toward Palestine 3842
American Relations with Turkey 1830-1930 3857
Americans and Oil in the Middle East 5107
Americans in Persia 3835

Title Index

American Zionism and United States Foreign Policy, 1942-1947 3852
Analytical Guide to the Bibliographies on Modern Egypt and the Sudan, An 6013
Analytical Guide to the Bibliographies on the Arab Fertile Crescent (with a Section on the Arab-Israeli Conflict), An 6011
Analytical Guide to the Bibliographies on the Arabian Peninsula, An 6012
Anatomy of Peace 4005
Anglo-Iranian Oil Dispute of 1951-1952, The p. 154, 5106
Angry Arabs, The 4001
An-Nahar Arab Report 6201
Annals of the American Academy of Political and Social Science, The 7102
Annotated Bibliography of Afghanistan 6050
Annotated Guide to Journals Dealing with the Middle East and North Africa 6023
Annuaire de L'Afrique Du Nord 6401
Annual Abstract of Statistics 1972 6406
Annual Index (NTIS) p. 165
Annual Statistical Bulletin 7308
Approaches to Peace in the Middle East p. 100, 4531
Arab and Israeli Elite Perceptions 4036
Arab Attitudes toward Israel 4034
Arab Awakening, The p. 10, 1103
Arab Ba'th Socialist Party, The 3201
Arab Bloc in the United Nations, The 1204
Arab Cold War, The p. 11, 1209
Arab Common Market, An 1215
Arab Cultural Nationalism in Palestine, 1919-1948 4603
Arab Culture and Society in Change 6036
Arab Federalists of the Ottoman Empire, The p. 12, 1218
Arab Guerilla Power, 1967-1972 4621
Arab Historical Writing, 1973 6001

Arabian Oil, America's Stake in the Middle East 5117
Arabian Peninsula, The 3112
Arabian Peninsula, The (U.S. Library of Congress. Orientalia Division) 6048
Arabian Peninsula, The (U.S. Library of Congress. Reference Department) 6049
Arabian Peninsula: Society and Politics, The 1304, 3105
Arab Intellectuals and the West p. 10, 1129
Arab Israel Conflict, an Indian Viewpoint, The 4042
Arab-Israel Conflict, The 4059
Arab-Israel Conflict: Documents and Comments, The 4039, 4205
Arab-Israeli Conflict: The 1967 Campaign, The 4736
Arab-Israeli Conflict: The Peaceful Proposals, 1948-1972, The 4520
Arab-Israeli Conflict in International Law, The 4029
Arab-Israeli Confrontation of June, 1967, The 4737
Arab-Israeli Dilemma, The p. 97, 4049
Arab-Israeli Military Balance since October, 1973, The 6508
Arab-Israeli Military Balance Today, The 6509
Arab-Israeli War, 1948, The 4713
Arab Looks at America, An 3817
Arab Middle East and Muslim Africa, The 1009
Arab Nationalism p. 11
Arab Nationalism, an Anthology 1114
Arab Nationalism and British Imperialism p. 10, 1121
Arab Oil, a Plan for the Future 5116
Arab Oil Question, The 5109
Arab Petroleum Congress, Papers and Discussions 7301
Arab Petroleum Directory 7302
Arab Political Encyclopedia 1503
Arab Politics in the Soviet Mirror 3734
Arab Rediscovery of Europe p. 10, 1101

Title Index

Arab Report and Record p. 167, 6202
Arab Resistance in Palestine, 1914-1948 4604
Arab Revival, The 1110
Arab Role in Africa, The 3602
Arabs and Israel, The 4744
Arabs and Israelis 4009
Arabs and Jews in Israel, The 4629
Arabs and the United Nations, The 1202
Arabs and the World, Nasser's Arab Nationalist Policy, The p. 12
Arabs and the World, The 1203
Arabs in Israel, The 4631
Arabs in Israel, 1948-1966, The 4618
Arabs' New Frontiers, The 1222
Arab States and the Arab League, a Documentary Record, The 1211
Arab Summit Conferences and the Palestine Problem (1936-1950), (1964-1966) p. 12, 1208
Arab-Turkish Relations and the Emergence of Arab Nationalism 1134
Arab Unity p. 12, 1219
Arab World, The 6409
Arab World and Israel, The 4051
Arab World Today, The 2003
Armageddon in the Middle East 4063
Armed Forces of the World 7215
Arms and Security 4749
Arms and Strategy 6506
Arms for the Third World 6505
Arms in the Persian Gulf 6510
Arms Sales to the Near East and South Asia 3831
Arms to Developing Countries, 1945-1965 6507
Arms Trade and International Systems, The p. 169, 6503
Arms Trade in International Relations, The 6502
Arms Trade with the Third World, The p. 168, 6504
Army p. 190, 7202
Army Officers in Arab Politics and Society p. 37, 2002
Art of the Possible, The p. 100, 4526

Ataturk p. 41
Ataturk: A Biography of Mustafa Kemal, Father of Modern Turkey 3402
Atlas of Middle Eastern Affairs, An 6414
Atlas of the Arab-Israeli Conflict 6404
Attitudes toward Jewish Statehood in the Arab World 4006
Aviation Week and Space Technology 7203

B

Backdrop to Tragedy p. 99, 4145
Background to the Middle East Situation 3501
Bahrein Islands 1302
Bahrein Islands, 750-1951, The 1311
Bahrain, Qatar and the United Arab Emirates 1325
Balfour Declaration, The 4158
Battle of Jerusalem, The 4748
Behind the Middle-East Conflict 4004
Behind the Silken Curtain 4112
Between Arab and Israeli p. 100, 4511
Between Enemies 4027
Between the Rock and the Hard Place 4041
Bibliography of Articles, Descriptive, Historical and Scientific, on Colonies and Other Dependent Territories, Appearing in American Geographical and Kindred Journals 6033
Bibliography of Articles on the Middle East, 1959-1967, A 6008
Bibliography of Iran 6015
Bibliography of Iran, A 6028
Bibliography of Libya, A 6016
Bibliography of Oman, 1900-1970, A 6020
Bibliography of Saudi Arabia, A 6042
Bibliography of the Arabian Peninsula 6024
Bibliography of the Foreign Relations of the Republic of Turkey 1919-1967 and Brief Biographies of Turkish Statesmen, A 6043

Title Index

Bibliography of Works about Arab Nationalism, A 6044
Bibliography of Works on Algeria Published in English since 1954, A 6022
Bidwell's Guides to Government Ministers 6102
Bi-National Idea in Palestine during Mandatory Times, The 4119
Birth of Israel; The Drama as I Saw It, The 4709
Birth of Israel: The Tousled Diplomatic Bed, The 3840
Bitter Harvest p. 101, 4614
Black September 4610
Bonn and Jerusalem--the Strange Coalition p. 40, 2615
Boundary Politics of Independent Africa, The 1411
BP Statistical Review of the World Oil Industry 7303
Bridge across the Bosporus p. 41, 3414
Brief: Middle East Highlights 6203
Britain and France in the Middle East and North Africa, 1914-1967 p. 9, 1032
Britain and Mesopotamia (Iraq to 1914) 1127
Britain and the Arabs 1112
Britain and the Middle East 3509
Britain and the Middle East from Earliest Times to 1963 3503
Britain, France and the Arab Middle East, 1914-1920 p. 11, 1124
Britain, India, and the Arabs, 1914-1921 3511
Britain's Moment in the Middle East, 1914-1956 3507
British Consulate in Jerusalem in Relation to the Jews of Palestine, 1838-1914, The 4204
British Defense Policy East of Suez 1947-1968 p. 69, 3504
British in Egypt, The 1120, 2311
British Interests in the Mediterranean and Middle East 3508
British Interests in the Persian Gulf 3510
British Politics in the Suez Canal p. 69, 3505

British Rule in Palestine 4130
Broken Sword of Justice, The 3838
Bulletin, Directory of Graduate and Undergraduate Programs and Courses in Middle East Studies in the United States, Canada and Abroad 6302

C

Cahiers de l'Orient Contemporain p. 167, 7002
Cairo Documents, The p. 38, 2306
Canal War, The p. 101, 4705
Challenge in the Middle East 3811
Changing Balance of Power in the Persian Gulf, The 1322
Changing Pattern of Political Power in Iraq, 1958-1971, The p. 38, 2505
Changing Patterns of the Middle East, The 1025
Chaos or Rebirth 1201
Chatham House Version and Other Middle-Eastern Studies, The p. 11, 1116
Clash of Destinies, A 4710
Colloquium on the Big Powers and the Present Crisis in the Middle East 4056
Communism and Nationalism in the Middle East p. 72, 3744
Communism in the Arab East p. 72, 3742
Communist China's Interaction with Arab Nationalists since the Bandung Conference p. 70, 3606
Communist Movement in Iran, The 3746
Communist Trade in Oil and Gas p. 153, 5002
Community of Oil Exporting Countries p. 155, 5203
Competitive Interference and Twentieth Century Diplomacy p. 70, 3834
Complete Diaries 4120
Conflict and Peace Data Bank (COPDAB) 6204
Conflict in the Middle East 4072
Confrontation 4761
Contemporary Arab Politics 1212
Contemporary Middle East, The 2008

Title Index

Contemporary Middle East 1948-1973, The p. 166, 6004
Cooperation and Conflict p. 189, 7103
Covenant and the Sword, The 4014
Crackle of Thorns, A 4134
Crescent and Star 4003
Crescent in Crisis, The 1205
Crisis: The Inside Story of the Suez Conspiracy 4730
Crisis and Conscience in the Middle East 4035
Crisis Decision-Making p. 39, 2652
Crisis in Lebanon 1023
Crisis of Diplomacy p. 100, 4512
Cromer in Egypt 1122
Crosscurrents in the Middle East 4073
Crossroads to Israel p. 98, 4161
Crude Oil Prices in the Middle East 5003
Current British Research in Middle Eastern Studies 6006
Current Foreign Policy 3872
Current History Annual 6205
Cursed Blessing, The 2650

D

Daily Report p. 168, 6219
David's Sling p. 40, 2640
Deadline Data p. 167, 6206
Dear Israelis, Dear Arabs p. 100, 4513
Decade of American Foreign Policy, A 3869
Decisions in Israel's Foreign Policy p. 6, 39, 2610
Defense Monitor, The 7204
Defense of the Middle East, Problems of American Policy 3807
Department of State Bulletin 3866, 3872
Desert Enterprise 5104
Dialogue with Ishmael 2627
Diary of the Sinai Campaign 4720
Dilemma of Israel, The 2622
Diplomacy in the Near and Middle East 1505
Diplomat among Warriors p. 6, 3820

Diplomatic History of Modern Iraq, A p. 38, 2506
Diplomatic History of Persia, 1917-1923 2405
Disinherited, The 4635
Dispossessed Majority, The 3847
Dissertation Abstracts 6039
Documents of the Xth Executive Committee Session of the Afro-Asian Peoples' Solidarity Organization, Damascus Syria, 23-24 June 1971 1507
Documents on American Foreign Relations 3832, 3864
Documents on International Affairs, 1962 1504
Documents on the Arab-Israel Conflict 4211
Documents on the Middle East p. 71, 3867
Documents on the Suez Crisis, 26 July to 6 November 1956 4213
Doubts and Dynamite p. 9, 1004
Dream and the Reality, a Jewish Critique, The 2654
Dulles over Suez, the Theory and Practice of His Diplomacy 3813, 4722
Dynamics of Neutralism in the Arab World, The 1220
Dynamics of World Power 3868

E

East and West of Suez 4721
Eastern Arabian Frontiers 3107
Economics and Politics of the Middle East, The 4012
Economics of Middle Eastern Oil, The p. 153, 5005
Edge of the Sword, The 4712
Egypt and Cromer 1128
Egypt and Nasser 2305
Egypt and Sinai 3502
Egypt and Sinai: External Battleground 1003
Egypt and the Fertile Crescent, 1516-1922 p. 12, 1206
Egypt and the Sudan 2302
Egypt and the United Nations 2308

Title Index

Egyptian Army in Politics, The 2313
Egypt's Struggle for Independence 2316
Egypt under Nasir 2304
Eisenhower Administration 1953-1961, The 3865
Embassies in Crisis 4739
Emergence of Arab Nationalism, The 1134
Emergence of Modern Turkey, The p. 41, 3410
Emergence of the Palestinian Arab National Movement, 1918-1929, The 4625
Empire by Treaty p. 69, 3512
Encounter with the Middle East, an Intimate Report on What Lies behind the Arab-Israeli Conflict 4740
Energy Crisis and U.S. Foreign Policy, The p. 154, 5124
English Bibliography of Iran 6035
Eternal Message of Muhammad, The 1001
Europe and the Maghreb 1406
Europe Leaves the Middle East, 1936-1954 p. 10, 1027
Europe's Need for Oil p. 154, 5123
Evasive Peace, The 4025
External Research: Middle East p. 165, 6046

F

Face of Defeat, The 4626
Facets of Arab Nationalism p. 11, 1133
Facts on File p. 167, 6207
Facts on File Master Index 6208
Faisal, King of Saudi Arabia 3102
Fall of Jerusalem, The 4062
Farewell to Arabia p. 42, 3104
Fedayeen: The Arab-Israeli Dilemma 4620
Fedayeen: The Story of the Palestinian Guerillas 4630
Fedayeen Action and Arab Strategy 4615
Financial Analysis of Middle Eastern Oil Concessions, A p. 153, 5009

First Ten Years, The 2624
Forbidden Frontiers 4704
Foreign Affairs p. 189, 7104
Foreign Aid and the Economic Development of the U.A.R. 2312
Foreign Investment in the Petroleum and Mineral Industries 5118
Foreign Policy p. 189, 7105
Foreign Policy Decision-Making p. 6
Foreign Policy of Iran, A Developing Nation in World Affairs, 1500-1941, The 2409
Foreign Policy System of Israel, The p. 39, 2611
Foreign Relations of Iran, a Developing State in a Zone of Great Power Conflict p. 13, 41, 2403
Foreign Relations of the United States, The 3875
Forgotten Ally, The 4164
Forgotten Friendship, The 2635
Foundations of British Policy in the Arab World p. 69, 3513
Foundations of Turkish Nationalism, the Life and Teachings of Ziya Gokalp 3406
Franco-British Rivalry in the Post-War Near East p. 11, 1107
French North Africa 1402
From Ankara to Marrakesh 2011
From Diplomacy to Resistance 4107
From Encroachment to Involvement 3723
From Haven to Conquest 4132
From Ottomanism to Arabism, Essays on the Origin of Arab Nationalism p. 10, 1108
From War to War 4061
Frontiers of a Nation, The 4146
Future of Palestine, The 4104

G

Game of Nations, The p. 6, 38, 2303
Games Nations Play p. 2
Genesis 1948 4711
Gentile Zionists, The 4149
German Path to Israel, The 2651
Government and Politics of the Middle East 2005

Title Index

Government and Politics of the Middle East in the Twentieth Century p. 37, 2009
Great Britain and Egypt, 1914-1951 1126
Great Britain and Palestine, 1915-1945 4150
Greater Israel 4147
Greater Maghreb, The 1408
Great Powers and the Near East, The 1502
Great Powers and the Near East, 1774-1923, The 1102
Green March, Black September 4609
Grooves of Change 4153
Growth of Films, The p. 154, 5010
Guerillas for Palestine 4628
Gulf, The 1312

H

Handbook: Oil and the Middle East 5301
Handbook to the Palestine Question, Questions and Answers, A 4602
Harvest in the Desert 4154
Has Israel Really Won 4017
Hate, Hope, and High Explosives 4708
High Dam at Aswan 2309
History of Modern Iran, The 2411
History of O.P.E.C., A 5206
History of Palestine from 135 A.D. to Modern Times, A 4143
History of the Israeli Army (1870-1974), A 2646
Holy City, The 4302
Holy Land under the Mandate, The 4102
Hussein, a Biography p. 39, 2705
Hussein of Jordan 2706

I

Idea of the Jewish State, The p. 40, 2625
Ideas of Arab Nationalism, The p. 11, 1125
L'Ideologie Palestinienne de Resistance p. 101, 4607

If I Forget Thee, O Jerusalem 3850
Impact of the October Middle East War, The 4767
Impact of U.S. Technical Aid on the Rural Development of Iran, The 2406
Imperialism and Nationalism in the Fertile Crescent 4101
Imperial Outpost-Aden 3506
Independent Iraq, 1932-58, a Study in Iraqi Politics 2503
Index Islamicus p. 166, 6017
Index Libycus 6037
India and the Persian Gulf Region, 1858-1907 p. 13, 1319
Indian and Pacific Oceans, The 1321
Indian Ocean: Its Political, Economic, and Military Importance, The 1316
Indian Ocean: Political and Strategic Future, The 1327
Indian Ocean: Towards a Peace Zone, The p. 12, 1317
Indian Ocean in Soviet Naval Policy, The 3711
Indo-Arab Relations 1320, 3601
Information and the Arab Cause 1011
Inside Pan-Arabia 1132
Insight on the Middle East War 4766
Institute for Defense Studies and Analyses Journal 7205
International Affairs 7106
International Affairs, A Journal of Political Analysis 7107
International and Comparative Law Quarterly 7108
International Conciliation, with Special Reference to the Work of the United Nations Conciliation Commission for Palestine 4516
International Defense Review 7206
International Documents on Palestine, 1967 4207
International Journal of Middle East Studies p. 190, 7003
International Organization 7109
International Peace Observation, a History and Forecast 4533
International Petroleum Encyclopedia 5302
International Problems 7110

Title Index

International Status of the Suez Canal 4727
International Studies Quarterly p. 189, 7111
Iran: The Impact of United States Interests and Policies, 1941-54 p. 70, 3836
Iran: The New Imperialism in Action p. 41, 2408
Iran, Afghanistan and Pakistan 2402
Iran Almanac, and Book of Facts 6405
Iranian Case, 1946, The 2412
Iranian Studies 7004
Iran Oil Journal 7304
Iran, the Arabian Peninsula, and the Indian Ocean 1308
Iran Who's Who 6103
Iraq: A Study in Political Development p. 38, 2502
Islam and International Relations 1216
Islam Inflamed 1123
Israel: A Colonial-Settler State? 4148
Israel: A Personal History 2606
Israel: Selected Annotated and Illustrated Bibliography 6002
Israel: Two Fateful Years, 1967-1969 4013
Israel: Years of Challenge 2607
Israel among the Nations p. 40, 2649
Israel and Elath p. 40, 2619
Israel and Her Neighbors 2620
Israel and Iran 2410
Israel and Negotiations 4501
Israel and Nuclear Weapons 2629
Israel and the Arabs 4060
Israel and the Arabs: Prelude to the Jewish State 4127
Israel and the Arabs: The June 1967 War 4747
Israel and the Arabs: The October 1973 War 4765
Israel and the Arab World 4202
Israel and the Arab World: The Crisis of 1967 4746
Israel and the Developing Countries 2636

Israel and the Holy Places of Christendom 4308
Israel and the Middle East 4026
Israel and the Palestine Arabs 2641, 4623
Israel and the Palestine Arabs 4623
Israel and the Palestinians 4010
Israel and the United Nations 2628
Israel and World Politics 4745
Israel et les Arabes, le 3^e Combat 4755
Israeli-American Relations 3846
Israeli-Arab Reader, The 4052
Israeli Campaign, 1967, The 4758
Israel in Paperback 6034
Israel in the World 2616
Israeli Withdrawal from Sinai 4714
Israel on the Road to Sinai p. 40, 2648
Israel's Armistice Agreements with the Arab States 4528
Israel's Peace Offers to the Arab States, 1948-1963 4208
Israel's Political-Military Doctrine p. 40, 2626
Israel-Syrian Armistice, The p. 100, 4503
Israel, the Arabs and the Middle East 4038
Israel, the Establishment of a State 4151
Israel, the Korean War, and China 2612
Israel without Zionists 2602

J

Jane's All the World's Aircraft 7210
Jane's Fighting Ships 7211
Jane's Weapons Systems 7212
Jerusalem: Keystone of an Arab-Israeli Settlement 4304
Jerusalem: Key to Peace 4307
Jerusalem: The Future of the Holy City for Three Monotheisms 4306
Jerusalem and the United Nations 4303
Jerusalem, Its Place in Islam and Arab History 4305

Title Index

Jerusalem Journal of International Relations 7112
Jerusalem Papers on Peace Problems 4043
Jerusalem Question, The 4301
Jewish Dilemma, The 4109
Jewish Observer and Middle East Review 7005
Jewish Social Studies p. 189, 7006
Jews among the Nations, The 2633
Jews and Arabs p. 98, 4117
Jordan, a Political Study p. 39, 2701
Jordan, Lebanon and Syria 6030
Jordan River Dispute, The 4403
Jordan River Partition 4404
Jordan Waters Conflict 4401
Journal of International Affairs 7113
Journal of Palestine Studies p. 102, 189, 7007
Journal of Peace Research 7114
Journey among Brave Men 2507
June 1967 Arab-Israeli War, The 4756
Just Peace in the Mideast, A 4044

K

Keesing's Archives p. 167, 6209
King-Crane Commission, The 4123
Kingdom of Oil, The 5131
Kissinger 3816
Kurdish War, The 2501
Kuwait and Her Neighbors p. 42, 3103

L

Land of the Hart p. 40, 2621
Latin America and the Palestine Problem 3604
Leadership and National Development in North Africa 1407
League of Arab States, The p. 12, 1214
Lebanese Crisis, 1958, The 1501
Lebanon: Improbable Nation p. 39, 2803
Legal Status of the Arabian Gulf States, The 1305

Letters and Non-Letters 3839
Letter to an Arab Friend p. 98, 4023
Level Sunlight 4155
Libyan Independence and the United Nations, a Case of Planned Decolonization 2902
Lightning War, The 4741
Long War, The 4701
Lost Soldiers 1117, 3605

M

Maghreb in the Modern World, The 1401
Maghreb/Machrek 6210
Major Middle Eastern Problems in International Law 1015
Making of a War, The 4018
Making of Foreign Policy, The p. 6
Making of Israel's Army, The p. 40, 2601
Mandate Memories, 1918-1948 4108
Mandates System, The 1105
Manual of Style, A p. 7
March Arabesque p. 9, 1005
Mediterranean, Its Role in America's Foreign Policy, The 3824
Memoirs (Samuel) 4153
Memoirs (Truman) p. 7, 3828
Memoirs of a Turkish Statesman, 1913-1919 3403
Memoirs of Sir Ronald Storrs, The 4159
M.E.N. Economic Weekly 7008
M.E.N. Weekly Review of World and Arab Affairs 7008
M.E.S.A. Bulletin p. 190, 7014
Middle East, The p. 189, 7009
Middle East: A Political and Economic Survey, The 6411
Middle East; A Selected Bibliography of Recent Works, The 6025
Middle East; Cauldron of International Politics, The 4045
Middle East: Its Governments and Politics, The p. 37, 2007
Middle East: Nations, Superpowers and Wars, The 4028
Middle East: Palestinians and Israel, The 4616

Title Index

Middle East; Problem Area in World Politics, The 1012
Middle East: Prospects for Peace, The 4524
Middle East: Quest for an American Policy, The 3818
Middle East: Some Basic Issues and Alternatives, The 4057
Middle East: Tricontinental Hub p. 166, 6045
Middle East: U.S. Policy, Israel, Oil and the Arabs, The 3809, 4024
Middle East and Islam p. 166, 6026
Middle East and North Africa, The (Economist) 6403
Middle East and North Africa, The (Vol. 5: Daily Report) 6219
Middle East and North Africa: A Bibliography for Undergraduate Libraries p. 166, 6027
Middle East and North Africa; Survey and Directory of Lands . . ., The 6410
Middle East and the Arab World, The 6512
Middle East and the European Common Market, The 1024
Middle East and the West, The p. 10, 1021
Middle East Annual Review 6412
Middle East Area Study Programs at American Universities and Colleges, 1970 6301
Middle East Conflict, The 4046
Middle East Crisis 4734
Middle East Crisis: Personal Interpretation, The 4032
Middle East Crisis: Test of International Law, The 4058
Middle East Diary, 1917-1956 4142
Middle East Dilemmas, the Background of United States Policy 3815
Middle-Eastern Oil and the Western World 5012
Middle Eastern Studies p. 190, 7015
Middle East in Crisis 1007
Middle East Information Series 7013
Middle-East Intelligence Survey 6212
Middle East International 7010

Middle East in the War, The 1018, 6217
Middle East in Transition, The p. 39, 2702
Middle East in World Affairs, The p. 9, 1020
Middle East in World Politics, The (Banerji) p. 9, 1002
Middle East in World Politics, The (Ismael) p. 9, 1013
Middle East Journal p. 166, p. 167, pp. 189-90, 7011
Middle East Monitor p. 168, 6213
Middle East 1945-1950, The 1019
Middle East, 1971, The 4071
Middle East, 1974, The 1030
Middle East Oil p. 154, 5126
Middle East, Oil, and the Great Powers, The p. 154. 5125
Middle East Oil and U.S. Foreign Policy 5112
Middle East Oil Crises and Western Europe's Energy Supplies 5115
Middle East Oil in United States Foreign Policy 5108
Middle East Petroleum Emergency of 1967, The 5130
Middle East Politics p. 37, 2006
Middle East Reader, A p. 97, 4031
Middle-East Record, 1968 6413
Middle-East Research and Information Project Reports 7012
Middle East Review 7013
Middle East Supply Centre, The 1033
Military and Politics in Israel 2642
Military Balance, The p. 190, 7208
Military Review p. 190, 7213
Mission in Palestine, 1948-1952 4502
Modern Egypt 2310
Modern History of Lebanon, The 2804
Modern Libya 2901
Modern Yemen: 1918-66 3116
Morocco, Algeria, Tunisia 1403
Moscow and Jerusalem p. 40, 2614
Most Important Country, The 4729
My Country 2617
My Mission in Israel--1948-1951 3844
My People Shall Live 4619
My Talks with Arab Leaders p. 100, 4504

Title Index

N

Nasser of Egypt 2315
Nasser's New Egypt 2314
Nationalism and Revolution in the Arab World, the Middle East and North Africa 1130
Nationalism in Iran 2404
Naval War College Review 7214
Near East and North Africa: A Selected Functional and Country Bibliography 6047
Near East and South Asia Series 3872
Near East and the Great Powers, The 1008
Near East Report 7016
Near East (South-West Asia and North Africa), The 6051
Negotiations with Nasser p. 100, 4505
New Horizons for the United States in World Affairs 3814
New Look at the Middle East 1028
New Middle East, The 7017
New Outlook p. 102, p. 189, 7018
New Perspectives on the Persian Gulf p. 13, 1328
News Dictionary, an Encyclopedic Summary of Contemporary History 6214
New York Times Index p. 167
Nisi Dominus 4106
No End of a Lesson 4725
Non-Alignment and the Afro-Asian States p. 9, 1014
North Africa 1113
North Africa in Regional and International Affairs 6029
North and Northeast Africa 6007

O

Objective: Egypt 1003
October War, Documents, Personalities, Analyses and Maps, The 4763
Offshore: The Journal of Ocean Business 7305
Oil and Arab Regional Development p. 155, 5207
Oil and Geopolitics in the Persian Gulf Area 1318
Oil and Petroleum International Yearbook, The 7306
Oil and Public Opinion in the Middle East 5201
Oil and the Persian Gulf 3707
Oil and the Persian Gulf in Soviet Policy in the 1970's 1306
Oil and the State in the Middle East 5202
Oil and World Power 5121
Oil Diplomacy 5103
Oil Imperialism 5105
Oil Import Question, The 5128
Oil in the Middle East p. 153, 5007
Oil Negotiations, OPEC and the Stability of Supply 5129
Oil, Politics, and Seapower 1303
Oil, Power and Politics 1301
Oil Producers and Consumers p. 154, 5122
Oil, the Middle East, and the World p. 154, 5110
O Jerusalem 4707
Oman since 1856 3108
On Arab Nationalism 1104
On the Rim of the Wilderness 4156
OPEC and the Petroleum Industry p. 155, 5205
OPEC and the Principle of Negotiation 5204
OPEC Oil p. 153, 5008
Orbis p. 189, 7115
Oriental and Asian Bibliography 6031
Oriente Moderno p. 99, 6215
Origins of Communism in Turkey, The 3743
Other Israel, The 2609
Other Side of the Coin, The 4053

P

Palestine: A Policy 4125
Palestine: A Search for Truth 4068
Palestine: A Study of Jewish, Arab, and British Policies p. 98, 4113

Title Index

Palestine: Concordance of the United Nations Resolutions, 1967-1971 4210
Palestine: Land of Promise 4139
Palestine: Star or Crescent? 4106
Palestine: The Arab Israeli Conflict 4634
Palestine and International Law 4019
Palestine and Israel 4067
Palestine and the Arab-Israeli Conflict p. 166, 6019
Palestine and the United Nations, Prelude to a Solution 4527
Palestine Deception, The 4128
Palestine Diary 2634, 4135
Palestine Diary, The 4129
Palestine Dilemma 4152
Palestine Entity, A 4624
Palestine Guerrillas p. 100, 4632
Palestine in Focus 4033
Palestine Is My Country p. 101, 4613
Palestine Mission 4111
Palestine or Israel 4521
Palestine Papers, 1917-1922 p. 99, 4206
Palestine Problem, The (Williams-Thompson) 4166
Palestine Problem, The (Hobeychi) 4037
Palestine Problem and Its Solution, The 4131
Palestine Question, The 4065
Palestine, the Arabs, and Israel 4020
Palestine the Reality 4128
Palestine, the Road to Peace 4021
Palestine through the Fog of Propaganda 4601
Palestine To-day and Tomorrow 4121
Palestine under the Mandate 4126
Palestinian Resistance Movement, The p. 101, 4608
Palestinian Resistance to Israeli Occupation, The 4605
Partition of Turkey, The p. 41, 3408
Passing of French Algeria, The 2202
Peace in the Middle East 4055
Peace in the Middle East: Reflections on Justice and Nationhood 4022

Peacekeeping by U.N. Forces from Suez to the Congo 4510
Peacemaking and the Immoral War 4070
People and Politics in the Middle East 4007
Persia and the Persian Question 1309
Persian Gulf, The (Burrell) 1307
Persian Gulf, The (Reich) p. 12, 1323
Persian Gulf; Iran's Role, The p. 13, 1324
Persian Gulf: Prospects for Stability, The 1315
Persian Gulf in the Twentieth Century, The p. 12, 1320
Persian Gulf States, The 1314
Persian Oil: A Study in Power Politics p. 154, 5102
Petroleum Economist, The p. 155, 7309
Political and Diplomatic History of the Arab World 6211
Political Dictionary of the Middle East in the Twentieth Century 6415
Political Dynamics in the Middle East (Hammond and Alexander) p. 9, 1010, 3823, 4012
Political Economy of International Oil and the Underdeveloped Countries, The p. 154, 5127
Political Economy of the Middle East 6010
Political Evolution in the Middle East 2010
Political Study of the Arab-Jewish Conflict, A 4115
Political Systems of the Middle East in the 20th Century 2001
Politics and Oil 5114
Politics and Oil, Moscow in the Middle East 3715
Politics and Petroleum 3806
Politics and the Military in Jordan: a Study of the Arab Legion, 1921-1957 p. 39, 2707
Politics and World Oil Economics, an Account of the International Oil Industry in Its Political Environment 5004

Title Index

Politics in Lebanon p. 39, 2801
Politics in North Africa 1409
Politics of Palestinian Nationalism, The p. 100, 4627
Politics of Peace-Keeping, The 4519
Politics of the Indian Ocean p. 12, 1326
Politics of the Third World, The 1022
Politics, Oil, and the Western Mediterranean 1404
Power Play p. 155, 5119
Precarious Republic, The 2802
Preface to Peace 4509
Prelude to Israel 4162
Present at the Creation p. 7, 3801
Present Tense p. 102, 7019
Price of Middle East Oil, The 5006
Pricing of Crude Oil, The 5011
Probe for Peace 4011
Problems of Commitment 3707
Problems of New Power 3001
Problems of Truce Supervision 4525
Promise and Fulfillment 4136
Proposed Expansion of U.S. Military Facilities in the Indian Ocean 1329
Prospects for an Economic Community in North Africa, The 1410
Protestant Diplomacy and the Near East 3862
Public Papers of the Secretaries-General of the United Nations 4201

Q

Quarterly Check-list of Oriental Studies 6032
Question of Palestine, 1914-1918, The p. 98, 4114

R

Rape of Palestine, The 4167
Reader's Guide to Contemporary History, A 6021
Realities of American-Palestine Relations, The 3845
Rebellion in Palestine 4140

Record of Israel at the United Nations, The 2644
Record of Political Opinions and Events in the Arab World 6216
Record of the Arab World 6216
Reflections on the Middle East Crisis 4054
Regional Arab Politics and Conflict with Israel 1210, 4047
Regional Development for Regional Peace 4728
Regional System and Political Development in the Arab World 1217
Les Relations Turco-Sovietiques et la Question des Destroits 3404
Religion in the Middle East p. 98, 4105
Report Presented by the Secretary of State for the Colonies to Parliament by Command of His Majesty, July, 1937 4118
Report to the General Assembly 4163
Report to the United States Government and His Majesty's Government in the United Kingdom 4103
Republican Iraq, a Study in Iraqi Politics since the Revolution of 1958 p. 38, 2504
Resolutions of the (year) Conference (OPEC) 7307
Return to Sinai p. 101, 4762
Review of Politics 7116
Revolt: Story of the Irgun, The 2605
Revolutionary Change and Modernization in the Arab World 3202
Revolutionary Warfare in the Middle East 4622
La Revolution Palestinienne et les Juifs p. 101, 4612
Revolutions and Military Rule in the Middle East p. 37, 2004
River Jordan, The 4402
River without Bridges, a Study of the Exodus of the 1967 Palestinian Arab Refugees p. 101, 4611
Road to Jerusalem: The Origins of the Arab-Israeli Conflict, 1967, The 4751
Road to Jerusalem: Zionism's Imprint on History 2637

Title Index

Road to Suez, The   1006
Role of Communications in the Middle East Conflict, The   4002
Round Table   p. 189, 7117
Russia and Britain in Persia, 1844-1914   p. 41, 2407
Russia and the West in Iran   3738
Russian Presence in Syria and Palestine, 1843-1914, The   3735
Russia's South Flank   3739

S

Sandstorm, The   4750
Saudi Arabia-Kuwait Neutral Zone, The   3101
Scientific Study of Foreign Policy, The   p. 4
Search for Peace in the Middle East (American Friends Service Committee)   4008
Search for Peace in the Middle East, The (Merlin)   p. 100, 4523
Seat of Pilate, The   4141
Second Arab Awakening, The   p. 9, 1017
Secret Battle for Israel, The   2632
Secure Boundaries and Middle East Peace in Light of International Law and Practice   2608
Select Bibliography: Asia, Africa, Eastern Europe, Latin America, A   6003
Select Chronology and Background Documents Relating to the Middle East, A   6220
Selected and Annotated Bibliography of Books and Periodicals in Western Languages Dealing with the Near and Middle East with Special Emphasis on Medieval and Modern Times, with Supplement, A   6009
Selected Bibliography of Articles Dealing with the Middle East, 1955-1958   6038
Selected Bibliography on Kuwait and the Arabian Gulf   6018
Selected Documents of the International Petroleum Industry   5303

Selected Rand Abstracts   p. 165
Seminar of Arab Jurists on Palestine   4029
Settler Regimes in Africa and the Arab World   4066
Seven Fallen Pillars   4133
Shades of Amber   3114
Shaping of the Arabs, The   1106
Sinai Campaign 1956, The   4726
Sinai Victory   4753
SIPRI Yearbook of World Armaments and Disarmaments   p. 190, 7207
Six Days in June   4743
Six Day War, The   4742
Soldiering for Peace   4517
Soldier with the Arabs, A   p. 39, 2703
Sources of Conflict in the Middle East   4040
Sources of Petroleum Statistical Information   5304
South Arabia   3109
Soviet Advances in the Middle East   3717
Soviet-American Rivalry in the Middle East   3708
Soviet Dilemma in the Middle East, The   3707
Soviet Involvement in the Middle East, The   3706
Soviet Involvement in the Middle East and the Western Response   3729
Soviet Middle East Studies   6005
Soviet Naval Developments   p. 72, 3725
Soviet Objectives in the Middle East   3726
Soviet Penetration into the Middle East   3710
Soviet Policies in the Indian Ocean Area   3719
Soviet Policy in the Middle East (Baczowski)   3701
Soviet Policy in the Middle East (Becker and Horelick)   p. 71, 3702
Soviet Policy toward the Middle East since 1970   3704
Soviet Presence in the Eastern Mediterranean, The   3733

Title Index

Soviet Russia and Asia, 1917-1927 p. 72, 3736
Soviet Russia and the Middle East 3712
Soviet-Third World Relations 3718
Soviet Union and the Arab East under Khrushchev, The 3724
Soviet Union and the Developing Nations, The 3727
Soviet Union and the Middle East, The p. 72, 3728
Soviet Union and the Muslim World, 1917-1958 p. 72, 3740
Soviet Union and the October 1973 Middle East War, The p. 71, 3713
Soviet Union in World Affairs, The 3714
Spirit of World Politics, with Special Studies of the Near East, The p. 11, 1115
State in the Making 4122
State Papers of Levi Eshkol 2623
States of North Africa in the 1970's, The 1412
Statistical Abstract of Israel 1974 6407
Statistical Yearbook 1972 6408
Statistical Yearbook of Turkey 1973 6416
Strategic Review 7216
Strategic Survey 7209
Struggle for Arab Independence, The p. 38, 3209
Struggle for Palestine, The p. 98, 4124
Struggle for Syria, The p. 12, 1221
Struggle for the Middle East, The p. 71, 3716
Sudanese-Egyptian Relations p. 38, 2301
Suez 4733
Suez: The Seven Day War 4716
Suez: The Twice-Fought War 4724
Suez: Ultra-Secret 2604, 4715
Suez and Sinai 4703, 4719
Suez Canal in World Affairs, The 4731
Suez Expedition, 1956, The 4717
Suez 1956, International Crisis and the Role of Law 4718
Suez Story 4723
Suez Ten Years After 4732
Sultans of Aden 3115
Summary of World Broadcasts p. 168
Sun Stood Still, The 4752
Super-Powers and the Balance of Power in the Arab World, The 1213
Superpowers and the Middle East, The p. 97, 4016
Superpowers in the Middle East 3705
Survey of American Interests in the Middle East, A 3819
Survey of International Affairs 6217
Survey of Northwest Africa, the Maghrib, A 6402
Survey of Palestine, A 4160
Survival p. 189, 7118
Survival or Hegemony? 2643
Swasia-North Africa pp. 167-68, 6218
Swiss Review of World Affairs p. 189, 7119
Syria p. 38, 3205
Syria and Lebanon pp. 38-39, 3204
Syrian Politics and the Military, 1945-1958 p. 39, 3207
Syrian Social Nationalist Party, The 3208
Syria under the Ba'th 1963-66 p. 39, 3206

T

Tacit Alliance, A p. 40, 2613, p. 70, 3603
Tanks of Tammuz, The 4757
Technical Assistance in Theory and Practice 2401
Tel Aviv-Bonn Axis and Poland, The 2653
Tensions in the Middle East 1029
Test: de Gaulle and Algeria, The 3607
There Could Have Been Peace 4050
Third Arab-Israeli War, The 4754
This Is Our Strength 2638
Three Days 4157
Times of Israel and World Jewish Review 7020

Title Index

To Jerusalem 4506
To the House of Their Fathers 4138
Toward the African Revolution 1109
To Whom Palestine? 4116
Transformation of Palestine, The p. 97, 4069
Treaties and Alliances of the World 1506
Trial and Error 4165
Troubled Alliance p. 41, 3405
Trucial States, The p. 13, 1313
Truman, the Jewish Vote and the Creation of Israel p. 70, 3851
Tsardom and Imperialism in the Far and Middle East, 1880-1914 3741
Tunisia, from Protectorate to Republic 1119, 3301
Turkey and the United Nations 3413
Turkey and the World 3409
Turkey at the Straits p. 41, 3412
Turkey, the Straits, and United States Policy 3858
Turkish Foreign Policy, 1939-1945 3401
Turkish Foreign Policy, 1943-1945 3416
Turkish Straits and NATO, The p. 41, 3415
Turkism and the Soviets 3407
Twentieth Century Petroleum Statistics p. 155, 7310

U

U.A.R. in Africa, The p. 38, 2307
U.N. entries. See United Nations
Uneasy Lies the Head p. 7, 2704
Unholy Land, The 4030
Unholy War, The 4636
United Nations and the Italian Colonies, The 2903
U.N. and the Middle East Crisis, 1967, The 4522
U.N. and the Palestinian Refugees, The 4606
United Nations and the Palestinians, The 4617
United Nations Emergency Force, The 4529
United Nations Emergency Force: Basic Documents 4209
United Nations Forces 4507
United Nations Peace-Keeping p. 100, 4508
United Nations Peacekeeping in the Middle East 4532
United Nations Peacekeeping, 1946-1967 p. 99, 4203
United Nations Peacemaking p. 100, 4514
United Nations Resolutions on Palestine, 1947-1972 4212
U.N. Secretary General and the Maintenance of Peace, The 4515
United States and International Oil, a Report for the Federal Energy Administration on U.S. Firms and Government Policy, The 5113
United States and Israel, The p. 70, 3848
United States and Its Role in the Middle East Conflict, The 3825
United States and Morocco, 1776-1956, The 3855
United States and North Africa, The 1111
U.S. and Soviet Policy in the Middle East, 1945-56 1031
U.S. and Soviet Policy in the Middle East, 1957-1966 3810
United States and the Arab World, The 3821
United States and the Jewish State Movement, The p. 70, 3849
United States and the Middle East 3803
United States and the Near East, The 3863
United States and the Palestinian People, The 3843
U.S. Foreign Policy and the Export of Nuclear Technology to the Middle East 3829
U.S. Foreign Policy for the 1970's, Shaping a Durable Peace 3876
United States Foreign Policy 1972, a Report of the Secretary of State 3870

Title Index

U.S. Interests in and Policy toward the Persian Gulf 3830
United States Interests in the Middle East p. 70, 3804
United States in the Middle East, The 3826
United States in World Affairs, The 3832, 3864
U.S. Naval Institute Proceedings p. 190, 7218
United States-Persian Diplomatic Relations, 1883-1921 3837
United States Policy and the Partition of Turkey, 1914-1924 3856
United States Policy in the Middle East 3823
United States Policy in the Middle East, Sept. 1956-June 1957 Documents 3871
United States Response to Turkish Nationalism and Reform 1914-1939, The 3859
United States, Turkey, and Iran, The 3827
Unity and Disunity in the Middle East 1207
USSR and Arab Belligerency, The 3709
USSR and Arabia, The 3720
USSR and the Arabs, The 3721
USSR and the Middle East, The p. 71, 3731
U.S.S.R. and the Middle East, The 3730
USSR and the Third World 3732
USSR Arms the Third World, The p. 71, 3722

V

Violent Truce, a Military Observer Looks at the Arab-Israeli Conflict 1951-1955 4518
Voice of Israel 2618

W

War Business, the International Trade in Armaments, The p. 169, 6511
War Diplomacy and the Turkish Republic 3411

War in Yemen, The 3111
Wary Partners: The Soviet Union and Arab Socialism p. 72, 3703
Weapons and Equipment of the Israeli Armed Forces 6501
We Fight for Oil 5101
We Need Not Fail 3853
West-Asian Crisis, The 4735
Western Civilization in the Near East p. 11, 1118
Western Mediterranean, The 1405
Western Powers and the Middle East, 1959, The 1026
Western Window in the Arab World 3854
West German Reparations to Israel 2603
When God Judged and Men Died 4764
Who Knows Better Must Say So 4015
Whose Jerusalem? 4064
Whose Land? 4144
Who's Who in Afghanistan 6101
Who's Who in Israel, and in the Work for Israel Abroad, 1973-74 6105
Who's Who in Lebanon, 1973-74 6106
Who's Who in the Arab World 6104
Wiener Library Bulletin, The 7021
Will the Middle East Go West? 3833
World Affairs 7120
World Armaments and Disarmaments, SIPRI yearbook p. 190, 7207
World Crisis in Oil 5120
World Event/Interaction Survey 6221
World Oil p. 155, 7311
World Petroleum Market, The p. 153, 5001
World Petroleum Report, an Annual Review of International Oil Operations 7312
World Politics 7121
World Today p. 189, 7122
World-Wide Military Expenditures p. 190, 7217

Y

Yearbook on International Communist Affairs 1972 3745

Title Index

Yemen: Imans, Rulers, and Revolutions, The 3106
Yemen: Unknown War, The 3113
Yemen and the Western World since 1571 3110
Yom Kippur War, The 4759
Yom Kippur War: Israel and the Jewish People, The 4760

Z

Zionism and Palestine before the Mandate 4168

Zionism, Israel, and Asian Nationalism 2631
Zionism Reconsidered 2647
Zionist Diplomacy, The 2645
Zionist Movement, The 4110
Zionist Movement in Palestine and World Politics, 1880-1918, The 4137

SUBJECT INDEX

This index is alphabetized letter by letter and underlined numbers refer to major entries on a topic. References are to entry numbers unless the number is preceded by a "p" (to indicate the reference is to a page number).

A

Abdullah, ibn-Husayn (King of Jordan) 3513
Aden 1131
Adenauer, Konrad 2651
Afghanistan
  bibliographies of 6050
  foreign relations and policy of by country 2101-2
    Russia 3736-37, 3739
Africa, North p. 3, 1401-12
  bibliographies of 6003, 6007, 6023, 6027, 6029, 6031, 6047, 6051
  chronologies of 6218
  colonialism in 1109
  economic policy of 1405, 1410
  foreign aid to 2630
  foreign relations and policy of by country 1401, 3602
    Egypt 2307
    U. S. 1111
  integration and unity in 1009, 1406, 1408-10
  nationalism in 1133
  petroleum industry in 1404-5
  yearbooks and atlases 6401-3, 6410
  See also Algeria; Libya; Morocco; Tunisia

Afro-Asianism 1014, 1016
Alami, Musa 4613
al-Fatah. See Fatah, al-
Algeria 1401, 1403, 1407, 1409
  bibliographies of 6022
  foreign relations and policy of by country 2201-4
    France 1117, 3605, 3607, 4732
  independence movements in 1111
  nationalism in 1113
  revolution (1954-62) 2203-4
  self-determination in 1202
  See also National Liberation Front
Anglo-American Committee of Inquiry on Palestine 4127
Anglo-Iranian Oil Co. 5102, 5106
Arab High Committee 4154
Arab-Israeli conflict p. 3, pp. 5-6, 1004, 1007, 1214, 2310, 2621, 2624, 2627, 3704, 3706, 3713, 3730, 3808, 3822, 3825, 3848, pp. 97-102, 4001-73, 5124
  bibliographies of 6011, 6019, 6034
  chronologies of 6202-3, 6205, 6209, 6218, 6220
  documents of 3871, p. 99, 4039,

Subject Index

    4052, 4056, 4059, <u>4201-13</u>, 4518, 4526
  economic implications of 4007
  history of pp. 98-99, 4101-68
  international law and 4019, 4029, 4058-59
  military engagements pp. 39-40, pp. 101-2, <u>4701-6</u>
    1948 war <u>4707-13</u>
    1967 war 2610, 2650, 2652, 2707, 3205, 4005, 4039, 4147, 4206, 4530, <u>4735-58</u>
    1973 war 2652, 3818, <u>4759-68</u>
  peacekeeping and negotiations pp. 99-100, 4017, 4036, 4043, 4056, 4060, 4070, 4208, <u>4501-33</u>
  periodicals 7007, 7013, 7018
  yearbooks and atlases 6404
  See also Jerusalem question; Jordan River dispute; Palestine, pre-1948; Palestinian question; Refugees, Arab; Suez Canal; West Bank
Arabs in America 4066
Arabs in Europe 4103
Arabs in Israel 2620, 2641, 4049, 4618, 4623, 4626, 4629, 4631
Arab Socialist Union 3703
Arab states 1012
  economic cooperation among 1215
  foreign relations and policy of by country 2002-4, 2011, 3104-5
    China 3606
    Great Britain 1112
    India 1320, 3601, 4042
    Israel 1210, 2620-22, 2628, 3709, 4602
    Palestine 4122
    Russia 1110, 3716, 3720, 3724, 3734
    U.S. 3112, 3821
    Western nations 3833
  history of 3115, 4001
  integration and unity among 1207, 1209, 1217-19, 1325, 2310, 2706, 3207
  military and defense policies of 4047, 4061, 6508-9

  nationalism in 1004, 1006, 1021, 1103, 1104, 1106, 1108, 1110, 1112, 1114, 1116, 1121, 1123, 1125, 1130, 1132-34, 1202-3, 1212, 1301, 2803, 3209, 4006, 4133, 4159, 4728, 6044
  politics in 1008, <u>1201-22</u>, 1304-5, 1312, 1328, 3110, 3805, 4017, 4026, 4031, 4047, 4061
  See also Federation of South Arabia; League of Arab States; names of specific Arab states
Aramco (oil company) 5118, 5301
Arbitration and mediation, international 4156, 4523. See also Arab-Israeli conflict
Arms. See Disarmament; Nuclear power and weapons; Weapons
Asia, foreign relations and policy of by country
  Israel 2631
  Palestine 4069
  See also Indo-China
Aswan Dam 2309
Atomic power. See Nuclear power and weapons; Nuclear sharing
Azcarate y Florez, Pablo de 4502

B

Baghdad Pact (1955) 3501, 3702, 3871, 4056. See also Central Treaty Organization
Bahrain Islands 1302, 1311, 1319, 1325
Balance of power 1213, 1322
Balfour Declaration (1917) 4019, 4104, 4109, 4114, 4126, 4153, 4158
Bandung Conference 1016, 1506
Ba'th Party 1221, 2504, 3201, 3206, 3703
Beaufre, Andre 4717
Begin, Menahem 2605
Ben-Gurion, David 4504
Bentwich, Helen 4108
Berger, Elmer 4015
Bosporus, Straits of 3404, 3412, 3414-15

Subject Index

Boundaries 2608
   African 1411
   Saudi Arabia-Trucial states disputes 1313
   See also Jurisdiction, territorial
Bourguiba, Habib 4523

C

Cairo Conference (1921) 3513
CENTO. See Central Treaty Organization
Central Treaty Organization p. 4, 1328, 1506. See also Baghdad Pact
China
   foreign relations and policy of by area 3732, 4728
      Arab states 1301, 3606
      Israel 2610, 2612
      Palestine 4043
      Russia 3705
   petroleum industry in 5127
   See also Maoism
Chouraqui, Andre 4023
Christianity in the Middle East 4105
Church and politics. See Christianity in the Middle East; Judaism; Missionaries; Mohammedanism; Religion and politics
Class conflict 3703
Cold war 1010, 1019, 2303, 2628, 2701, 3701, 3802, 3807, 3848, 4060
Collective security 1015, 3867
Colonialism p. 10, p. 11, 1002, 1019, 1032, 1109, 1118, 1131-32, 1205, 1325, 3106, 3204, 4148
Commerce, statistics 1020, 1215
Communism 1216, 3716, 3730, 3740, 3742-46, 4728
   nationalism and p. 11, 1133, p. 72, 3742
   See also Class conflict; Maoism; Marxism; Socialism
Conciliation, international. See Arbitration and mediation, international
Constantinople Convention 1506
Crimean War 1102

Cromer, Lord 1122, 1128
Culture
   impact of Western on Arab states 1101
   Iranian 3835
   Middle Eastern 2008, 3708, 3804, 3860, 3863
Czechoslovakia
   Egyptian foreign relations and policy 2315, 3722
   military assistance to Israel 2635

D

Decision-making in Middle Eastern politics pp. 5-7, 2652, 3812. See also Game theory in Middle Eastern politics
de Gaulle, Charles 3607
Democracy, in the Arab states 1110
Detente 3702, 3713, 4063
Dhofar War 1328
Diplomacy
   in the Arab-Israeli conflict 4107, 4113, 4127, 4154, 4512, 4730, 4739-40, 4742
   by country
      Algeria 2204
      Canada 4730
      Great Britain 3512
      Iran 2405
      Israel 2607, 2645
      Morocco 3854-55
      Palestine 4154
      Persian Gulf states 1315
      Russia 3716
      Turkey 3402, 3408
      U. S. 3856, 3858-59
   documents of 1505
   history of 2005, 2010, 3863
   in petroleum concessions 5105
   See also Foreign policy and relations
Disarmament 4749. See also Nuclear power and weapons; Weapons
Dulles, John Foster 3813, 4722, 4724

Subject Index

E

Eban, Abba 2616
Economic assistance 1202. See also Military aid; Technical assistance
Economic change, in the Maghreb 1401
Economic development
  of occupied areas 4049
  of the United Arab Republic 2312
Economic policy
  of the Arab states 1215
  of the North African states 1405, 1410
  of Russia 3708, 3716, 3804, 3807, 3811
  of the U. S. 3708, 3804, 3807, 3811, 3826, 3856-57
Economics
  by country
    Iran 3827
    Israel 2611
    Lebanon 2904
    Palestine 4154, 4156, 4160
    Turkey 3410, 3827
  statistics 2007-8
  See also Petroleum, economics of
Eden, Anthony 4725
Egypt
  Army 2313
  bibliographies of 6013
  foreign relations and policy of by country p. 3, 2301-16, 4705
    Africa 2307
    Czechoslovakia 2315, 3722
    France 1101
    Great Britain 1120, 1126, 2311, 2316, 3502, 4725, 4729
    Israel 2643
    Lebanon 1023
    Russia 2648, 3706, 3710, 3728
    Sudan 2301-2
    Syria 1221, 3206-7
  nationalism in 1115, 1128
  politics in 1112, 4064
  role in regional politics p. 12
  world politics and 1003

See also Suez Canal; Nasser, Gamal Abdel; United Arab Republic
Eisenhower, Dwight 4505, 4724
Eisenhower Doctrine 1006, 1121, 2802, 3501, 3865, 4056
Embargo. See Petroleum, embargo of
England. See Great Britain
Eshkol, Levi 2623
Ethiopia 1310
Europe
  economic cooperation with African states 1405
  foreign relations and policy of by area 1018-19, 1027, 1125, 1205
    Arab states 1132, 1206, 3204
    Iraq 1127
    Israel 2622
    U. S. 3861
  role in petroleum trade 5002, 5115, 5121, 5123
European Economic Community 1024

F

Faisal Ibn Abdul-Aziz al Saud 3102, 3209, 3513
Fatah, al- 4062, 4612, 4632
Fedayeen 3703, 4072, 4615, 4620, 4622, 4630, 4633
Federation. See Arab states, integration and unity of; League of Arab States
Federation of South Arabia 3109, 3113
Fertile Crescent 1206, 4101
  bibliographies of 6011
  foreign relations and policy of pp. 38-39
  nationalism in 1133
  See also Iraq; Israel; Jordan; Lebanon; Palestine; Syria
FLN. See National Liberation Front
Foreign aid
  Israeli 2630
  Egyptian 2312
  See also Economic assistance; Military aid
Foreign policy and relations pp. 37-41, 2001-11

Subject Index

comparative   pp. 4-5
by country
  Afghanistan   2101-2, 3736-37
  Africa   1401, 2307, 3602
  Algeria   1117, 2201-4, 3605, 3607, 4732
  Arab states   1110, 1112, 1210, 2002-4, 2011, 2620-22, 2628, 3104-5, 3109, 3112, 3601, 3606, 3716, 3720, 3724, 3734, 3833, 4122, 4602
  Asia   2631, 4069
  China   2610, 2612, 3606, 3732, 4043, 4728
  Czechoslovakia   2315, 3722
  Egypt   1023, 1101, 1120, 1126, 1221, p. 38, 2301-16, 2648, 3206, 3502, 3706, 3710, 3728, 4705, 4725, 4729
  Europe   1018, 1027, 1125, 1127, 1132, 1206, 2622, 3861
  Fertile Crescent   pp. 38-39
  France   1032, 1101, 1107, 1118, 1124, 1401-2, 2631, 3209, 3603, 3605, 3607, 3854, 4732
  Germany   2101-2, 2603, 2615, 2651, 2653
  Great Britain   p. 12, p. 13, 1026, 1032, 1107, 1112, 1118, 1120-21 1124, 1126-27, 1131, 1304, 1309, 1319, 1320, 2101, 2311, 2316, 2407, 2502, 3209, p. 69, 3501-13, 3835, 4113-14, 4119, 4122, 4130, 4133, 4149-50, 4158-59, 4161, 4167-68, 4206, 4725, 4729, 4731, 4733, 5101
  India   1317, 3601, 4735
  Indian Ocean states   3719
  Iran   1302, 1304, 1308, 1310, 1319, 1324, 1328, 2401-12, 3705, 3736-39, 3827, 3834-37, 4735
  Iraq   1112, 1127, 1221, 2501-7, 3710
  Israel   1008, 1030, 1210, 1310, pp. 39-40, 2410, 2601-54, 3603, 3709, 3802, 3838-53, 4602, 4705
  Jordan   2701-7
  Kuwait   3101, 3103
  Lebanon   2801-4, 3204
  Libya   2901-3
  Morocco   3001, 3854-55
  Northern Tier states   pp. 40-41, 2004, 3716
  Palestine   3735, 3838, 3842, 3845, 3850, 3853, 4043, 4111, 4113, 4119, 4122, 4129-30, 4149-50, 4158-59, 4161, 4167-68, 4206
  Persian Gulf states   p. 12, p. 13, 1304, 1306, 1309, 1315, 1319, 1320, 1324, 1328, 3510-11, 3830
  Russia   1008, 1018, 1023, 1028, 1030-31, 1301, 1306, 1315, 1319, 1405, 2101, 2407, 2412, 2614, 2648, 3404-5, 3407, pp. 71-72, 3701-42, 3804, 3807-8, 3810-11, 3822, 3835, 4043, 4061, 4705, 4728, 4735, 6411
  Saudi Arabia   3103-5, 3107
  Soviet-bloc nations   2635
  Syria   3201-9, 3735
  Tunisia   3301
  Turkey   2011, 3401-16, 3705, 3736, 3824, 3827, 3856-59, 4735
  U. S.   1008, 1019, 1023, 1028, 1030-31, 1111, 1203, 1315, 1320, 1327-29, 1405, 2401, 2408, 2622, 3112, 3116, 3405, 3409, pp. 70-71, 3712-13, 3801-76, 4024, 4060-61, 4067, 4073, 4111-12, 4129, 4705, 4735, 5101, 5108, 5112, 5124, 6411, 6510
  Western nations   1006, 1101, 3833
  Yemen   3106, 3110, 3116
documents of   3864-76
periodicals   7104-5
petroleum and   1404
See also Cold war; Colonialism; Diplomacy; Imperialism;

235

Subject Index

France
  foreign relations and policy by area 1032, 1107, 1118, 1124
    African states 1401-2
    Algeria 1117, 3605, 3607, 4732
    Arab states 1124
    Egypt 1101
    Great Britain 1107
    Israel 2613, 3603
    Morocco 3858
    Syria 3209
Friedlander, Saul 4009
Front de Liberation National. See National Liberation Front

G

Game theory in Middle Eastern politics pp. 5-6, 4530. See also Decision-making in Middle Eastern politics
Gas, natural. See Natural gas industry
Germany, foreign relations and policy of by country
  Afghanistan 2101-2
  Israel 2603, 2615, 2651, 2653
Gokalp, Ziya 3406
Great Britain
  foreign relations and policy of by area 1032, 1107, 1118, p. 69, 3501-13, 4114, 4731, 4733
    Arab states 1026, 1112, 1121, 1124, 1131, 4133
    Bahrain 1302
    Egypt 1120, 1126, 1128, 2311, 3502, 4725, 4729
    France 1107, 1124
    Iran 1302, 2407, 3835
    Iraq 1127
    Palestine 4113, 4119, 4122, 4130, 4149-50, 4158-59, 4161, 4167-68, 4206
    Persian Gulf states p. 12, p. 13, 1304, 1309, 1319, 1320, 3510-11
    Syria 3209
    U. S. 1320, 5101

World politics and the Middle East
  role in petroleum trade 5101
  See also Balfour Declaration; Mandate system
Guerrilla warfare. See al-Fatah; Fedayeen; Palestinian question, guerrilla movement
Gulf states. See Persian Gulf states

H

Hammarskjold, Dag 4201, 4510
Herzel, Theodor 4120
Holy Land. See Jerusalem question; Palestine, pre-1948; Palestinian question
Hussein, ibn Talal (King of Jordan) 2704-6

I

Imperialism 1021, 1115, 1121, 1125, 1129, 2408, 2643, 3741, 3847, 4101. See also Colonialism
India
  British rule of 3511
  foreign relations and policy of by area 1317, 4735
    Arab states 1320, 3601, 4042
Indian Ocean states p. 3, p. 12, 1303, 1310, 1316-17, 1321, 1326-27, 1329, 3719. See also names of specific Indian Ocean states
Interest groups, in American foreign policy 3849
International law
  Arab-Israeli conflict and 4019, 4029, 4058-59
  periodicals 7101, 7108
International organization, periodicals 7109
International organizations 2506. See also Mandate system; names of specific organizations
International politics. See World politics and the Middle East
Iran p. 13, 1019
  bibliographies of 6015, 6028, 6035

Subject Index

biographical directories of 6103
communism in 3746
foreign relations and policy of by
    country 1308, 1310, <u>2401-12</u>, 4735
  Bahrain 1302, 1319
  Great Britain 1302, 2407
  Israel 2410
  Persian Gulf states 1304, 1319, 1324, 1328,
  Russia 2407, 2412, 3705, 3736-39
  U. S. 2408, 3827, <u>3834-37</u>
nationalism in 2404
periodicals 7004
petroleum industry in 3801, 3836, 5102-3, 5106, 5111, 5118
politics in 3827, 3834-36
technical assistance to 2401, 2406
yearbooks and atlases 6405
See also Tudeh Party
Iraq
  foreign relations and policy of by
    country <u>2501-7</u>
  Europe 1127
  Great Britain 2502
  Russia 3710
  Syria 1221
  nationalism in 2505
  petroleum industry in 2504, 5127, 5201
  politics in 1112
  yearbooks and atlases 6406
  See also Kurdish-Iraq War
Irgun 2605
Islam. See Mohammedanism
Israel 1017, 1205
  Arab population of 2620, 2641, 4049, 4618, 4623, 4626, 4629, 4631
  bibliographies of 6002, 6034, 6040
  biographical directories of 6105
  creation of 1012, 1027, 2625, 2632, 3812, 3828, 3838, 3840-41, 3851, 4157
  dependence on foreign aid 4101
  foreign aid to Africa 2630
  foreign relations and policy of by
    country 1030, <u>pp. 39-40</u>, <u>2601-54</u>

  Arab states 1210, 2620-22, 2628, 3709, 4602
  Asia 2631
  China 2610, 2612
  Egypt 2643
  Europe 2622
  France 2613, 3603
  Germany 2603, 2615, 2653
  Iran 1310, 2410
  Soviet-bloc nations 2635
  Soviet Union 2614, 3709
  U. S. 1008, 2622, 3802, <u>3838-53</u>
intelligence service 4754
military and defense policies 2601, 2611, 2626, 2629, 2640, 2642, 2646, 4061, 6501, 6504, 6508-9
military assistance to 2635
nationalism in 4007
periodicals 7020
politics in 4064
technical assistance programs of 2636
See also Arab-Israeli, conflict; Balfour Declaration (1917); Jerusalem question; Irgun; Palestine; Palestinian question; Zionism
Israeli-Lebanon Armistice Agreement 4014
Israeli Socialist Organization 2609

J

Jerusalem question 2610, 2628, 4043, <u>4301-8</u>, 4737. See also Palestinian question
Jews in America
  as a political interest group 3849-50
  Zionist activities of 4162
Jews in Arab lands 4054
Jews in Europe 4103
Jews in Great Britain, Zionist activities of 4162
Jews in Palestine 2632, 2634, 4103, 4118, 4121, 4135, 4156, 4164, 4204

Subject Index

Jordan
   bibliographies of 6030
   civil war (1970) 3816
   foreign relations and policy of
      2701-7
   military and defense policies of
      2707
   nationalism in 2701
   politics in 1112, 2701, 2707
   yearbooks and atlases 6408
   See also West Bank
Jordan River dispute 2610, 2616, 4029, 4401-4. See also West Bank
Judaism 4105
Jurisdiction, territorial 1015. See also Boundaries

K

Kemal, Mustafa (Ataturk) 3402, 3743
Khaled, Leila 4619
Khrushchev, Nikita 3724
King-Crane Commission 4123
Kissinger, Henry 3816
Korean War (1950-53) 2610, 2612
Kurdish-Iraq War 2501, 2507
Kuwait
   bibliographies of 6018
   foreign relations and policy of 3101, 3103
   petroleum industry in 1304, 3101
Kuwait Fund for Arab Economic Development 1222

L

Labor Party (Australia) 1303
Landownership, Arab/Jewish statistics of 4021
Latin America
   petroleum industry in 5120
   support for Palestine 3604
League of Arab States p. 3, pp. 11-12, 1211, 1214, 1302, 1506, 4115
League of Nations 2505, 2625, 3413, 4115

Lebanon
   bibliographies of 6030
   biographical directories of 6106
   civil war (1958) 1023, 1501, 3820, 4519
   foreign relations and policy of
      2801-4, 3204
   politics in 2801-3
Libya
   bibliographies of 6016, 6037
   foreign relations and policy of
      2901-3
   self-determination in 1202

M

McDonald, James Grover 3844
Maghreb, the. See Africa, North; Algeria; Libya; Morocco; Tunisia
Mandate system 1105, 1116, 1124, 2502, 2602, 2605, 2634, 2802, 3204, 3513, 3838, pp. 98-99, 4029, 4050, 4066, 4069, 4102, 4106, 4108, 4110, 4113, 4115, 4118-19, 4124-26, 4129, 4131, 4135, 4145-47, 4160, 4166-67, 4202, 4613-14, 4627. See also Protectorates
Maoism 3716
Marxism
   Arab-Israeli conflict explained in terms of 4051, 4148
   Arab socialist theory and 3703
   See also Class conflict; Communism
Mass media, treatment of Arab and Israeli in U.S. 4737
Mediation, international. See Arbitration and mediation, international
Meinertzhagen, Richard 4142
Mesopotamia. See Iraq
Middle East pp. 1-7
   area studies programs 6301-18
   bibliographies and indexes of
      pp. 165-66, 6001-51
   biographical directories of 6101-6
   chronologies of pp. 167-68, 6201-21

Subject Index

definition p. 2
economic development of 4012
history of 3863, 4133
periodicals pp. 189-90, 7001-21, 7101-22
in world politics 1001-33, 4028, 4070
yearbooks and atlases 6401-16
See also Africa, North; Arab states; Fertile Crescent; Indian Ocean states; Northern Tier states; Persian Gulf states; Trucial states; names of specific countries
Middle East Supply Center 3824
Military aid 6507
    Czechoslovakian 2635
    Russian 6505
    See also Weapons
Military policies and forces 4049, 4061
    by area
        Egypt 2313
        Indian Ocean 1308, 1310, 1316, 1319, 1326, 1329, 3725
        Israel 2601, 2607, 2626
        Jordan 2707
        Palestine 4616
        Russia 1308, 1310, 3702, 3707, 3710, 3725
        U. S. 1308, 1310, 1329, 3804, 3807, 3826
    intervention in domestic policies 2002, 2004, 2006
    periodicals 7201-18
    strategy and tactics 2204
    See also Arab-Israeli conflict, military engagements; Sea power
Missionaries, historical role in foreign policy 3862
Mohammedanism 1009, 1216, 1403, 2202
    nationalism and 1104, 1114, 1125, 1133-34
    political ideology and 1129
    public affairs and 1001
Morocco 1401, 1403, 1407
    foreign relations and policy of by country 3001

France 3854
U. S. 3854-55
independence movements in 1111
nationalism in 1113
self-determination in 1202
Mossadegh, Mohammed 3836
Murphy, Robert D. 3820

N

Nasser, Gamal Abdel p. 12, 1203, 1209, 2302-7, 2310, 2314-15, 4505, 4725, 4740
Nationalism pp. 10-11, 1002, 1009, 1101-34, 1118, 1129, 1216, 3504, 3744, 4004, 4059, 4101
    by area
        Arab states p. 11, 1004, 1006, 1021, 1103, 1104, 1106, 1108, 1110, 1112, 1114-16, 1121, 1123, 1125, 1130, 1132-34, 1202-3, 1212, 1301, 2803, 3209, 3742, 4006, 4133, 4159, 4728, 6044
        Asia 2631
        Egypt 1128
        Iran 2404
        Iraq 2505
        Israel 4007
        Jordan 2701
        North Africa 1113
        Palestinian 1017, 1115, pp. 100-101, 4007, 4038, 4521, 4601-36
        Syria 1104, 1308
        Turkey 3406, 3859
    See also Self-determination, national
National Liberation Front 3703
National security 2641, 4623, 5128
NATO. See North Atlantic Treaty Organization
Natural gas industry, economics of 5002. See also Petroleum
Naval policies and forces. See Military policies and forces; Sea power
Near East. See Middle East
Neutrality
    Arab states 1220

Subject Index

Egypt p. 12, 1203, 2314
Turkey 3411
North Africa. See Africa, North
North Atlantic Treaty Organization
   3413-15, 3729, 3862
Northern Tier states p. 4
   foreign relations and policy of by
      country pp. 40-41
      Palestine 2004
      Russia 3716
   See also Afghanistan; Iran; Turkey
Nuclear power and weapons
   Israel's capacity for 2616, 2629
   proliferation of 3702
   sharing 1030, 3829
   Soviet Union use of 3714
   See also Weapons

O

OAPEC. See Organization of Arab
   Petroleum Exporting Countries
Ocean bed. See Seabed
Oil. See Petroleum
Oman
   bibliographies of 6020
   foreign relations and policy of
      3108
OPEC. See Organization of Petroleum Exporting Countries
Organization for European Economic
   Cooperation 5123
Organization of Arab Petroleum
   Exporting Countries p. 4,
   5125, 5203
Organization of Petroleum Exporting
   Countries p. 4, 5008,
   5010, 5124-25, 5129, 5201,
   5203-6
Ottoman Empire p. 10, 1021, 1108,
   1206, 1218, 3862, 4613
Ottomanism, political ideology of
   1129

P

Palestine, pre-1948 1115, 4069,
   4116, 4131-32, 4139-40,
   4146, 4152-54, 4156, 4166

foreign relations and policy toward
   by area
   Arab states 4122
   Great Britain 4113, 4119,
      4122, 4129-30, 4149-50,
      4158-59, 4161, 4167-68,
      4205
   Russia 3735
   U. S. 3838, 3842, 3845,
      3850, 3853, 4111, 4129
   history of 4102, 4104, 4110, 4114,
      4124-26, 4128, 4136, 4141-
      45, 4160
   Jews in 2632, 2634, 4118, 4121,
      4135, 4156, 4164, 4204
   See also Balfour Declaration (1917);
      Mandate system
Palestinian question 1008, 1010,
   1015, 1027-28, 1202, 2701,
   3818, 4017, 4033, 4037,
   4044, 4050-51, 4055, 4063-
   65, 4071, 4104, 4402, 4527,
   6411
   bibliographies of 6019, 6040
   documents concerning 1507, 4212
   guerrilla movement 4621, 4626,
      4628, 4632, 4634
   nationalism and 1017, pp. 100-101,
      4007, 4038, 4521, 4601-36
   periodicals 7006-7
   support for 2004, 3604
   See also al-Fatah; Arab-Israeli
      conflict; Fedayeen; Jerusalem
      question; Refugees, Arab;
      West Bank
Palestinians
   alienation of in the Arab world
      4066
   assimilation into Jordan 2707
   attitudes toward Israel 4001, 4003,
      4006, 4036
   as a political entity 4054
Palestinian War 1019
Pan-Arabism. See League of Arab States;
   Arab states, nationalism
Pan-Turanism. See Turkey, nationalism
Paris Peace Conference (1919) 4854
Peace, periodicals 7114
Peace Corps 3862
Peace treaties 4043

Subject Index

Peel Report 4118
Persian Gulf states p. 3, p. 12, <u>1301-29</u>, 4071
   development problems of 1322,
   foreign relations and policy of by country 1324
      Great Britain 1309, 1320, 3510-11
      Russia 3707
      U. S. 1320, 3830
   petroleum industry in 1304-5, 1307-8, 1318, 1320, 1324, 5124
   politics in 1307, 1312, 1328,
   See also Bahrain Islands; Iraq; Kuwait; Qatar; Saudi Arabia
Petroleum 1324, 2504, 3804, 3809, 4521, 4761, 6411
   concessions and agreements 1313, 1321, 1505, 3101, 3801, 5007, 5009, 5102, 5105, 5107, 5118, 5125, 5202, 5301, 6403
   economics of 1405, pp. 153-54, <u>5001-12</u>, 5110, 5120, 5125, 5127, 5202, 5206-7
   embargo of 1030, 5130
   maps 6403
   nationalization of 5102-3, 5106, 5111
   periodicals <u>7301-12</u>
   producer-consumer relations 1008, 1010, 1012-13, 1027, 1301, 1303-4, 1307-8, 1318, 1320, 1328, 1404, 3707, 3715, 3802, 3806, 3836, 4024, 4063, 5004, 5011, pp. 154-55, <u>5101-31</u>
   reference books p. 155, 5301-4
   relations among producers p. 155, <u>5201-7</u>
   statistics 1020, 1328, 7310
   See also Natural gas industry
Point Four Program 3862
Poland, Israeli politics and 2653
Political parties. See Ba'th Party; Social Nationalist Party (Syria)
Politics. See Regional politics and relations; Religion and politics; World politics and the

Middle East
Population, Arab/Jewish statistics 4021
Press. See Mass media
Protectorates 1131, 3301. See also Mandate system
Public opinion, in Middle Eastern affairs 1011

Q

Qassem, Abd al-Karim 2504, 5201
Qatar 1326

R

RCD. See Regional Cooperation for Development
Refugees, Arab 1010, 2624, 2628, 2641, 3843, 4030, 4048-49, 4053, 4069, 4606, 4611, 4623, 4626, 4635, 4738, 4747
   documents of 3871, 4210
   See also Palestinian question
Regional Cooperation for Development p. 4
Regional politics and relations p. 2, pp. 3-4, <u>pp. 9-13</u>, <u>1001-33</u>, <u>1101-34</u>, <u>1201-22</u>, <u>1301-29</u>, <u>1401-12</u>, <u>1501-7</u>, 2006, 2628, 3708, 3811, 3863, 3867, 4047, 4071, 5110
Religion and politics 3735, 3860.
   See also Christianity in the Middle East; Judaism; Missionaries; Mohammedanism
Reparations 2603, 2610, 2651
Rogers, William 3822
Roosevelt, Franklin 3849

S

Samuel, Herbert Louis 4153
Saud, King 3849
Saudi Arabia
   bibliographies of 6042
   boundary disputes 1313, 3107
   foreign relations and policy of 3101-2, 3107
   petroleum industry in 1304, 3101

Subject Index

Seabed, rights to 1313
Sea power 1303. See also Waterways, conflicts over
Security. See Collective security; National security
Self-determination, national 1202. See also Nationalism
Shi'ites 1214
Sinai Campaign (1956). See Suez Canal
Socialism 2004, 3716, 4022
    Arab theory of 3703, 3721
    See also Communism; Israeli Socialist Organization
Social Nationalist Party (Syria) 3208
Soviet Union
    economic policy of 3708, 3716, 3804, 3807, 3811
    foreign relations and policy by area 1008, 1018, 1028, 1030-31, pp. 71-72, 3701-42, 3810, 3822, 4705, 4728, 6411
        Afghanistan 2101
        Africa, North 1405
        Arab states 1110, 1301, 3720, 3724, 3734
        China 3705
        Egypt 2648, 3706, 3728
        Indian Ocean states 3719
        Iran 2407, 2412, 3738, 3835
        Lebanon 1023
        Palestine 3735, 4043
        Persian Gulf states 1306, 1315, 1319
        Turkey 3404-5, 3407
        U. S. 1007, 1308, 1310, 1312, 1404, 2701, 3708, 3804, 3807-8, 3811, 3818, 4061, 4735
    military and defense policies of 3702, 3707, 3711, 3725, 6505
    role in the petroleum trade 5002, 5114, 5121, 5131
Storrs, Ronald 4159
Sudan
    bibliographies of 6013
    foreign policy and relations with Egypt 2301-2

Suez Canal 1003, 1006, 1012, 2604, 2618, 2648, 3501, 3505, 3813, 3820, 3865, 4071, 4201, 4206, 4213, 4511, 4519, 4703, 4714-34
Summit conferences 1208, 3704
Sunnis 1214
Sykes-Picot Agreement 4109
Syria
    bibliographies of 6030
    foreign relations and policy of by country 3201-9
        Egypt 3206-7
        Europe 3209
        Russia 3735
    Iraqi-Egyptian rivalry in 1221
    nationalism in 1104, 1115, 1307
    politics in 1112, 3204, 3206-7
    See also Ba'th Party; Social Nationalist Party (Syria)

T

Technical assistance
    in Iran 2401
    in underdeveloped countries 2636
    See also Economic assistance; Military aid
Territory, national. See Boundaries; Jurisdiction, territorial
Terrorist groups. See al-Fatah; Fedayeen; Irgun; Israel, creation of; Palestinian question, guerrilla movement
Third World, independence movements in 1014, 1016, 1022, 2628. See also Underdeveloped countries
Trade. See Commerce
Treaties, mutual defense 1322. See also Peace treaties
Tripartite Convention (1950) 3501
Trucial states 1313. See also Union of Arab Emirates
Truman, Harry 3828, 3851
Truman Doctrine 3824
Tudeh Party 3746
Tunisia 1401, 1403, 1407, 1409

Subject Index

foreign relations and policy of 3301
independence movements in 1111
nationalism in 1113
as a protectorate 1119
self-determination in 1202
Turkey 1019
  bibliographies of 6403
  communism in 3743
  foreign relations and policy by country 2011, <u>3401-16</u>, 4735
    Russia 3404, 3407, 3705, 3736, 3739
    U. S. 3405, 3409, 3824, 3827, <u>3856-59</u>
  nationalism in 1125, 3406, 3859
  neutrality of 3411
  partition of 3408, 3856
  politics in 3410, 3827
  yearbooks and atlases 6416
  See also Ottoman Empire

U

Underdeveloped countries
  role in petroleum trade 5203
  technical assistance to 2636
  See also Third World
Union of Arab Emirates 1325. See also Trucial states
Union of Soviet Socialist Republics. See Russia
United Arab Republic, formation of the 1221. See also Egypt
United Nations pp. 3-4, 1013, 2608
  Arab-Israeli conflict and the 4019, 4049, 4056, 4127, 4129, 4151, 4155, 4163, 4201, 4203, 4207, 4209-12, 4303, 4307, 4502, 4506-12, 4514, 4519, 4522, 4524-27, 4529, 4532-33, 4606, 4617, 4709, 4716, 4718, 4730, 4742, 4747
  documents of 3868
  involvement by country
    Arab states 1202, 1204
    Bahrain Islands 1302

Egypt 2308
Iran 1302, 5106
Iraq 2506
Israel 2622, 2625, 2628, 2639, 2644
Latin America 3604
Lebanon 1023
Libya 2901-3
Palestine 3604
Turkey 3413
petroleum politics and the 5106
United States
  economic policy of the 3708, 3804, 3807, 3811, 3826, 3856-57
  foreign relations and policy by area 1019, 1028, 1030-31, pp. <u>70-71</u>, 3712-13, <u>3801-33</u>, <u>3860-76</u>, 4024, 4060, 4067, 4073, 4112, 4705, 4735, 5108, 5111, 5124, 6411
    Afghanistan 2101
    Africa 1111, 1405
    Arab states 3112, 3821, 3833
    Egypt 1203
    Europe 3861
    Great Britain 1320, 5101
    Indian Ocean states 1327, 1329
    Iran 2401, <u>3834-37</u>
    Israel 1008, 2622, 3802, <u>3838-53</u>
    Lebanon 1023
    Morocco <u>3854-55</u>
    Palestine 3838, 3842, 3845, 3850, 3853, 4110, 4129
    Persian Gulf states 1315, 1320, 1328, 3830, 6510
    Russia 1007, 1308, 1310, 1312, 1404, 2701, 3708, 3804, 3807-8, 3811, 3818, 4061
    Turkey 3405, 3409, 3824, <u>3856-59</u>
    Yemen 3116
  military and defense policies of the 1308, 1310, 1329, 3826
  role in the petroleum trade 5012, 5101, 5107-9, 5112-13,

Subject Index

5115, 5117, 5121, 5124, 5128-30
technical assistance by the 2401, 2406
weapons technology of the 3702

W

War
  economics of 4530
  limited 4706
  unconventional 2204
  See also Arab-Israeli conflict; Korean War (1950-53); World War I; World War II
Waterways, conflicts over 1015, 1020, 4059. See also Jordan River dispute
Weapons pp. 168-69, 6501-12
  international agreements 3722
  sales and transfers of 1328, 2613, 2616, 2632, 2646, 3603, 3831, 4063, 6502, 6510-11
  technology and 3702, 6503-4
  See also Disarmament; Military aid; Nuclear power and weapons
Weizmann, Chaim 4155, 4165
West Bank 2650. See also Arab-Israeli conflict; Jordan River dispute; Palestinian question
Western nations
  foreign relations and policy 1006, 1101

imperialism and 1021, 1129
White Paper (1939) 4109
Wilson, Woodrow 3856, 3862
World politics and the Middle East 1001-33, 4028, 4070, 5124
  periodicals 7101-23
World War I 1107
World War II 1018, 1033, 3411, 3416, 4127. See also Reparations

Y

Yemen 1131, 4519, 4533
  civil war 3111, 3113, 3805
  establishment of 3109
  foreign relations and policy of 3106, 3110, 3116
  politics in 3106

Z

Zionism 2609, 2621, 2631, 2634, 2637, 2643, 2645, 2647, 2654, 3817, 3839, 3842, 3847, 3849, 3852, pp. 98-99, 4002, 4010, 4044, 4066, 4069, 4102, 4107, 4109-13, 4116, 4120-21, 4124-25, 4128-33, 4135-39, 4147, 4149, 4152, 4155, 4159, 4161-62, 4165, 4168, 4603

Ref
Z
6465
N35
S38